Everyman's Book
of English Love Poems

Everyman's Book of English Love Poems

Edited by

John Hadfield

J M Dent & Sons Ltd
London Melbourne Toronto

First published 1980
Selection, introduction and notes © J M Dent & Sons Ltd, 1980
All rights reserved. No part of this
publication may be reproduced, stored in
a retrieval system, or transmitted, in any form or by
any means, electronic, mechanical, photocopying,
recording or otherwise, without the prior
permission of
J M Dent & Sons Ltd

This book is set in 12/14pt VIP Baskerville by
D P Media Ltd, Hitchin, Hertfordshire

Printed in Great Britain by
Billing & Sons Ltd, Guildford, London, Oxford, Worcester for
J M Dent & Sons Ltd
Aldine House, Welbeck Street, London

British Library Cataloguing in Publication Data

Everyman's book of English love poems
  1. Love poetry, English
  I. Hadfield, John, *b.1907*
  821'.008'0354   PR1184

ISBN 0-460-04445-1

Contents

Erratum

The date of publication of Elizabeth Barrett Browning's *Sonnets from the Portuguese* is given as 1830 instead of 1850, and the poems are therefore misplaced in the sequence of the book. The date is also incorrectly given in the introduction on page 28 and in the biographical note on page 381.

The Triple Fool

I am two fools, I know,
For loving, and for saying so
   In whining poetry;
But where's that wise man that would not be I,
If she would not deny?
   Then as th' earth's inward narrow crooked lanes
Do purge sea-water's fretful salt away,
   I thought, if I could draw my pains
Through rhyme's vexation, I should them allay.
    Grief brought to numbers cannot be so fierce,
    For he tames it, that fetters it in verse.

But when I have done so,
Some man, his art and voice to show,
   Doth set and sing my pain,
And, by delighting many, frees again
Grief, which verse did restrain.
   To Love and Grief tribute of Verse belongs,
But not of such as pleases when 'tis read;
   Both are increasëd by such songs:
For both their triumphs so are publishëd,
    And I, which was two fools, do so grow three;
    Who are a little wise, the best fools be.

John Donne

Introduction

This book has a two-fold purpose: first, to provide a representative selection of the lyric poetry of love; and, second, to illustrate through poetry the different attitudes to love adopted by English men and women during the past four hundred years.

The success or failure of the book in its first purpose is a matter of opinion and subjective judgment. Lyric poetry is – with the English country house and the English garden – among the most notable contributions made by the English people to Western culture. And love was, from the sixteenth to the late eighteenth century, the chief theme of the lyric poets. To express preferences within the huge output of lyric verse during that period is to invite argument. Who is to decide with any finality which of Shakespeare's or Spenser's sonnets is to have the preference? How does it come about that such great English poets as Milton, Shelley and Wordsworth are so scantily represented in the book, whereas minor writers like Sir Charles Sedley and George Granville are represented by five and seven poems respectively? The answer to this question, setting aside editorial prejudice, is that the great writers mentioned wrote very little lyric verse about love, whereas Sedley and Granville wrote about little else.

I have made no conscious attempt to include or to exclude love poems that have achieved common acceptance through repetition in other anthologies. Nor have I included the work of outstanding poets simply because they are outstanding. It may seem surprising that so eloquent a lyric poet as Keats is not represented at all. But Keats was far more interested in other aspects of life and nature than he was in love: the very titles of his odes and sonnets are evidence of this. And perhaps the finest poet produced by America, Emily Dickinson, hardly wrote at all in personal terms about human love.

Readers may well disagree with me over the omission of this or that poet, or my preference for one poem over another. What I think can be claimed for this book, in the pursuance of the first of its aims, is that it presents quite a large number of authors – such as Fulke Greville, William Cavendish, Richard Leigh and Soame Jenyns – whose work is little known today, and a number of poems of anonymous authorship which have been seldom reprinted. Quantitatively, also, this volume contains a much more extensive collection of English love poems than has appeared in any other recent anthology.

The second aim of the book is one that emerged almost accidentally from the assembly of a vast amount of love poetry. Placing the poems in roughly the chronological order in which they were written and published it became evident to me that, regardless of their literary merits, they were of significant interest as reflecting the amatory and sexual *mores* of the differing societies that produced them. There are always exceptions to any classifications, but I have deliberately grouped my selection under the headings of Elizabethan (1558–1603), Jacobean and Cavalier (1603–60), Restoration (1660–1714), Georgian (1714–1830), Victorian (1830–1901) and Modern (1901 onwards). I suggest that in broad terms these periods were distinguished not only by political, aesthetic and social changes, but also by changing attitudes to love and sex, attitudes which are reflected in the lyric poetry they produced.

Before attempting to indicate the differing attitudes which characterized these periods I should perhaps point out one constant factor that ran through almost the whole of the four hundred years under review, though it has been less evident latterly. This is the close relationship between love poems and music. Much of the best of the poetry was set to music, to be sung. Many of the poems of the Elizabethan and Restoration periods originated as songs interpolated into plays. And the printed sources of many of the Georgian lyrics have no titles other than the single word 'Song'.

The musical element was less predominant in those Victorian poems which are worthy of reprinting, but it should not be forgotten that throughout Victoria's reign one of the most popular recreations was listening to 'songs at the piano' in drawing room or parlour. The theme of most of these ballads was love, though death, disaster and military activity were also favourite subjects. In the twentieth century, moreover, the chief form of expression of love and sexual attraction has been the popular song, whether from a musical play or the dance floor. For this reason I have included, in the final section of the book, a few examples of love lyrics – and one satirical cabaret song – that have had wide musical popularity and show some originality and finesse in verbal expression. It is unfortunate that so many of the best tunes of today are accompanied by words of total banality.

The Elizabethans

The continuing musical popularity of the madrigal and part song has, I fancy, caused many people to suppose that most Elizabethan love poetry is of an Arcadian artlessness, expressing sentiments of pastoral simplicity to an accompaniment of hey-nonny-nonnies and fal-la-las. There was much of that sort of thing – the equivalent of the Edwardian musical comedy song or the pop music of today – though curiously, it did not reach its zenith until the Stuart period (the age of metaphysical poetry!) But the best of Elizabethan verse, even in its purely lyrical moods, is by no means simple in style, and is far from unsophisticated in sentiment.

It has been interesting, in arranging this selection, to see how two elements – the singing note and the intellectual conceit – run side by side through the period, gradually merging in the best of the songs set by Campion, Dowland, and – the musician with the most metaphysical tastes of any of them – Robert Jones.

The singing note, of course, had sounded through the Middle Ages, and there is nothing specifically Elizabethan about 'Fain would I have a pretty thing' or 'Love me little, love me long'. As early as 1572, however, we find George Gascoigne making an odd marriage of simplicity and sophistication in his 'Lullaby of a Lover'. With Sir Philip Sidney, whose poems were mostly written ten or more years before their appearance in print, a complex, highly civilized intelligence enters the poetic field. At the same time his friend Fulke Greville, Lord Brooke, was composing metaphysical love poems which are the unmistakable predecessors of Donne's.

The love poetry of the 1580s and 1590s, until the lutenists entered the field, was largely dominated by the sonnet form, by sentiments and ideas derived from foreign sources such as Petrarch and Desportes, and by the baroque conventions of the Court. 'As we read' – I quote what C. S. Lewis has said of *Arcadia* – 'we must have in mind the ruffs, the feathers, the tapestries, the rich earrings, the mannered gardens, the elaborate courtesies.' Typical of the courtly lover's vision of his loved one are Thomas Watson's lines:

> I saw the object of my pining thought
>   Within a garden of sweet Nature's placing,
> Wherein an arbour, artificial wrought,
>   By workman's wondrous skill the garden gracing,
> Did boast his glory . . .

Much of the love poetry is merely 'artificial wrought', but even the most elaborate structures of verbal antithesis, embroidered metaphor and fulsome compliment, are apt to be lit by brilliant shafts of purely lyrical sunshine.

Genius apart – and twenty years which saw the writing of the sonnets of Sidney, Spenser and Shakespeare, and the love poems of Donne, carried no inconsiderable freight of genius – the Elizabethan love lyric is the consequence of fresh appetites and eager tempers discovering for the first time the stylistic and intellectual vistas of the Renaissance. 'Its inspiration', wrote Sir Edmund Chambers, 'is in the lust of the eyes and the pride of life. It hymns the splendour of a palace, and passes in like spirit to dwell on the simpler felicities of the Spring.' Because life in the palace was fraught with hazard, rivalry and treachery, and because Winter and death were no less real to the poets than love and Spring, there was a singular lack of sentimentality even in the most anguished outpouring of tender sentiment.

The metaphysical element reached its apogee in the love poems of John Donne. Although most of these were not published until 1633 I have included them in the Elizabethan section since they were all written between 1598 and 1602. It is to be assumed that most of them were addressed to Ann More, niece of Sir Thomas Egerton, Lord Keeper of the Great Seal, to whom Donne was secretary from 1598 to 1602. Donne's secret marriage to her in 1601 cost him his post. Some of the more tender poems, such as 'Love's Infiniteness', were almost certainly written after his marriage.

Donne's poems heralded the high noon of English love poetry. They have none of the artless charm of early Elizabethan verse, and their artificiality is not merely decorative, as was that of such predecessors as Thomas Watson or the Earl of Oxford, but the result of artifice working upon complex thoughts and emotions. As Sir Herbert Grierson wrote, in the Introduction to his edition of Donne's poems: 'Hot-blooded and passionate he was, with a passion in which body and soul are sometimes inextricably blended . . . Not sensual nor sensuous but passionate is the note of the young Donne and his verse, an intense susceptibility to the fascination of sex, a fascination that at once allures and repels, enthralls and awakens a spirit of scornful rebellion. He ranges through the whole gamut of passion from its earthliest to its most abstractedly detached moods.'

But Donne, although the most profound of the Elizabethan love poets, was not representative of his period. Poetically his place is amongst the metaphysical writers (many of them inspired by religion, as Donne was in his later years) of the mid-seventeenth century. Meanwhile, as the Elizabethan age drew to its close, song book after song book issued from the presses, and England became, to its musical glory, 'a nest of singing birds'.

To save the arbour of artifice from becoming, as it might

have done in an increasingly self-conscious age, a temple of metaphysics, a musical discipline was imposed by the lutenists, who filled their song books with such lyrics as lent themselves to the singing voice. Lyrics which were to be sung had to retain some of the simplicity, directness and spontaneity of the Arcadian age. The singing note struck from their lutes and orpharions by Dowland, Campion, Jones and their fellows continued to sound through English love poetry for over a hundred years.

Jacobeans and Cavaliers

The first few years of the seventeenth century were a fertile age for the drama, and it is not surprising that many of the best love lyrics of the time were introduced as songs in plays by Ben Jonson, Thomas Heywood and lesser writers such as Nathaniel Field and Peter Hausted. These inevitably tended to be literary trifles, to fill gaps in the dramatic action or allow changes of scene or cast. But some of them, especially those written by Ben Jonson, such as 'Drink to me only with thine eyes', have achieved lasting fame.

Meanwhile, the output of song books continued, and yielded some of the most beautifully conceived and finely turned love lyrics in our literature. It is extraordinary that the authorship of so many of them has never been discovered. The credit for their survival must go entirely to the lutenists. Thomas Campion is known to have written his own words, but 'Anon' is the author of most of the songs set to music by John Dowland, Francis Pilkington and Robert Jones, whose *Musical Dreame* (1609) and *The Muse's Gardin for Delights* (1610) are rich quarries for lyric verse.

The poets who wrote for publication in print rather than performance with music came into their own with the accession of Charles I. It is perhaps dangerous to link the personality of a monarch with the poetic attitude of his or her reign, but there is little doubt that much of the love poetry written in Court circles during the reign of Elizabeth I was deliberately intended to refer to the Virgin Queen. And the personal image created by Charles I undoubtedly coloured the general outlook of what may be called, as a group, the Cavalier Poets of his reign – Thomas Carew and Sir John Suckling (who were close friends) and Richard Lovelace. All were connected with the Court, of which the head was a monarch of high purpose and natural dignity, a man of culture and a connoisseur of the arts. The Court poets represented, as it were, an aristocracy of elegant refinement, with total belief in themselves, just as their monarch believed in the divine right of kings.

Their poetry reflected this self-confidence. It is characteristic that one of Carew's poems is entitled 'Mediocrity in Love Rejected' and another 'Boldness in Love'. As most of his and his friends' poems were concerned with love, and all three of them were very talented versifiers, it is hardly surprising that this period has been described as the Golden Age of the love lyric. One poem, 'A Rapture', here reprinted in full, has come to stand beside Donne's 'Going to Bed' as a classic of erotic poetry.

Lovelace, the rather younger contemporary of Carew and Suckling, added to the Cavalier characteristics of boldness and style a soldierly recognition that only martial duty or loyalty to a cause can claim greater allegiance than love.

Meanwhile, down in Devon, the pastoral tradition was being 'nobly' maintained by the Reverend Robert Herrick. Not only did he

> Sing of brooks, of blossoms, birds and bowers
> Of April, May, of June and July flowers

but he also celebrated unashamedly his delight in the physical charms of his younger female parishioners.

The reign of Charles I also saw the emergence of another Royalist whose adventures in politics were paralleled by adventures in love. Edmund Waller's polished love lyrics included 'Go, lovely rose'. Abraham Cowley, a younger man, who was for a time cipher-secretary to Queen Henrietta Maria in exile, published *The Mistress* in 1647; and another supporter of the Royalist cause, William Cavendish, paid court to, and married, a maid-in-waiting to the Queen, and wrote a collection of exquisite love-poems for her, which remained in manuscript for over three hundred years.

This Golden Age of love poetry was brought to a violent end with the execution of Charles I in 1649 and the triumph of the Puritans. Carew had died a debauchee in 1639, Suckling had fled to France and was said by John Aubrey to have committed suicide in Paris. Lovelace was twice imprisoned and died a bankrupt in 1658. Henry King, who had written pleasant love lyrics early in the reign of Charles I and a moving Exequy on his dead wife, was deprived of the Bishopric of Chichester by the Parliamentarians.

During the period of the Commonwealth the only two poets of consequence who had official recognition were Milton, whose single lyric poem about personal love was the touching tribute to his dead wife written in 1658, and Andrew Marvell, who became tutor to Cromwell's ward.

Herrick and Cowley were still alive, but the only poet I have discovered who published a volume of love lyrics of any merit during the Commonwealth was the obscure Nicholas Hookes, whose delightful verses in praise of Amanda (1653) seem to have been ignored by most literary historians. The effect of the Puritan régime during the 1650s was as disastrous to the Art of Love, and its celebration, as it was to the interior decoration of innumerable churches throughout Britain.

The Restoration Wits

'This morning, before I was up,' wrote Samuel Pepys in his diary on 30 January 1659/60, 'I fell a-singing of my song, "Great, good and just, &c.," and put myself thereby in mind that this was the fatal day, now ten year since, his Majesty died.' Meanwhile clerks and apprentices, setting about their day's work, were quoting lewd doggerel about the Grandees of the Rump. London was restive and ill at ease. From lip to lip was passed the significant couplet:

> 'Tis hoped before the month of June
> The birds will sing another tune.

The hope was vouchsafed. On 29 May of that same year Charles II entered London, 'with a triumph of above twenty thousand horse and foot, brandishing their swords and shouting with inexpressible joy; the ways strewed with flowers, the bells ringing, the streets hung with tapestry, fountains running with wine'. Not only the birds, but all England burst into a new tune.

When he heard of the Restoration Sir Thomas Urquhart is said to have died of laughing. That was an apt, if over-emphatic, comment on the change which now spread across the face of his country.

The return of the Black Boy meant a restoration of wit, a resurgence of gaiety and song. Just as moralists painted Charles II even darker than his raven locks, so sentimentalists invested with an unreal glamour the gallantries of his Court. There was much that was merely bestial in the frolics of the town. Rochester was painting his own picture when he wrote the lines attributed to him:

> Room, room for a Blade of the Town,
>   That takes delight in roaring,
> And daily rambles up and down
>   And at night in the street lies snoring.
> That for the noble name of Spark
>   Dares his companions rally;
> Commits an outrage in the dark,
>   Then slinks into an alley.

Admittedly, dirt, disease and violence had characterized earlier ages, but certain accepted rules of formality and grace that had governed the poetry of the Elizabethans and Jacobeans were undoubtedly relaxed in the Restoration period as a reaction to Puritanism.

The group of Wits which included Sir Charles Sedley and Charles Sackville, Lord Buckhurst (later the Earl of Dorset), was chiefly responsible for setting the tone of fashionable morality and social behaviour. Reacting against the solemn didacticism of the Commonwealth, they turned to the sensuous pleasures of a pagan philosophy:

> Let us enjoy the joys we know
> Of music, wine and love.
> We're sure of what we find below,
> Uncertain what's above.

Many of their excesses and escapades – such as the appearance of Sedley, Buckhurst and Sir Thomas Ogle stark naked on the balcony of the Cock Tavern, where Sedley delivered a blasphemous mock sermon to a crowd of over a thousand people – were the equivalent of undergraduate 'rags' in our own time. A few of the Wits, like Rochester, pursued their mad course until they were overtaken by disease and remorse. It is significant, however, that of the trio who enraged the Puritans by their unseemly pranks at the Cock Tavern, one, Sir Thomas Ogle, became a sober Governor of Chelsea College; another, Buckhurst, was soon happily married; and Sedley became a responsible Member of Parliament. All three grew old gracefully and lived into the eighteenth century. Etherege was the only notable figure amongst the Wits who continued his Rake's Progress to the end.

If we regard the Court poets of the Restoration as high-spirited undergraduates, reacting against an older generation, and living in a world where cruelty and the grosser appetites were taken for granted, the sensuality and inconstancy of their sentiments may be understood, if not forgiven. And what they lacked in decorum and constancy was made up in ardour and wit.

There were, of course, other poets capable of more profound emotions. The 'poor, suffering heart' of Dryden's song was no mere image of the mind. I think many readers who know Dryden best in his longer periods will be surprised at the depth of feeling revealed in some of his songs. As Peter Quennell has said, 'their texture sometimes recalls a brocaded fabric, heavily ornamented and yet supple to the touch'. There is, however, something more than poetic mastery in such songs as 'Secret

Love', and the song from *Cleomenes*, with its final superb, double-edged couplet:

> Time and Death shall depart, and say, in flying,
> Love has found out a way to live by dying.*

Etherege is the inconstant lover in excelsis, but even he, for all his scepticism, has an underlying tenderness of feeling:

> Cloris, at worst you'll in the end
> But change your lover for a friend.

Sedley, perhaps, never went quite out of his emotional depth, but I confess to finding a real, if autumnal, feeling in his song to 'Cloris' when it is realized that it was addressed to the young Ann Ayscough who was destined to become his wife in every sense except that of law.

Dorset is perhaps the most engaging personality of them all. His levity was counterbalanced by his tenderness, his sensuality by his kindness. 'My Lord Dorset might do anything,' said Rochester, 'yet was never to blame.' How agreeable, at a time when men worship Security, is the bold statement that

> My love is full of noble pride,
>   And never will submit
> To let that fop Discretion ride
>   In triumph over Wit.

I take the year 1672 to be the high noon of the Restoration – or (should I say?) the midnight of the Rakes. This was the year which saw the publication of Kemp's *Collection of Poems* – a major source-book of the English lyric – *Covent Garden Drollery*, Robert Veal's *New Court-Songs*, and the second part of *Westminster Drollery*. In the following year appeared that interesting and largely unexplored miscellany called by the first line of Dorset's 'Methinks the Poor Town . . .'.

After this date the fever of the love lyric gradually declined. There were, of course, exceptions, such as the heart-cries of

---

* 'Dying' was the seventeenth- and eighteenth-century euphemism for an orgasm.

that mysterious jilt, 'Ephelia', and the plunging passions of the only poet amongst them all to approach the stature of Dryden – John Wilmot, Earl of Rochester. For all his fantastic irreverence, one can imagine Rochester, spent with excesses, echoing on his death-bed those lines of Vaughan:

> I played with fire, did counsel spurn,
>   Made life my common stake;
> But never thought that fire would burn,
>   Or that a soul could ache.

For the rest, the mainstream of the lyrical impulse was gradually diverted into a variety of rivulets. Some flowed into obscurity, like the exquisite metaphysical conceits of Richard Leigh or the intellectual antitheses of Philip Ayres – both of whom are restored in this collection to a position worthier of their merits. Thomas Heyrick is another thoughtful writer in the minor key who has his own peculiar talent and charm, and deserves some reconsideration.

The light-hearted gallantry of Dorset, Sedley, and Etherege was fitfully sustained by John Sheffield, Duke of Buckingham, and George Granville, Lord Lansdowne, both of whom have been curiously neglected by anthologists. With the Glorious Revolution, however, wit and scepticism finally triumphed over ardour. To John Oldmixon – a prose hack but an accomplished versifier – love was a game, a convention. William Walsh's cynicism is only surpassed by that of Congreve, of whom F. W. Bateson wrote: 'It is no inconsiderable achievement to contemplate sex under the dry light of irony.' With Congreve we enter the Age of Reason, when even the transports of love savoured of that unfashionable attribute, Enthusiasm, and when Honest Merry Harry Carey, who was capable of so sweet a sentimentality as 'Sally in our Alley', nevertheless sang:

> If she does not love you, make her;
> When she loves you, then – forsake her;
> 'Tis the modish way of wooing.

Yet, though the mode of wooing may seem to have changed, though the lyrical impulse was now fired by a new fashion, one element had remained constant through the years – the rule of song. Earlier I quoted Samuel Pepys: he, as everyone knows, found his chief delight in song. At the accession of Charles II, the day after the King's proclamation 'against drinking, swearing and debauchery' was, with a charming irony, read to the ships' companies in the Fleet, the Admiral, Lord Sandwich, called for the lieutenant's cittern and, with two candlesticks filled with money for cymbals, he and Samuel Pepys made 'barber's musique, with which my Lord was much pleased'. This is but one of a thousand examples of the rule of song in Restoration England.

In every household, every tavern or ale-house, it was customary to gather in the evening to sing glees or catches. In 1678 a small-coal merchant, Thomas Britton, began to give concerts in a loft above his warehouse in Clerkenwell. There, every night for forty years, could be heard the finest music in London. On the walls of barbers' shops hung citterns and guitars – as one might find copies of the weekly magazines today. Almost everyone could play some musical instrument. A special pride was taken in mastering the various graces affected by the lutenist – the Back-fall, the Elevation, the Relish, the Slide, or the Springer. Between 1651 and 1702 no less than two hundred and fifty song-books were published in London. Many of the Restoration songs I have included in this book recur again and again in those collections, set to music by such composers as Dr Blow, John Eccles, Henry Lawes, and Henry and Daniel Purcell.

Music, indeed, was no less an inspiration to the poets of the Restoration than love. The two yielded a literature which, though it may rest a little below the peaks of lyrical achievement, has a lingering beauty of phrase and an undying reality for the restless heart. The swains who dallied with their nymphs beneath the willow trees, the gallants who ogled orange girls in the Pit, the goddesses who 'gave ambrosia in a kiss', or the ageing sceptics who simply asked 'to love and live in quiet' – all were students at that Academy of Compliments which taught them to shape their passions in gracious words and sing them to the music of the viol, the harpsichord or the lute.

The Georgians

In the eighteenth century verse was employed – rather like the novel today – as a maid of all work. Verse was the common form of literary expression – for describing the wool industry in John Dyer's *The Fleece*, for celebrating the economics of *The Sugar-Cane*, even for examining the scientific delights of *The Botanic Garden*.

It is a mistake, however, to assume that all or most of the poetry of the Georgian epoch was didactic, satirical, topographical, or otherwise governed by 'unpoetic' influences. Throughout the century – and particularly the first half of it – there was an outpouring of 'occasional' love lyrics; inconspicuous, unconsidered trifles, which were not rated highly in their time (popular though they were), and have mostly been forgotten since. In the journals and monthly magazines, in the song-books and miscellanies, and in countless modest volumes of *Poems on Several Occasions*, they tripped into print – polite playthings, literary toys, which nonetheless reflected with sparkling clarity the spirit of their age.

These 'songs', as they were usually called, as distinct from more elaborate and formal poems, were true lyrics. Like the 'songs' of the Restoration, they were written to be sung. They were set to music by such composers as the Arnes and William Boyce; they were interpolated in plays; they were warbled by buxom contraltos or boy sopranos in the pleasure gardens of Vauxhall, Ranelagh and Marylebone. They were sung, too, by Ladies of Quality, to the accompaniment of the harpsichord or the German flute, in the withdrawing rooms of country houses or the crescents of Bath, Tunbridge Wells and York. Judging by the frequency with which they were reprinted in the successive song-books of the time – which were graced by such names as *The Lark*, *The Bull-Finch* or *The British Songster* – it was the now-forgotten love lyrics by dimly recognized authors which enjoyed the longest popularity.

It would be idle to claim that many of these songs scaled the heights of imagination or plumbed the depths of emotion. I do claim, however, that they possessed some agreeable merits, and deserve to be better known than they are. Their gaiety and finesse, their polished conceits and neat antitheses, were charming manifestations of the taste which enjoyed the conversation pieces of Gainsborough or Zoffany, the furniture of Chippendale, Chelsea porcelain, *The School for Scandal*, the minuet, the masquerade, the snuff-box and the fan.

To enter upon a critical discussion of the form and imagery of the Georgian love lyric would be as otiose as to analyse the physical properties of a bubble. Its form is usually simple; its imagery clear and controlled. Ambrose Philips, a skilful craftsman despite his Namby-Pamby reputation, criticized his more eminent predecessors, Donne and Cowley, for what he called 'redundancy of wit'. He complained that 'the reader's attention is dazzled by the continual sparkling of their imagination'. To Ambrose Philips and his contemporaries clarity, exactness and polish were of greater consequence than imaginative power or originality. 'Wit and fine writing,' said Addison, paraphrasing Boileau, 'doth not consist so much in advancing things that are new as in giving things that are known an agreeable turn.'

The love songs in the eighteenth-century section of this book give some 'agreeable turn' to that most ancient of known experiences – the fluttering of the heart. Most of the lyrical verse of the period was dedicated to Cupid, and was concerned with the praise of Delia, Chloe, Belinda and other fair charmers in patches and hoop-petticoats. The forms and imagery of the lyrics, though restricted by polite convention (a convention, I must add, which allowed a liberal latitude in morality), were peculiarly suited to the exercise of wit. Readers coming fresh to these trifles after the passionate complexities of Donne may find them insincere. Many of them (but not all) do lack sincerity, or rather, express that qualified sincerity which is summed up in Samuel Boyce's graceful declaration:

> Then while I can I'll be sincere
> As turtles to their mates:
> This moment's yours and mine, my dear!
> The next, you know, is Fate's.

For the artificiality of the verse no apologies need be made. Of 'The Landskip', a typical lyric by that bachelor amorist, William Shenstone, the late Iolo Williams aptly wrote that 'it breathes the truest spirit of artifice, and fills us with admiration and amusement at once'. That might be said of most of the poems I have chosen to represent this period. Their artificiality is deliberate, and is among their chief merits. The expression of amorous sentiments was an elaborate game, which had to be played according to the rules. The worth of a love lyric was measured less by the depth of its feeling than by its surface smoothness and wit. If these qualities evoke amusement as readily as they command admiration, *tant mieux*. Although it was often seemly for the Georgian poet to strike an attitude of despair, this was only a move in the game. The art of love was regarded essentially as an exercise in pleasure – the pleasure of persuasion, anticipation and gratification.

Within this pleasure garden, this landskip of artifice, what a variety of sentiments, conceits and verbal felicities the poets contrived! The very self-discipline of the forms and conventions heightened their pleasure and increased their skill. 'A song loses all its lustre', wrote Ambrose Philips in his Introduction to *The Hive*, 'if it be not polished with the greatest accuracy; the smallest blemish in it, like a flaw in a jewel, takes off the whole value of it. A song is, as it were, a little image in enamel, that requires all the nice touches of the pencil, a gloss and a smoothness, with those delicate finishing strokes which would be superfluous and thrown away upon larger figures.' Not every one of the Georgian love songs in this book is a precious stone, but all have a certain gloss and smoothness, or some pencil-touch of wit and fancy.

In exploring this particular foothill of Helicon one must not look for, or expect to find, great poets. Few authors of the front rank are represented here. Collins, Fielding, Gay, Goldsmith, Cowper, Sheridan, Burns: probably that is all. One or two of the others were, perhaps, better poets than we have yet recognized. Soame Jenyns had a pretty diction and an engagingly cynical wit; I cannot understand why he has never come into vogue. His verses are as amusing and limpid in their clarity of conceit as the paintings of Arthur Devis. (How perfectly one can imagine Arthur Devis illustrating that exquisite conversation piece, 'Chloe Angling'!) Most of the other poets, however, were craftsmen of undistinguished talent who now and again rose above their mediocrity and fashioned a little gem.

Glance, for instance, at Barton Booth's 'Sweet are the charms of her I love'. Here is a poem of remarkably rich and well-ordered imagery, abounding in lines that ring memorably in the ear. Nobody would be surprised to come upon this poem in the pages of *The Oxford Book of English Verse*; yet it is one of only a few poems of merit written by an actor who published no book of verse in his lifetime.

Amongst the more conventional poems, I would draw attention to 'The Confession' by Samuel Boyce, Matthew Concanen's 'The Theft', Robert Dodsley's 'The Parting Kiss', and the songs by Joseph Thurston and Leonard Welsted. None of these authors has yet been – or ever will be – crowned with laurels, but the poems I have mentioned unite felicity of idea and deftness of expression with a success that surely claims a place in an anthology. Some of the songs I have chosen from the writings of Broome, Lyttelton and Parnell are a little more widely known, but even they have hardly yet been assured of their niche in the Georgian Assembly Room.

The anonymous poems which are scattered through the many miscellanies and song-books present tricky problems, not only of the identification of the authors but also the dating of the poems, which continued to be reprinted throughout the century. In spite of the efforts of scholars in recent years there are still poems of outstanding merit whose authorship is by no

25

means established. For instance, several of the fine lyrics in Lewis's two miscellanies of 1726 and 1730 are believed to have been written by David Lewis himself, who certainly contributed some of his own work to these collections; but I am not aware of any conclusive proof that these poems are his. I have, however, stumbled upon the authorship of another poem, 'The Fan', which is among the most accomplished lyrics of the century, and has hitherto appeared in anthologies as an anonymous work. Here it appears – for the first time, I think, since the eighteenth century – under the name of its author, Robert Lloyd, the friend of Wilkes and Charles Churchill.

I wish I could report more success in attribution. But I cannot, and there remains an interesting assembly of lyrical verse which is obstinately anonymous. One or two lyrics have a familiar ring, or an echo of a known style, but I decline to venture on suppositious ascriptions. They may many of them be 'trifles, but I feel that their emergence from scarce and long-forgotten miscellanies and song-books is one of the minor justifications of this collection. What is otherwise one of the most admirable selections of *English Love Poems* I know, that edited by Sir John Betjeman and the late Geoffrey Taylor, totally ignores this vast output of anonymous verse of the eighteenth century.

Perhaps the Georgian lover was not sufficiently profound. But he *enjoyed* love. He had his mode and his manners; and his disinclination to take himself, his audience, or his passion too seriously is a characteristic of his age – the age not only of *The Beggar's Opera* and Fanny Hill, but also of *She Stoops to Conquer* and Lord Chesterfield's letters to his (illegitimate) son. As Samuel Butler wrote:

> She that with poetry is won
> Is but a desk to write upon,
> And what men say of her they mean
> No more than on the thing they lean.

But even if the Georgian lover did not always mean what he said, his verse sounded as though he meant it, ardently, unmis-

takably, unblushingly. It was not until the last quarter of the
century, when Conscience began to rear its awkward head,
that reverend poets like Richard Graves began to counsel
prudence:

> Then would'st thou merit Waller's fame,
>   And ev'n to Pope's aspire?
> Let Reason check thy amorous flame
>   And Virtue tune thy lyre.

A surprising number of reverend poets appear in this period.
Reason, one might say, was their religion but most of them
were as eager as the fops or the beaux to prove the heat of their
amorous flames.

'How pleased we are with importunity', said Lamira in *The
Fatal Friendship*; 'that makes our own desires seem condescen-
sion.' What more can woman want? Much, maybe; but that
will come after the song is ended, when the German flute is laid
aside, and only the echoes of the harpsichord, whispering
behind panelled walls and gilded mirrors, recall the flutter of
Cupid's wings.

However, a new mood developed during the last quarter of
the eighteenth century. This arose from the discovery of
Nature and of Sentiment. The discovery of Nature could
perhaps be traced back to William Collins's 'Ode to Evening',
published in 1747, and the discovery of Sentiment to Henry
Mackenzie's novel, *The Man of Feeling*, in 1771; though Sterne –
in other respects a typical Georgian philanderer – had used the
title *A Sentimental Journey* in 1768.

The cult of Nature, encouraged by such romantic water-
colourists of the late eighteenth century as J. R. Cozens and
Francis Towne, culminated in the collaboration of Words-
worth and Coleridge in *Lyrical Ballads* in 1798. Although the
rich and aristocratic continued through the Regency period
and thereafter to follow much the same set of rules as the
Restoration Rakes, the poets began to reflect the new conven-
tions of Sensibility. Young women in long muslin dresses
draped themselves over garden urns, like Charlotte in *The*

Sorrows of Young Werther. Sex gave way to Sentiment, and love became pure, idealistic and frequently rejected or fatal.

There are poems in this collection by Cowper and the Rev. Samuel Bishop which express real sentiment, but most of the major poets of the Romantic Period – Wordsworth, Coleridge, Keats and Shelley – trained their gaze on higher, nobler and less personal objects than women. Women played a large part in Byron's life, but a surprisingly small part in his poetry.

It is not to be supposed that women had lost interest in love, but their literary tastes were now largely catered for by sentimental novels, and their 'lower natures' by lurid romances about rape in ruined abbeys by lascivious monks.

The Victorians

To this section of the book I have added the brief reign of William IV because (although the Sailor King had, in true Georgian fashion, fathered ten children on his mistress, Mrs Jordan) the year of his accession, 1830, saw the publication of the most significant volume of the love poetry that we now regard as essentially Victorian, *Sonnets from the Portuguese* by Elizabeth Barrett Browning.

The Brownings in their lives and in their verse reflect the most admirable aspects of early Victorian sexual *mores*. Elizabeth Barrett was a true romantic, her deep feelings perhaps heightened by physical illness; and she had a most sensitive command over words and rhythm. Robert was not only the quintessential Man of Feeling, but he had an intellectual grasp of poetic imagery and meaning which carries his love poems right out of their own time.

These two very fine poets, with Tennyson and Matthew Arnold, sent the Victorian era off to a magnificent start in the reflection of romantic love in verse. On different levels, at the same time, there were the simple but poignant expressions of youthful passion and lost love by the 'peasant poet', John Clare, and the drawing-room ballads of Thomas Haynes Bayly: these latter continued the tradition of love lyrics to music, this time in songs at the piano.

It was not until mid-century that the attitude of the Victorian poets to love became more equivocal and sometimes sour. To what extent this was due to the general repressiveness and double morality of the time is an interesting question. But, in comparison with the *Sonnets from the Portuguese* or *Maud* or Arnold's 'Absence', a sometimes sinister question mark seems to hang over much of the later Victorian love poetry. Coventry Patmore wrote effusively in praise of marriage but I find his *Angel in the House* (1863) unconvincing and ambiguous, lacking the spontaneity of his little early lyric 'Eros'.

Much the most significant love poem of the mid-century is, I suggest, George Meredith's sonnet sequence, *Modern Love* (1862), from which I have space for only five examples. There are passages in this which grate a little on the modern ear but it remains a marvellously perceptive and profound examination of a love that turned sour and a marriage that foundered. Here is a truly modern sensibility considering the implications of love. The Georgians and the Restoration poets would not have been able to make head or tail of it. John Donne might.

In the wake of Meredith came a host of lesser writers who were obsessed by unrequited love, infidelity and fatal attachments. Some, like Arthur O'Shaughnessy or Lord de Tabley, seem to have got involved in what we now call a love-hate relationship; other poets appeared to turn to love, like deaths in infancy or railway accidents, just because they wanted 'a good cry'. And finally, in the 'nineties, the Decadents could only find comfort in the arms of prostitutes where

> I have been faithful to thee, Cynara! in my fashion.

From these strictures on the frustrated and tearful lesser writers I exempt the earlier and much more plangent distress calls of Emily Brontë. Whether or not these reflected life or the recesses of her imagination I do not know.

It would be wrong to leave the Victorians with the impression that all of them failed to follow Blake's advice that

> . . . he who kisses the joy as it flies
> Lives in eternity's sun rise.

In the same year as Meredith was struggling with the complexities of *Modern Love*, Christina Rossetti published some love lyrics of such simplicity and pure feeling that one could not doubt that *her* heart was 'like a singing bird'. Her brother, Dante Gabriel, almost alone amongst the Victorians, made it abundantly clear, in several wonderfully eloquent lyrics, that

This hour be her sweet body all my song.

There can be no doubt of Dante Gabriel Rossetti's straightforward physical passions; but some of the most eloquent hymns to sexual love were composed by a friend of Rossetti's who apparently had curious sexual tastes and never seems to have established any satisfactory relationship with a woman, Algernon Charles Swinburne. There are, I suggest, two answers to this puzzle. The first is that Swinburne had superb poetic facility: in ideas, in his gift for words, and in his melodic genius. The other is that he – like Dowson and Arthur Symons and other poets of the 'nineties – represented the inverse side of mid-Victorian propriety – the sexual indulgence and various manifestations of 'decadence' that respectable citizens preferred to drape, like the legs of their pianos. Swinburne's peculiar 'excesses' obviously provided sufficient impulse to release his extraordinary creative gifts.

The sheer eloquence of Swinburne, his almost bardic gift for expressing passion in memorable lines and phrases, was shared by a poet who has to be regarded as a Victorian, since his most famous love poems were written in the 1880s and 1890s, but whom we still tend to think of as a modern. W. B. Yeats, of course, needs no commentary. His pellucid verses speak for themselves.

The Moderns

The erotic complications and marital complexities to which I have drawn attention in discussing the mid-Victorians are still more evident in much of the poetry of the twentieth century. Few modern poets have influenced their young contemporaries more than Thomas Hardy, and it is significant that his most beautiful love poems were written in his seventy-second year, after the death of his first wife, from whom he had been estranged.

It is by no means easy to find in twentieth-century poetry the straightforward celebration of passionate love and uninhibited sexual attraction that came so readily to the Elizabethans, the Cavaliers, and even the self-indulgent Restoration Rakes. A lyric with the unequivocal, vivid impact of Laurie Lee's 'First Love' is a rarity. There is immediacy and intensity of emotion in a remarkable poem, 'Passional', by Edmund John, but it clearly celebrates a homosexual love.

Although his personal relationships were, to say the least, stormy and complex, the fact remains that the truest and most straightforward expressions of sexual love in our day are those of D. H. Lawrence. Among the most sensitive and understanding expressions of marital love are those of that much underestimated poet, John Freeman.

I have tried to show the continuance of the alliance of words and music in our century by including the lyrics of well-known songs by Rodgers and Hart, Cole Porter, Noël Coward and Lerner and Loewe. The Cole Porter joke, 'Let's Do It', was, of course, made famous by its elaboration in performance by Noël Coward. I have printed the original version. Of the innumerable song lyrics about love in our time the most subtle, evocative and ingeniously expressed, in my opinion, are those of Eric Maschwitz, for 'These Foolish Things'.

With the poems by Harold Monro, W. H. Auden, Conrad Aiken and George Barker, the complex and often very pessimistic outlook on love and sex which is characteristic of our century is demonstrated; Dorothy Parker sums it up with devastating irony in her famous little aphorism.

It is interesting to compare – and only in a collection such as this could it be done – the wartime attitudes of Alun Lewis in the twentieth century and Richard Lovelace in the seventeenth. The poems by Louis MacNeice and John Betjeman, however, are wholly based in the social framework of our own time, as also is the vivid setting of Laurence Whistler's deeply felt poem.

If it becomes obvious that the twentieth century is no Golden Age of Love there is at least some consolation in the fact that its poets are the first (apart from the seventeenth-century Lady Dyer, and William Cowper in the eighteenth century) to recognize and put into words the old age of love and affection. It is perhaps fitting to end the selection with Ralph Hodgson's poignant 'Silver Wedding', Patrick Kavanagh's poem 'In Memory of My Mother', Philip Larkin's recognition of marital constancy, and the vivid domestic detail of F. Pratt Green's 'The Old Couple'.

1980   John Hadfield

Textual Note

To some extent the selection of poems for part of this book is based on volumes of *Georgian Love Songs*, *Restoration Love Songs* and *Elizabethan Love Songs* which I edited for publication in small limited editions in 1949, 1950 and 1955. I have quoted in the Introduction to this book some passages from the Introductions to those volumes.

I wish to express my indebtedness to the work of the late Norman Ault, whose collections of *Elizabethan Lyrics* (1925, 1949), *Seventeenth Century Lyrics* (1928, 1950) and *Treasury of Unfamiliar Lyrics* (1938) are rich sources of information to anyone attempting a selection of English lyric verse. I also express my gratitude to the late John Hayward for the stimulus and help given to me in this field not only by him personally but also by his books.

The poems here included have all been collated with their original appearance in print, or, in a few cases, with the manuscript sources. The source is given (in the original spelling) at the end of each poem. The spelling and punctuation of the poems, however, have been modernized (in which task I gratefully acknowledge the help of Penelope Miller). The titles of the poems, where given, are those to be found in the original publication, though I have omitted such purely descriptive headings as 'Song' or 'Sonnet'.

The order in which the poems are printed is the order in which they were first published or were written (if publication occurred some time later). The only exception to this is that where an author is represented by more than one poem all his poems are grouped together, following the date of the earliest one quoted.

Indexes of authors and of first lines, and some biographical notes on the authors, will be found at the end of the book.

J. H.

The
Elizabethans

Attributed to
Queen Elizabeth I

When I was fair and young and favour gracèd me,
Of many was I sought, their mistress for to be:
But I did scorn them all, and answered them therefore,
  'Go, go, go, seek some other where:
      Importune me no more.'

How many weeping eyes I made to pine with woe,
How many sighing hearts, I have no skill to show:
Yet I the prouder grew, and answered them therefore,
  'Go, go, go, seek some other where:
      Importune me no more.'

Then spake fair Venus' son, that proud victorious boy,
And said, 'Fine dame, since that you be so coy,
I will so pluck your plumes that you shall say no more,
  "Go, go, go, seek some other where:
      Importune me no more." '

When he had spake these words, such change grew in my
  breast
That neither night nor day, since that, I could take any rest:
Then lo, I did repent that I had said before,
  'Go, go, go, seek some other where:
      Importune me no more.'

Bodleian MS. Rawl. Poet. 85
(supposed to have been written *c.* 1561)

Anonymous

Fain would I have a pretty thing
  To give unto my lady:
I name no thing, nor I mean no thing,
  But as pretty a thing as may be.

Twenty journeys would I make,
    And twenty ways would hie me,
To make adventure for her sake
    To set some matter by me.
        But I would fain have a pretty thing, etc.

Some do long for pretty knacks,
    And some for strange devices:
God send me that my lady lacks,
    I care not what the price is.
        Thus fain, etc.

Some go here, and some go there,
    Where gazes be not geason*;
And I go gaping everywhere
    But still come out of season.
        Yet fain, etc.

I walk the town, and tread the street,
    In every corner seeking
The pretty thing I cannot meet
    That's for my lady's liking.
        Fain, etc.

The mercers pull me going by,
    The silk-wives say, 'What lack ye?'
'The thing you have not', then say I,
    'Ye foolish fools, go pack ye!'
        But fain, etc.

It is not all the silk in Cheape,
    Nor all the golden treasure,
Nor twenty bushels on a heap
    Can do my lady pleasure.
        But fain, etc.

The gravers of the golden shows
    With jewels do beset me:
The seamsters in the shops, that sews,
    They do no thing but let me.
        But fain, etc.

*geason] uncommon

But were it in the wit of man
   By any means to make it,
I could for money buy it then,
   And say, 'Fair lady, take it!'
     Thus fain, etc.

O lady, what a luck is this:
   That my good willing misseth
To find what pretty thing it is
   That my good lady wisheth!

Thus fain would I have had this pretty thing
   To give unto my lady:
I said no harm, nor I meant no harm,
   But as pretty a thing as may be.

    A Handefull of Pleasant Delites, 1584 (written 1566–7)

Anonymous

Love me little, love me long,
Is the burden of my song.
Love that is too hot and strong
   Burneth soon to waste:
Still I would not have thee cold,
Not too backward, nor too bold;
Love that lasteth til 'tis old
   Fadeth not in haste.
    Love me little, love me long,
    Is the burden of my song.

If thou lovest me too much,
It will not prove as true as touch;
Love me little, more than such,
   For I fear the end:
I am with little well content,
And a little from thee sent
Is enough, with true intent

To be steadfast friend.
Love me little, love me long,
Is the burden of my song.

Say thou lov'st me while thou live,
I to thee my love will give,
Never dreaming to deceive
　Whiles that life endures:
Nay, and after death, in sooth,
I to thee will keep my truth,
As now when in my May of youth;
　This my love assures.
　　Love me little, love me long,
　　Is the burden of my song.

Constant love is moderate ever,
And it will through life persèver:
Give me that, with true endeavour
　I will it restore.
A suit of durance let it be
For all weathers that for me
For the land or for the sea,
　Lasting evermore.
　　Love me little, love me long,
　　Is the burden of my song.

Winter's cold or summer's heat,
Autumn's tempests, on it beat,
It can never know defeat,
　Never can rebel:
Such the love that I would gain,
Such the love, I tell thee plain,
Thou must give, or woo in vain:
　So to thee farewell.
　　Love me little, love me long,
　　Is the burden of my song.

Extracts from the Registers of the Stationers' Company, 1848
(registered 1569–70)

George Gascoigne

The Lullaby of a Lover

Sing lullaby, as women do,
  Wherewith they bring their babes to rest,
And lullaby can I sing too,
  As womanly as can the best.
With lullaby they still the child,
And if I be not much beguiled,
Full many wanton babes have I
Which must be stilled with lullaby.

First lullaby my youthful years,
  It is now time to go to bed,
For crooked age and hoary hairs
  Have won the haven within my head.
With lullaby then, youth, be still,
With lullaby content thy will,
Since courage quails, and comes behind,
Go sleep, and so beguile thy mind.

Next lullaby my gazing eyes,
  Which wonted were to glance apace,
For every glass may now suffice
  To show the furrows in my face.
With lullaby then wink a while,
With lullaby your looks beguile:
Let no fair face, nor beauty bright,
Entice you eft with vain delight.

And lullaby my wanton will,
  Let reason's rule now reign thy thought,
Since all too late I find by skill
  How dear I have thy fancies bought.
With lullaby now take thine ease,
With lullaby thy doubts appease,
For trust to this, if thou be still,
My body shall obey thy will.

Eke lullaby my loving boy,
    My little Robin, take thy rest,
Since age is cold, and nothing coy,
    Keep close thy coin, for so is best.
With lullaby be thou content,
With lullaby thy lusts relent,
Let others pay which have more pence,
Thou art too poor for such expense.

Thus lullaby my youth, mine eyes,
    My will, my ware, and all that was,
I can no more delays devise,
    But welcome pain, let pleasure pass.
With lullaby now take your leave,
With lullaby your dreams deceive,
And when you rise with waking eye,
Remember Gascoigne's lullaby.

Ever or Never

A Hundreth Sundrie Flowres, 1572

Thomas Churchyard

*The Lover, deceived by his Lady's Inconstancy,
writeth unto her as followeth*

The heat is past that did me fret,
    The fire is out that nature wrought:
The plants of youth that I did set
    Are dry and dead within my thought:
The frost hath slain the kindly sap
    That kept the heart in lively state,
The sudden storm and thunder clap
    Hath turnëd love to mortal hate.

The mist is gone that bleared mine eyes,
   The louring clouds I see appear:
Though that the blind eat many flies,
   I would you knew my sight is clear:
Your sweet, deceiving, flattering face
   Did make me think that you were white:
I muse how you had such a grace –
   To seem a hawk, and be a kite.

Where precious ware is to be sold,
   They shall it have, that giveth most:
All things, we see, are won with gold,
   Few things is had where is no cost:
And so it fareth now by me,
   Because I press to give no gifts,
She takes my suit unthankfully,
   And drives me off with many drifts.

Is this the end of all my suit:
   For my good will, to have a scorn?
Is this of all my pains the fruit:
   To have the chaff, instead of corn?
Let them that list possess such dross,
   For I deserve a better gain:
Yet had I rather leave with loss
   Than serve and sue, and all in vain.

In *A Gorgious Gallery of Gallant Inventions*, 1578

Sir Philip Sidney

Come sleep, O sleep, the certain knot of peace,
   The bathing place of wits, the balm of woe,
The poor man's wealth, the prisoner's release,
   The indifferent judge between the high and low;

With shield of proof shield me from out the prease*
   Of those fierce darts despair at me doth throw;
O make in me those civil wars to cease;
   I will good tribute pay, if thou do so.
Take thou of me smooth pillows, sweetest bed,
   A chamber deaf to noise and blind to light,
A rosy garland and a weary head;
   And if these things (as being thine in right)
      Move not thy heavy grace, thou shalt in me,
      Livelier than elsewhere, Stella image see.

*prease] press   *Astrophel and Stella*, 1591 (written *c*.1580)

My true Love hath my heart, and I have his,
   By just exchange, one for the other given:
I hold his dear, and mine he cannot miss;
   There never was a better bargain driven.
His heart in me keeps me and him in one,
   My heart in him his thoughts and senses guides:
He loves my heart, for once it was his own;
   I cherish his because in me it bides.
His heart his wound receivëd from my sight,
   My heart was wounded, with his wounded heart;
For as from me, on him his hurt did light,
   So still methought in me his hurt did smart.
      Both, equal hurt, in this change sought our bliss:
      My true Love hath my heart, and I have his.

The Countesse of Pembroke's Arcadia, 1598 (written 1580–5)

Lock up, fair lids, the treasure of my heart:
   Preserve those beams, this age's only light:
To her sweet sense, sweet sleep, some ease impart,
   Her sense too weak to bear her spirit's might.

And while, O sleep, thou closest up her sight
  (Her sight where Love did forge his fairest dart),
O harbour all her parts in easeful plight:
  Let no strange dream make her fair body start.

But yet, O dream, if thou wilt not depart
  In this rare subject from thy common right,
  But wilt thyself in such a seat delight,
Then take my shape, and play a lover's part:
  Kiss her from me, and say unto her sprite,
  Till her eyes shine, I live in darkest night.

The Countesse of Pembroke's Arcadia, 1598 (written 1580–5)

O words, which fall like summer dew on me!
  O breath, more sweet than is the growing bean!
O tongue, in which all honeyed liquors be!
  O voice, that doth the thrush in shrillness stain!
    Do you say still this is her promise due,
    That she is mine, as I to her am true.

Gay hair, more gay than straw when harvest lies!
  Lips, red and plump, as cherry's ruddy side!
Eyes, fair and great, like fair great ox's eyes!
  O breast, in which two white sheep swell in pride!
    Join you with me, to seal this promise due,
    That she be mine, as I to her am true.

But thou white skin, as white as curds well pressed,
  So smooth as, sleekstone-like, it smooths each part!
And thou dear flesh, as soft as wool new dressed,
  And yet as hard as brawn made hard by art!
    First four but say, next four their saying seal;
    But you must pay the gage of promised weal.

The Countesse of Pembroke's Arcadia, 1598 (written 1580–5)

Anonymous

If love be like the flower that in the night,
  When darkness drowns the glory of the skies,
Smells sweet and glitters in the gazer's sight,
  But when the gladsome sun begins to rise,
    And he that views it would the same embrace,
    It withereth and loseth all his grace:

Why do I love and like the cursèd tree,
  Whose bud appears, but fruit will not be seen?
Why do I languish for the flower I see,
  Whose root is not, when all the leaves be green?
    In such a case it is a point of skill
    To follow chance, and love against my will.

*Fedele and Fortunio, or The Two Italian Gentlemen, c.*1584

Thomas Watson

Come, gentle Death! *Who calls?* One that's oppressed.
  What is thy will? That thou abridge my woe
By cutting off my life. *Cease thy request:*
  I cannot kill thee yet. Alas, why so?
    Thou want'st thy heart. Who stole the same away?
    Love, whom thou serv'st. Entreat him, if thou may.

Come, come, come, Love? *Who calleth me so oft?*
  Thy vassal true, whom thou should'st know by right.
What makes thy cry so faint? My voice is soft,
  And almost spent by wailing day and night.
    Why then, what's thy request? That thou restore
    To me my heart, and steal the same no more.

And thou, O Death, when I possess my heart,
   Dispatch me then at once. *Why so?*
By promise thou art bound to end my smart.
   Why, if thy heart return, then what's thy woe?
     That, brought from cold, it never will desire
     To rest with me, which am more hot than fire.

      The Hekatompathia or Passionate Centurie of Love, 1582

I saw the object of my pining thought
   Within a garden of sweet Nature's placing,
Wherein an arbour, artificial wrought,
   By workman's wondrous skill the garden gracing,
Did boast his glory, glory far renowned,
   For in his shady boughs my mistress slept,
And, with a garland of his branches crowned,
   Her dainty forehead from the sun ykept.
Imperious Love upon her eyelids tending,
   Playing his wanton sports at every beck,
And into every finest limb descending,
   From eyes to lips, from lips to ivory neck;
     And every limb supplied, and t' every part
     Had free accèss, but durst not touch her heart.

The Tears of Fancie, or, Love Disdained, 1593 (written before 1592)

George Peele

O gentle Love, ungentle for thy deed,
   Thou mak'st my heart
   A bloody mark
With piercing shot to bleed.

Shoot soft, sweet Love, for fear thou shoot amiss,
   For fear too keen
   Thy arrow's been,
And hit the heart where my belovèd is.

Too fair that fortune were, nor never I
    Shall be so blessed,
    Among the rest,
That Love shall seize on her by sympathy.

Then since with Love my prayers bear no boot,
    This doth remain,
    To cease my pain,
I take the wound, and die at Venus' foot.

The Araygnement of Paris, 1584

What thing is love? for, well I wot, love is a thing:
It is a prick, it is a sting,
It is a pretty, pretty thing;
It is a fire, it is a coal,
Whose flame creeps in at every hole;
And, as my wit doth best devise,
Love's dwelling is in ladies' eyes,
From whence do glance Love's piercing darts
That make such holes into our hearts;
And all the world herein accord
Love is a great and mighty lord,
And when he list to mount so high,
With Venus he in heaven doth lie,
And evermore hath been a god
Since Mars and she played even and odd.

The Hunting of Cupid, *c*.1591 (Drummond MSS, vol. vii)

Anthony Munday

Fedele's Song

I serve a mistress whiter than the snow,
    Straighter than cedar, brighter than the glass,
Finer in trip and swifter than the roe,
    More pleasant than the field of flowering grass;

More gladsome to my withering joys that fade,
Than winter's sun or summer's cooling shade.

Sweeter than swelling grape of ripest wine,
    Softer than feathers of the fairest swan,
Smoother than jet, more stately than the pine,
    Fresher than poplar, smaller than my span,
Clearer than beauty's fiery pointed beam,
Or icy crust of crystal's frozen stream.

Yet is she curster than the bear by kind,
    And harder-hearted than the aged oak,
More glib than oil, more fickle than the wind,
    Stiffer than steel, no sooner bent but broke.
Lo! thus my service is a lasting sore;
Yet will I serve, although I die therefore.

Fedele and Fortunio, 1585

Fulke Greville, Lord Brooke

You little stars that live in skies,
    And glory in Apollo's glory,
In whose aspècts conjoinëd lies
    The Heaven's will and Nature's story,
Joy to be likened to those eyes,
    Which eyes make all eyes glad or sorry:
For, when you force thoughts from above,
These overrule your force by love.

And thou, O Love, which in these eyes
    Hast married reason with affection,
And made them saints of beauty's skies,
    Where joys are shadows of perfection,
Lend me thy wings that I may rise
    Up not by worth but thy election:
For I have vowed, in strangest fashion,
To love, and never seek compassion.

Caelica, in *Certaine Learned and Elegant Workes*, 1633 (written before 1586)

Eyes, why did you bring unto me those graces,
   Graced to yield wonder out of her true measure,
Measure of all joys, stay to fancy traces,
   Module of pleasure?

Reason is now grown a disease in reason,
   Thoughts knit upon thoughts free alone to wonder;
Sense is a spy, made to do fancy treason;
   Love go I under.

Since then eyes pleasure to my thoughts betray me,
   And my thoughts reasons-level have defacëd,
So that all my powers to be hers obey me,
   Love be thou gracëd.

Gracëd by me, Love? No, by her that owes me;
   She that an angel's spirit hath retained
In Cupid's fair sky, which her beauty shows me,
   Thus have I gained.

Caelica, in *Certaine Learned and Elegant Workes*, 1633 (written before 1586)

Cynthia, whose glories are at full for ever,
   Whose beauties draw forth tears and kindle fires,
Fires which kindled once are quenchëd never,
   So beyond hope your worth bears up desires!
Why cast you clouds on your sweet-looking eyes?
   Are you afraid they show me too much pleasure?
Strong Nature decks the grave wherein it lies:
   Excellence can never be expressed in measure.
Are you afraid, because my heart adores you,
   The world will think I hold Endymion's place?
Hippolytus, sweet Cynthia, kneeled before you;
   Yet did you not come down to kiss his face?
     Angels enjoy the heavens' inward choirs;
     Star-gazers only multiply desires.

Caelica, in *Certaine Learned and Elegant Workes*, 1633 (written before 1586)

I with whose colours Myra dressed her head,
　　I that wear posies of her own hand-making
I that mine own name in the chimneys read
　　By Myra finely wrought ere I was waking –
Must I look on, in hope time coming may
With change bring back my turn again to play?

I that on Sunday at the church stile found
　　A garland sweet, with true-love knots in flowers,
Which I to wear about mine arm was bound,
　　That each of us might know that all was ours –
Must I now lead an idle life in wishes,
And follow Cupid for his loaves and fishes?

I that did wear the ring her mother left,
　　I for whose love she gloried to be blamed,
I with whose eyes her eyes committed theft,
　　I who did make her blush when I was named –
Must I lose ring, flowers, blush, theft, and go naked,
Watching with sighs till dead love be awakëd?

I that when drowsy Argus fell asleep,
　　Like jealousy o'erwatchëd with desire,
Was even warnëd modesty to keep,
　　While her breath, speaking, kindled Nature's fire –
Must I look on a-cold, while others warm them?
Do Vulcan's brothers in such fine nets arm them?

Was it for this that I might Myra see
　　Washing the water with her beauties white?
Yet would she never write her love to me.
　　Thinks wit of change, while thoughts are in delight?
Mad girls must safely love, as they may leave;
No man can print a kiss: lines may deceive.

Caelica, in *Certaine Learned and Elegant Workes*, 1633 (written before 1586)

Robert Greene

Fair is my Love, for April in her face;
  Her lovely breasts September claims his part;
And lordly Jùly in her eyes takes place;
  But cold December dwelleth in her heart:
Blessed be the months that set my thoughts on fire!
Accursed that month that hindreth my desire!

Like Phoebus' fire, so sparkle both her eyes;
  As air perfumed with amber is her breath;
Like swelling waves her lovely teats do rise;
  As earth her heart, cold, dateth me to death:
Ay me, poor man, that on the earth do live,
When unkind earth death and despair doth give!

In pomp sits mercy seated in her face;
  Love 'twixt her breasts his trophies doth imprint;
Her eyes shine favour, courtesy, and grace
  But touch her heart, ah, that is framed of flint!
That 'fore my harvest in the grass bears grain
The rock 'twill wear, washed with a winter's rain.

Perimedes the Blacke-smith, 1588

Like to Diana in her summer weed,
  Girt with a crimson robe of brightest dye,
      Goes fair Samela.

Whiter than be the flocks that straggling feed,
  When washed by Arethusa faint they lie,
      Is fair Samela.

As fair Aurora in her morning gray,
  Decked with the ruddy glister of her love,
      Is fair Samela.

Like lovely Thetis on a calmëd day,
Whenas her brightness Neptune's fancy move,
      Shines fair Samela.

Her tresses gold, her eyes like glassy streams,
Her teeth are pearl, the breasts are ivory
      Of fair Samela.

Her cheeks, like rose and lily, yield forth gleams,
Her brows, bright arches framed of ebony:
      Thus fair Samela

Passeth fair Venus in her bravest hue,
And Juno in the show of majesty –
      For she's Samela –

Pallas in wit: all three if you well view,
For beauty, wit, and matchless dignity,
      Yield to Samela.

Menaphon, 1589

John Lyly

My Daphne's hair is twisted gold,
Bright stars apiece her eyes do hold;
My Daphne's brow enthrones the Graces,
My Daphne's beauty stains all faces;
On Daphne's cheek grow rose and cherry,
On Daphne's lip a sweeter berry;
Daphne's snowy hand but touched does melt,
And then no heavenlier warmth is felt;
My Daphne's voice tunes ail the spheres,
My Daphne's music charms all ears.
Fond am I thus to sing her praise;
These glories now are turned to bays.

Midas, in *Sixe Court Comedies*, 1632 (written 1589)

Henry Constable

My lady's presence makes the roses red,
  Because to see her lips they blush for shame.
  The lily's leaves, for envy, pale became,
And her white hands in them this envy bred.
The marigold the leaves abroad doth spread,
  Because the sun's and her power is the same.
  The violet of purple colour came,
Dyed in the blood she made my heart to shed.
In brief, all flowers from her their virtue take;
  From her sweet breath their sweet smells do proceed;
The living heat which her eyebeams doth make
  Warmeth the ground, and quickeneth the seed.
    The rain, wherewith she watereth the flowers,
    Falls from mine eyes, which she dissolves in showers.

Diana, 1594 (written 1589)

Dear to my soul, then leave me not forsaken!
  Fly not! my heart within thy bosom sleepeth:
Even from my self and sense I have betaken
  Me unto thee for whom my spirit weepeth;
And on the shore of that salt teary sea,
  Couched in a bed of unseen seeming pleasure,
Where in imaginary thoughts thy fair self lay,
  But being waked, robbed of my life's best treasure,
I call the heavens, air, earth, and seas to hear
  My love, my truth, and black disdained estate;
Beating the rocks with bellowings of despair,
  Which still with plaints my words reverberate;
    Sighing, 'Alas, what shall become of me?'
    Whilst Echo cries, 'What shall become of me?'

Diana, 1594

Christopher Marlowe

The Passionate Shepherd to His Love

Come live with me, and be my Love,
And we will all the pleasures prove
That valleys, groves, hills and fields,
Woods, or steepy mountain yields.

And we will sit upon the rocks,
Seeing the shepherds feed their flocks
By shallow rivers, to whose falls
Melodious birds sing madrigals.

And I will make thee beds of roses
And a thousand fragrant posies,
A cap of flowers, and a kirtle
Embroidered all with leaves of myrtle.

A gown made of the finest wool,
Which from our pretty lambs we pull,
Fair linèd slippers for the cold,
With buckles of the purest gold.

A belt of straw and ivy buds
With coral clasps and amber studs:
And if these pleasures may thee move,
Come live with me, and be my Love.

The shepherds' swains shall dance and sing
For thy delight each May morning:
If these delights thy mind may move,
Then live with me, and be my Love.

In *Englands Helicon*, 1600 (written *c*.1589)

Thomas Lodge

Rosalynde's Description

Like to the clear in highest sphere,
   Where all imperial glory shines,
Of selfsame colour is her hair,
   Whether unfolded, or in twines:
     Heigh ho, fair Rosalynde!
Her eyes are sapphires set in snow,
   Refining heaven by every wink;
The gods do fear whenas they glow,
   And I do tremble when I think,
     Heigh ho, would she were mine!

Her cheeks are like the blushing cloud,
   That beautifies Aurora's face,
Or like the silver crimson shroud,
   That Phoebus' smiling looks doth grace:
     Heigh ho, fair Rosalynde!
Her lips are like two budded roses
   Whom ranks of lilies neighbour nigh,
Within which bounds she balm encloses,
   Apt to entice a deity:
     Heigh ho, would she were mine!

Her neck like to a stately tower,
   Where Love himself imprisoned lies,
To watch for glances every hour
   From her divine and sacred eyes:
     Heigh ho, fair Rosalynde!
Her paps are centres of delight,
   Her breasts are orbs of heavenly frame,
Where Nature moulds the dew of light
   To feed perfection with the same:
     Heigh ho, would she were mine!

With orient pearl, with ruby red,
  With marble white, with sapphire blue,
Her body every way is fed,
  Yet soft in touch and sweet in view:
    Heigh ho, fair Rosalynde!
Nature herself her shape admires;
  The gods are wounded in her sight;
And Love forsakes his heavenly fires,
  And at her eyes his brand doth light:
    Heigh ho, would she were mine!

Then muse not, Nymphs, though I bemoan
  The absence of fair Rosalynde!
Since for her fair there is fairer none,
  Nor for her virtues so divine:
    Heigh ho, fair Rosalynde;
Heigh ho, my heart! would God that she were mine!

Rosalynde, 1590

Turn I my looks unto the skies,
Love with his arrows wounds mine eyes:
If so I gaze upon the ground,
Love then in every flower is found:
Search I the shade, to fly my pain,
He meets me in the shade again:
Wend I to walk in secret grove,
Even there I meet with sacred Love:
If so I bain me in the spring,
Even on the brink I hear him sing:
If so I meditate alone,
He will be partner of my moan:
If so I mourn, he weeps with me,
And where I am, there will he be.
Whenas I talk of Rosalynde,
The god from coyness waxeth kind,
And seems in selfsame flames to fry,
Because he loves as well as I;

Sweet Rosalynde, for pity, rue!
For why than Love I am more true:
He, if he speed, will quickly fly;
But in thy love I live and die.

Rosalynde, 1590

Rosalynde's Madrigal

Love in my bosom like a bee
   Doth suck his sweet;
Now with his wings he plays with me,
   Now with his feet.
Within mine eyes he makes his nest,
His bed amidst my tender breast;
My kisses are his daily feast,
And yet he robs me of my rest:
   Ah, wanton, will ye?

And if I sleep, then percheth he
   With pretty flight,
And makes his pillow of my knee
   The livelong night.
Strike I my lute, he tunes the string;
He music plays if so I sing;
He lends me every lovely thing;
Yet cruel he my heart doth sting:
   Whist, wanton, still ye! –

Else I with roses every day
   Will whip you hence,
And bind you, when you long to play,
   For your offence.
I'll shut mine eyes to keep you in,
I'll make you fast it for your sin,
I'll count your power not worth a pin –
Alas! what hereby shall I win
   If he gainsay me?

What if I beat the wanton boy
   With many a rod?
He will repay me with annoy,
   Because a god.
Then sit thou safely on my knee,
And let thy bower my bosom be;
Lurk in mine eyes, I like of thee!
O Cupid, so thou pity me,
   Spare not, but play thee!

Rosalynde, 1590 (text from 1592 edition)

Love guards the roses of thy lips
   And flies about them like a bee;
If I approach he forward skips,
   And if I kiss he stingeth me.

Love in thine eyes doth build his bower,
   And sleeps within their pretty shine;
And if I look the boy will lour
   And from their orbs shoots shafts divine.

Love works thy heart within his fire,
   And in my tears doth firm the same;
And if I tempt it will retire,
   And of my plaints doth make a game.

Love, let me cull her choicest flowers;
   And pity me, and calm her eye;
Make soft her heart, dissolve her lours;
   Then will I praise thy deity.

But if thou do not, Love, I'll truly serve her
In spite of thee, and by firm faith deserve her.

Phillis, 1593

59

Nicholas Breton

Sweet birds, that sit and sing amid the shady valleys,
And see how sweetly Phillis walks amid her garden alleys,
Go round about her bower, and sing as ye are bidden:
To her is only known his faith that from the world is hidden.
And she among you all that hath the sweetest voice,
Go chirp of him that never told, yet never changed, his choice.

And not forget his faith that lived for ever loved,
Yet never made his fancy known, nor ever favour moved;
And ever let your ground of all your grace be this –
'To you, to you, to you the due of love and honour is,
On you, on you, on you our music all attendeth,
For as on you our Muse begun, in you all music endeth.'

Brittons Bowre of Delights, 1591

I would thou wert not fair, or I were wise;
I would thou hadst no face, or I no eyes;
I would thou wert not wise, or I not fond;
Or thou not free, or I not so in bond.

But thou art fair, and I cannot be wise:
Thy sun-like face hath blinded both mine eyes;
Thou canst not but be wise, nor I but fond;
Nor thou but free, nor I but still in bond.

Yet am I wise to think that thou art fair;
Mine eyes their pureness in thy face repair;
Nor am I fond, that do thy wisdom see;
Nor yet in bond, because that thou art free.

Then in thy beauty only make me wise;
And in thy face the Graces guide mine eyes;
And in thy wisdom only see me fond;
And in thy freedom keep me still in bond.

So shalt thou still be fair, and I be wise;
Thy face shine still upon my clearëd eyes;
Thy wisdom only see how I am fond;
Thy freedom only keep me still in bond.

So would I thou wert fair, and I were wise;
So would thou hadst thy face, and I mine eyes;
So would I thou wert wise, and I were fond,
And thou wert free and I were still in bond.

In *The Strange Fortunes of Two Excellent Princes*, 1600

Samuel Daniel

My spotless love hovers with white wings
   About the temple of the proudest frame,
Where blaze those lights, fairest of earthly things,
   Which clear our clouded world with brightest flame.
My ambitious thoughts, confinëd in her face,
   Affect no honour but what she can give me:
My hopes do rest in limits of her grace;
   I weigh no comfort unless she relieve me.
For she that can my heart imparadise
   Holds in her fairest hand what dearest is;
My fortune's wheel the circle of her eyes,
   Whose rolling grace deign once a turn of bliss.
     All my life's sweet consists in her alone,
     So much I love the most unloving one.

Delia, 1592

Fair is my Love, and cruel as she's fair;
   Her brow shades frowns, although her eyes are sunny:
Her smiles are lightning, though her pride despair,
   And her disdains are gall, her favours honey.
A modest maid, decked with a blush of honour,
   Whose feet do tread green paths of youth and love;
The wonder of all eyes that look upon her,
   Sacred on earth, designed a saint above.
Chastity and beauty, which were deadly foes,
   Live reconcilëd friends within her brow;
And had she pity to conjoin with those,
    Then who had heard the plaints I utter now?
      For had she not been fair, and thus unkind,
      My Muse had slept, and none had known my mind.

Delia,1592

Ah, I remember well – and how can I
But ever more remember well – when first
Our flame began, when scarce we knew what was
The flame we felt; when as we sat and sighed,
And looked upon each other, and conceived
Not what we ailed, yet something we did ail,
And yet were well, and yet we were not well,
And what was our disease we could not tell.
Then would we kiss, then sigh, then look: and thus
In that first garden of our simpleness
We spent our childhood: but when years began
To reap the fruit of knowledge, ah, how then
Would she with graver looks, with sweet stern brow,
Check my presumption and my forwardness;
Yet still would give me flowers, still would me shew
What she would have me, yet not have me, know.

Hymen's Triumph, 1615

Giles Fletcher

In time the strong and stately turrets fall,
  In time the rose and silver lilies die,
In time the monarchs captives are, and thrall,
  In time the sea and rivers are made dry;
The hardest flint in time doth melt asunder;
  Still living fame in time doth fade away;
The mountains proud we see in time come under;
  And earth, for age, we see in time decay.
The sun in time forgets for to retire
  From out the east where he was wont to rise;
The basest thoughts we see in time aspire,
  And greedy minds in time do wealth despise.
    Thus all, sweet Fair, in time must have an end,
    Except thy beauty, virtues, and thy friend.

Licia, or Poemes of Love, 1593

My Love was masked, and armëd with a fan,
  To see the sun so careless of his light;
Which stood and gazed, and, gazing, waxëd wan,
  To see a star himself that was more bright.
Some did surmise she hid her from the sun,
  Of whom in pride she scorned for to be kissed,
Or feared the harm by him to others done;
  But these the reason of this wonder missed:
Nor durst the sun, if that her face were bare,
  In greatest pride presume to take a kiss;
But she, more kind, did show she had more care
  Than with her eyes eclipse him of his bliss.
    Unmask you (sweet) and spare not dim the sun:
    Your light's enough, although that his were done.

Licia, or Poemes of Love, 1593

Barnabe Barnes

Soft, lovely, rose-like lips, conjoined with mine,
   Breathing out precious incense such,
Such as, at Paphos, smokes to Venus' shrine,
   Making my lips immortal with their touch,
My cheeks, with touch of thy soft cheeks divine,
   Thy soft warm cheeks which Venus favours much;
Those arms, such arms, which me embraced,
   Me with immortal cincture girding round,
   Of everlasting bliss, then bound
With her enfolded thighs in mine entangled,
And both in one self-soul placed,
   Made a hermaphrodite with pleasure ravished.
There heat for heat's, soul for soul's empire wrangled;
   Why died not I with love so largely lavished?
     For waked (not finding truth of dreams before)
     Its secret vexeth ten times more.

Parthenophil and Parthenophe, 1593

Anonymous

Those eyes which set my fancy on a fire,
   Those crispèd hairs which hold my heart in chains,
Those dainty hands which conquered my desire,
   That wit which of my thoughts doth hold the reins!
Those eyes for clearness do the stars surpass;
   Those hairs obscure the brightness of the sun;
Those hands more white than ever ivory was;
   That wit even to the skies hath glory won.
O eyes that pierce our hearts without remorse,
   O hairs of right that wear a royal crown,
O hands that conquer more than Caesar's force,
   O wit that turns huge kingdoms upside down!
     Then Love be judge, what heart may thee withstand,
     Such eyes, such hair, such wit, and such a hand.

In *The Phoenix Nest*, 1593

Edward de Vere, Earl of Oxford

What cunning can express
  The favour of her face,
To whom in this distress
  I do appeal for grace?
    A thousand Cupids fly
    About her gentle eye,

From whence each throws a dart
  That kindleth soft sweet fire
Within my sighing heart,
  Possessèd by desire:
    No sweeter life I try
    Than in her love to die.

The lily in the field,
  That glories in his white,
For pureness now must yield
  And render up his right:
    Heaven pictured in her face
    Doth promise joy and grace.

Fair Cynthia's silver light,
  That beats on running streams,
Compares not with her white,
  Whose hairs are all sunbeams:
    Her virtues so do shine
    As day unto mine eyne.

With this there is a red
  Exceeds the damask rose,
Which in her cheeks is spread,
  Whence every favour grows:
    In sky there is no star
    That she surmounts not, far.

When Phoebus from the bed
　　Of Thetis doth arise,
The morning blushing red
　　In fair carnation wise,
　　　　He shows it in her face
　　　　As queen of every grace.

This pleasant lily white,
　　This taint of roseate red,
This Cynthia's silver light,
　　This sweet fair Dea spread,
　　　　These sunbeams in mine eye,
　　　　These beauties make me die.

In *The Phoenix Nest*, 1593

Sir Walter Raleigh
A Description of Love

Now what is love, I pray thee tell?
It is that fountain and that well
Where pleasure and repentance dwell.
It is perhaps that sauncing bell
That tolls all in to heaven or hell:
And this is love, as I hear tell.

Yet what is love, I pray thee say?
It is a work on holy day.
It is December matched with May,
When lusty bloods in fresh array
Hear ten months after of the play:
And this is love, as I hear say.

Yet what is love, I pray thee sain?
It is a sunshine mixed with rain.
It is a tooth-ache or like pain;
It is a game where none doth gain;
The lass saith No, and would full fain:
And this is love, as I hear sain.

Yet what is love, I pray thee say?
It is a yea, it is a nay,
A pretty kind of sporting fray;
It is a thing will soon away;
Then take the vantage while you may:
And this is love, as I hear say.

Yet what is love, I pray thee show?
A thing that creeps, it cannot go;
A prize that passeth to and fro;
A thing for one, a thing for mo;
And he that proves must find it so:
And this is love, sweet friend, I trow.

In *The Phoenix Nest*, 1593

As you came from the holy land
  Of Walsingham,
Met you not with my true Love
  By the way as you came?

'How shall I know your true Love,
  That have met many one,
As I went to the holy land,
  That have come, that have gone?'

She is neither white nor brown,
  But as the heavens fair;
There is none hath a form so divine
  In the earth or the air.

'Such an one did I meet, good sir,
    Such an angelic face,
Who like a queen, like a nymph, did appear
    By her gate, by her grace.'

She hath left me here all alone,
    All alone, as unknown,
Who sometimes did me lead with her self,
    And me loved as her own.

'What's the cause that she leaves you alone,
    And a new way doth take,
Who loved you once as her own,
    And her joy did you make?'

I have loved her all my youth;
    But now old, as you see,
Love likes not the falling fruit
    From the withered tree.

Know that Love is a careless child,
    And forgets promise past;
He is blind, he is deaf when he list,
    And in faith never fast.

His desire is a dureless content,
    And a trustless joy:
He is won with a world of despair,
    And is lost with a toy.

Of womenkind such indeed is the love,
    Or the word love abused,
Under which many childish desires
    And conceits are excused.

But love is a durable fire,
    In the mind ever burning,
Never sick, never old, never dead,
    From itself never turning.

Bodleian MS. Rawl. Poet. 85 (written before 1600: part of the
second stanza is quoted in *Hamlet*)

Sir Walter Raleigh

The Nymph's Reply to the Shepherd
[A rejoinder to Marlowe]

If all the world and love were young,
And truth in every shepherd's tongue,
These pretty pleasures might me move
To live with thee, and be thy love.

Time drives the flocks from field to fold,
When rivers rage and rocks grow cold;
And Philomel becometh dumb;
The rest complain of cares to come.

The flowers do fade, and wanton fields
To wayward winter reckoning yields:
A honey tongue, a heart of gall,
Is fancy's spring, but sorrow's fall.

Thy gowns, thy shoes, thy beds of roses,
Thy cap, thy kirtle, and thy posies
Soon break, soon wither, soon forgotten,
In folly ripe, in reason rotten.

Thy belt of straw and ivy buds,
Thy coral clasps and amber studs,
All these in me no means can move
To come to thee, and be thy love.

But could youth last, and love still breed,
Had joys no date, nor age no need,
Then these delights my mind might move
To live with thee, and be thy love.

In *Englands Helicon*, 1600

Michael Drayton

The glorious sun went blushing to his bed
   When my soul's sun from her fair cabinet
Her golden beams had now discoverëd,
   Lightening the world eclipsëd by his set.
Some mused to see the earth envy the air,
   Which from her lips exhaled refinëd sweet,
A world to see, yet how he joyed to hear
   The dainty grass make music with her feet.
But my most marvel was when from the skies
   So comet-like each star advanced her light,
As though the heaven had now awaked her eyes,
   And summoned angels to this blessed sight.
      No cloud was seen, but crystalline the air,
      Laughing for joy upon my lovely Fair.

Ideas Mirrour, 1594

My Fair, look from those turrets of thine eyes
   Into the ocean of a troubled mind,
Where my poor soul, the barque of sorrow, lies,
   Left to the mercy of the waves and wind.
See where she floats, laden with purest love,
   Which those fair islands of thy looks afford,
Desiring yet a thousand deaths to prove,
   Than so to cast her ballast overboard.
See how her sails be rent, her tacklings worn,
   Her cable broke, her surest anchor lost;
Her mariners do leave her all forlorn,
   Yet how she bends towards that blessed coast.
      Lo! where she drowns in storms of thy displeasure,
      Whose worthy prize should have enriched thy treasure.

Ideas Mirrour, 1594

To His Coy Love: a Canzonet

I pray thee leave, love me no more,
  Call home the heart you gave me!
I but in vain that Saint adore
  That can but will not save me.
These poor half-kisses kill me quite;
  Was ever man thus servëd,
Amidst an ocean of delight
  For pleasure to be starvëd?

Show me no more those snowy breasts
  With azure riverets branchëd,
Where, whilst mine eye with plenty feasts,
  Yet is my thirst not stanchëd.
O Tantalus, thy pains ne'er tell!
  By me thou art prevented:
'Tis nothing to be plagued in Hell,
  But thus in Heaven tormented!

Clip me no more in those dear arms,
  Nor thy life's comfort call me!
O these are but too powerful charms,
  And do but more enthral me.
But see, how patient I am grown
  In all this coil about thee!
Come, nice thing, let thy heart alone!
  I cannot live without thee.

Odes, with Other Lyric Poesies, 1619

Edmund Spenser

Coming to kiss her lips (such grace I found)
   Meseemed I smelt a garden of sweet flowers,
That dainty odours from them threw around
   For damsels fit to deck their lovers' bowers.
Her lips did smell like unto gillyflowers,
   Her ruddy cheeks like unto roses red,
Her snowy brows like budded belamours,
   Her lovely eyes like pinks but newly spread;
Her goodly bosom like a strawberry bed,
   Her neck like to a bunch of columbines,
Her breast like lilies ere their leaves be shed,
   Her nipples like young blossomed jessamines.
      Such fragrant flowers do give most odorous smell;
      But her sweet odour did them all excel.

Amoretti and Epithalamion, 1595

One day I wrote her name upon the strand,
   But came the waves and washëd it away:
Again I wrote it with a second hand,
   But came the tide, and made my pains his prey.
'Vain man', said she, 'that dost in vain essay
   A mortal thing so to immortalize,
For I myself shall like to this decay,
   And eke my name be wipëd out likewise.'
'Not so,' quoth I, 'let baser things devise
   To die in dust, but you shall live by fame;
My verse your virtues rare shall eternize,
   And in the heavens write your glorious name,
      Where, whenas death shall all the world subdue,
      Our love shall live, and later life renew.'

Amoretti and Epithalamion, 1595

Fair bosom, fraught with virtue's richest treasure,
  The nest of love, the lodging of delight,
The bower of bliss, the paradise of pleasure,
  The sacred harbour of that heavenly sprite!
How was I ravished with your lovely sight,
  And my frail thoughts too rashly led astray,
Whiles, diving deep through amorous insight,
  On the sweet spoil of beauty they did prey,
And 'twixt her paps, like early fruit in May
  Whose harvest seemed to hasten now apace,
They loosely did their wanton wings display,
  And there to rest themselves did boldly place.
    Sweet thoughts, I envy your so happy rest,
    Which oft I wished, yet never was so blessed.

Amoretti and Epithalamion, 1595

William Shakespeare

So sweet a kiss the golden sun gives not
  To those fresh morning drops upon the rose,
As thy eye-beams, when their fresh rays have smote
  The night of dew that on my cheeks down flows:
Nor shines the silver moon one half so bright
  Through the transparent bosom of the deep,
As doth thy face through tears of mine give light:
  Thou shin'st in every tear that I do weep;
No drop but as a coach doth carry thee,
  So ridest thou, triumphing in my woe:
Do but behold the tears that swell in me,
  As they thy glory through my grief will show:
But do not love thyself; then thou wilt keep
My tears for glasses, and still make me weep.
    O Queen of queens! how far dost thou excel,
    No thought can think, nor tongue of mortal tell.

Loves Labors Lost, 1598 (written 1594–5)

73

Who is Silvia? What is she,
　　That all our swains commend her?
Holy, fair, and wise is she;
　　The heaven such grace did lend her,
That she might admirëd be.

Is she kind as she is fair?
　　For beauty lives with kindness.
Love doth to her eyes repair,
　　To help him of his blindness;
And, being helped, inhabits there.

Then to Silvia let us sing,
　　That Silvia is excelling;
She excels each mortal thing,
　　Upon the dull earth dwelling:
To her let us garlands bring.

The Two Gentlemen of Verona, 1623 (written 1594–5)

O mistress mine, where are you roaming?
O stay and hear! your true Love's coming,
　　That can sing both high and low:
Trip no further, pretty sweeting;
Journeys end in lovers' meeting,
　　Every wise man's son doth know.

What is love? 'tis not hereafter;
Present mirth hath present laughter;
　　What's to come is still unsure:
In delay there lies no plenty:
Then come kiss me, sweet-and-twenty,
　　Youth's a stuff will not endure.

Twelfth Night, 1623 (written 1599–1600)

Shall I compare thee to a summer's day?
  Thou art more lovely and more temperate:
Rough winds do shake the darling buds of May,
  And summer's lease hath all too short a date:
Sometime too hot the eye of heaven shines,
  And often is his gold complexion dimmed;
And every fair from fair sometime declines,
  By chance or nature's changing course untrimmed;
But thy eternal summer shall not fade,
  Nor lose possession of that fair thou owest,
Nor shall death brag thou wand'rest in his shade,
  When in eternal lines to time thou growest;
    So long as men can breathe, or eyes can see,
    So long lives this, and this gives life to thee.

Shake-speares Sonnets, 1609 (written before 1600)

Farewell! thou art too dear for my possessing,
  And like enough thou know'st thy estimate:
The charter of thy worth gives thee releasing;
  My bonds in thee are all determinate.
For how do I hold thee but by thy granting?
  And for that riches where is my deserving?
The cause of this fair gift in me is wanting,
  And so my patent back again is swerving.
Thyself thou gav'st, thy own worth then not knowing,
  Or me, to whom thou gav'st it, else mistaking;
So thy great gift, upon misprision growing,
  Comes home again, on better judgment making.
    Thus have I had thee, as a dream doth flatter,
    In sleep a king, but, waking, no such matter.

Shake-speares Sonnets, 1609 (written before 1600)

Let me not to the marriage of true minds
  Admit impediments: love is not love
Which alters when it alteration finds,
  Or bends with the remover to remove.
O no! it is an ever-fixèd mark,
  That looks on tempests and is never shaken;
It is the star to every wandering barque,
  Whose worth's unknown, although his height be taken.
Love's not Time's fool, though rosy lips and cheeks
  Within his bending sickle's compass come;
Love alters not with his brief hours and weeks,
  But bears it out even to the edge of doom.
    If this be error, and upon me proved,
    I never writ, nor no man ever loved.

Shake-speares Sonnets, 1609 (written before 1600)

Thine eyes I love, and they, as pitying me,
  Knowing thy heart torments me with disdain,
Have put on black, and loving mourners be,
  Looking with pretty ruth upon my pain.
And truly not the morning sun of heaven
  Better becomes the grey cheeks of the East,
Nor that full star that ushers in the even,
  Doth half that glory to the sober West,
As those two mourning eyes become thy face:
  O let it then as well beseem thy heart
To mourn for me, since mourning doth thee grace,
  And suit thy pity like in every part.
    Then will I swear beauty herself is black,
    And all they foul that thy complexion lack.

Shake-speares Sonnets, 1609 (written before 1600)

How oft, when thou, my music, music play'st
  Upon that blessed wood whose motion sounds,
With thy sweet fingers when thou gently sway'st
  The wiry concord that mine ear confounds,
Do I envy those jacks that nimble leap
  To kiss the tender inward of thy hand;
Whilst my poor lips, which should that harvest reap,
  At the wood's boldness by thee blushing stand:
To be so tickled, they would change their state
  And situation with those dancing chips,
Oer whom thy fingers walk with gentle gait,
  Making dead wood more blessed than living lips.
    Since saucy jacks so happy are in this,
    Give them thy fingers, me thy lips, to kiss.

Shake-speares Sonnets, 1609 (written before 1600)

Come away, come away, death,
  And in sad cypress let me be laid;
Fly away, fly away, breath;
  I am slain by a fair cruel maid.
My shroud of white, stuck all with yew,
  O prepare it!
My part of death, no one so true
  Did share it.

Not a flower, not a flower sweet,
  On my black coffin let there be strewn;
Not a friend, not a friend greet
  My poor corpse, where my bones shall be thrown:
A thousand thousand sighs to save,
  Lay me, O! where
Sad true lover never find my grave,
  To weep there.

Twelfth Night, 1623 (written 1599–1600)

Take, O take, those lips away,
  That so sweetly were forsworn;
And those eyes, the break of day,
  Lights that do mislead the morn:
But my kisses bring again
Bring again:
Seals of love but sealed in vain,
– Sealed in vain!

Measure for Measure, 1623 (written 1604)

Bartholomew Griffin

Fair is my Love that feeds among the lilies,
  The lilies growing in that pleasant garden
Where Cupid's Mount that well-belovëd hill is,
  And where that little god himself is warden.
See where my Love sits in the beds of spices,
  Beset all round with camphor, myrrh and roses,
And interlaced with curious devices
  Which her from all the world apart encloses!
There doth she tune her lute for her delight,
  And with sweet music makes the ground to move,
Whilst I, poor I, do sit in heavy plight,
  Wailing alone my unrespected love:
    Not daring rush into so rare a place,
    That gives to her, and she to it, a grace.

Fidessa, 1596

Sir John Davies

From *Orchestra, a Poem of Dancing*

What makes the vine about the elm to dance
  With turnings, windings, and embracements round?
What makes the lodestone to the North advance
  His subtle point, as if from thence he found
  His chief attractive virtue to redound?
Kind nature first doth cause all things to love;
Love makes them dance, and in just order move.

. . .

Thus when at first Love had them marshallèd,
  As erst he did the shapeless mass of things,
He taught them rounds and winding *hays* to tread,
  And about trees to cast themselves in rings;
  As the two Bears, whom the first mover flings
With a short turn about heaven's axle-tree,
In a round dance for ever wheeling be.

. . .

Thus Love taught men, and men thus learned of Love
  Sweet music's sound with feet to counterfeit;
Which was long time before high-thundering Jove
  Was lifted up to heaven's imperial seat;
  For though by birth he were the prince of Crete
Nor Crete nor heaven should that young prince have seen
If dancers with their timbrels had not been.

. . .

This is true Love, by that true Cupid got,
  Which danceth galliards in your amorous eyes,
But to your frozen heart approacheth not;
  Only your heart he dares not enterprize;
  And yet through every other part he flies,
And everywhere he nimbly danceth now,
That in yourself, yourself perceive not how.

For your sweet beauty, daintily transfused
  With due proportion throughout every part,
What is it but a dance where Love hath used
  His finer cunning and more curious art;
  Where all the elements themselves impart,
And turn, and wind, and mingle with such measure,
That th' eye that sees it, surfeits with the pleasure?

Love in the twinkling of your eyelids danceth;
  Love danceth in your pulses, and your veins;
Love, when you sew, your needle's point advanceth,
  And makes it dance a thousand curious strains
  Of winding rounds, whereof the form remains,
To show that your fair hands can dance the *hay*,
Which your fine feet would learn as well as they.

And when your ivory fingers touch the strings
  Of any silver-sounding instrument,
Love makes them dance to those sweet murmurings,
  With busy skill and cunning excellent.
  Oh, that your feet those tunes would represent
With artificial motions to and fro,
That Love, this art in every part might show!

Orchestra, or a Poem of Dancing, 1596

Robert Tofte

As burnished gold, such are my Sovereign's hairs;
  A brace of stars divine her blackish eyes,
Like to the fairest black the raven bears,
  Or fairer, if you fairer can devise;
So likewise fair's the beauty of her breasts,
Where pleasure lurks, where joy still dallying rests.

This Venus' bower you rightly may compare
  To whitest snow that ere from heaven fell,
Or to the mines of alabaster fair.
  Woe's me, 'tis sweet to sleep in Cupid's cell,
Whilst he the heart makes surfeit with delight
Through golden hair, black eyes, and breast most white.

Laura, 1597

Anonymous

Dear, if you change, I'll never choose again:
  Sweet, if you shrink, I'll never think of love;
Fair, if you fail, I'll judge all beauty vain;
  Wise, if too weak, moe wits I'll never prove.
Dear, sweet, fair, wise, change, shrink, nor be not weak;
And, on my faith, my faith shall never break.

Earth with her flowers shall sooner heaven adorn;
  Heaven her bright stars through earth's dim globe shall
    move.
Fire, heat shall lose; and frosts of flames be born;
  Air, made to shine, as black as hell shall prove.
Earth, heaven, fire, air, the world transformed shall view,
Ere I prove false to faith, or strange to you.

In John Dowland's First Booke of Songes or Ayres, 1597

Anonymous

Sleep, wayward thoughts, and rest you with my love:
  Let not my Love be with my love displeased.
Touch not, proud hands, lest you her anger move,
  But pine you with my longings long diseased.
Thus, while she sleeps, I sorrow for her sake:
So sleeps my Love, and yet my love doth wake.

But O the fury of my restless fear!
  The hidden anguish of my flesh desires!
The glories and the beauties that appear
  Between her brows, near Cupid's closèd fires!
Thus, while she sleeps, moves sighing for her sake:
So sleeps my Love, and yet my love doth wake.

My love doth rage, and yet my Love doth rest:
  Fear in my love, and yet my Love secure;
Peace in my Love, and yet my love oppressed,
  Impatient yet of perfect temperature.
Sleep, dainty Love, while I sigh for thy sake:
So sleeps my Love, and yet my love doth wake.

In John Dowland's First Booke of Songes or Ayres, 1597

Anonymous

Come away, come, sweet Love!
  The golden morning breaks;
All the earth, all the air,
  Of love and pleasure speaks.
Teach thine arms then to embrace,
  And sweet rosy lips to kiss,
  And mix our souls in mutual bliss.
Eyes were made for beauty's grace,
  Viewing, rueing, love's long pain,
  Procured by beauty's rude disdain.

Come away, come, sweet Love!
  The golden morning wastes
While the sun, from his sphere,
  His fiery arrows casts,
Making all the shadows fly,
  Playing, staying in the grove,
  To entertain the stealth of love.
Thither, sweet Love, let us hie,
  Flying, dying in desire,
  Winged with sweet hopes and heavenly fire.

Come away, come, sweet Love!
  Do not in vain adorn
Beauty's grace, that should rise
  Like to the naked morn.
Lilies on the river's side.
  And fair Cyprian flowers new-blown,
  Desire no beauties but their own:
Ornament is nurse of pride.
  Pleasure measure love's delight
  Haste then, sweet Love, our wishëd flight!

In John Dowland's *First Booke of Songes or Ayres*, 1597

George Chapman

Epithalamion Teratos

Come, come, dear Night! Love's mart of kisses,
  Sweet close of his ambitious line,
The fruitful summer of his blisses,
  Love's glory doth in darkness shine.

O come, soft rest of cares! come, Night!
  Come naked virtue's only tire,
The reapëd harvest of the light
  Bound up in sheaves of sacred fire.

      Love calls to war;
        Sighs his alarms,
      Lips his swords are,
        The field his arms.

Come, Night, and lay thy velvet hand
  On glorious Day's outfacing face;
And all thy crownëd flames command
  For torches to our nuptial grace.

Love calls to war;
  Sighs his alarms,
Lips his swords are,
  The field his arms.

No need have we of factious Day,
  To cast, in envy of thy peace,
Her balls of discord in thy way:
  Here beauty's day doth never cease.
    Day is abstracted here,
    And varied in a triple sphere,
Hero, Alcmane, Mya, so outshine thee,
Ere thou come here, let Thetis thrice refine thee.

Love calls to war;
  Sighs his alarms,
Lips his swords are,
  The field his arms.

Hero and Leander, 1598

Anonymous

Lady, the silly flea, of all disdained
Because it hath complained,
I pity that poor creature,
Both black and small of stature:
Were I a flea in bed, I would not bite you,
But search some other way for to delight you.

In Giles Farnaby's *Canzonets to Foure Voyces*, 1598

Sir Edward Dyer

The lowest trees have tops, the ant her gall,
  The fly her spleen, the little sparks their heat:
And slender hairs cast shadows, though but small,
  And bees have stings, although they be not great;
    Seas have their source, and so have shallow springs:
    And love is love, in beggars and in kings.

Where waters smoothest run, there deepest are the floods;
  The dial stirs, yet none perceives it move;
The firmest faith is found in fewest words;
  The turtles do not sing, and yet they love.
    True hearts have ears and eyes, no tongues to speak;
    They hear and see and sigh, and then they break.

Bodleian MS. Rawl. Poet. 148, dated 1598 (a slightly different version
was printed in *A Poetical Rapsody*, 1602)

John Lilliat

When love on time and measure makes his ground,
  Time that must end, though love can never die,
'Tis love betwixt a shadow and a sound,
  A love not in the heart but in the eye;
A love that ebbs and flows, now up, now down,
A morning's favour, and an evening's frown.

Sweet looks show love, yet they are but as beams;
  Fair words seem true, yet they are but as wind:
Eyes shed their tears, yet are but outward streams;
  Sighs paint a sadness in the falsest mind.
Looks, words, tears, sighs, show love when love they leave;
False hearts can weep, sigh, swear, and yet deceive.

In Robert Jones's *First Booke of Songes and Ayres*, 1600

Anonymous

Farewell, dear Love, since thou wilt needs be gone:
Mine eyes do show my life is almost done.
        Nay, I will never die
        So long as I can spy;
        There be many moe
        Though that she do go:
  There be many moe, I fear not.
Why then, let her go, I care not.

Farewell, farewell, since this I find is true,
I will not spend more time in wooing you.
        But I will seek elsewhere
        If I may find her there.
        Shall I bid her go?
        What and if I do?
  Shall I bid her go and spare not?
O, no, no, no, no, I dare not.

Ten thousand times farewell! Yet stay a while,
Sweet, kiss me once; sweet kisses time beguile.
        I have no power to move:
        How now, am I in love?
        Wilt thou needs be gone?
        Go then, all is one.
  Wilt thou needs be gone? O hie thee!
Nay; stay, and do no more deny me.

Once more farewell! I see 'Loath to depart'
Bids oft adieu to her that holds my heart.
        But, seeing I must lose
        Thy love which I did choose,
        Go thy ways for me,
        Since it may not be.
  Go thy ways for me: but whither?
Go, oh but where I may come thither.

What shall I do? My Love is now departed.
She is as fair as she is cruel hearted.

She would not be entreated
With prayers oft repeated.
If she come no more
Shall I die therefore?

If she come no more, what care I?
Faith, let her go, or come, or tarry.

In Robert Jones's *First Booke of Songes and Ayres*, 1600

John Donne

The Bait

Come live with me, and be my Love,
And we will some new pleasures prove,
Of golden sands and crystal brooks,
With silken lines and silver hooks.

There will the river whispering run
Warmed by thy eyes more than the sun.
And there the enamoured fish will stay,
Begging themselves they may betray.

When thou wilt swim in that live bath,
Each fish which every channel hath
Will amorously to thee swim,
Gladder to catch thee, than thou him.

If thou to be so seen beest loath
By sun or moon, thou darkenest both,
And if myself have leave to see,
I need not their light, having thee.

Let others freeze with angling reeds,
And cut their legs with shells and weeds,
Or treacherously poor fish beset
With strangling snare or windowy net.

Let coarse bold hands from slimy nest
The bedded fish in banks out-wrest,
Or curious traitors, sleave-silk flies,
Bewitch poor fishes' wandering eyes.

For thee, thou needst no such deceit,
For thou thyself art thine own bait;
That fish that is not catched thereby,
Alas, is wiser far than I.

Poems, 1633 (written *c*. 1600)

The Sun Rising

Busy old fool, unruly Sun,
    Why dost thou thus,
    Through windows, and through curtains, call on us?
Must to thy motions lovers' seasons run?
    Saucy, pedantic wretch, go chide
Late schoolboys and sour prentices;
    Go tell Court huntsmen that the King will ride;
Call country ants to harvest offices.
    Love, all alike, no season knows, nor clime,
    Nor hours, days, months, which are the rags of time.

Thy beams so reverend, and strong,
    Why should'st thou think?
    I could eclipse and cloud them with a wink,
But that I would not lose her sight so long:
    If her eyes have not blinded thine
Look, and tomorrow late, tell me
    Whether both the Indias of spice and mine
Be where thou left them, or lie here with me.
    Ask for those kings whom thou sawst yesterday,
    And thou shalt hear, All here in one bed lay.

She is all states, and all princes I;
   Nothing else is.
Princes do but play us; compared to this
All honour's mimic, all wealth alchemy.
   Thou Sun art half as happy as we,
In that the world's contracted thus;
   Thine age asks ease, and since thy duties be
To warm the world, that's done in warming us.
   Shine here to us, and thou art everywhere;
   This bed thy centre is, these walls thy sphere.

Poems, 1633 (written *c*.1600)

The Good-Morrow

I wonder, by my troth, what thou and I
   Did, till we loved? Were we not weaned till then?
But sucked on country pleasures, childishly?
   Or snorted we in the Seven Sleepers' den?
'Twas so: but this, all pleasures fancies be;
If ever any beauty I did see,
Which I desired, and got, 'twas but a dream of thee.

And now good-morrow to our waking souls,
   Which watch not one another out of fear;
For love all love of other sights controls,
   And makes one little room an everywhere.
Let sea-discoverers to new worlds have gone;
Let maps to other, worlds on worlds have shown;
Let us possess one world; each hath one, and is one.

My face in thine eye, thine in mine appears,
   And true plain hearts do in the faces rest;
Where can we find two better hemispheres
   Without sharp North, without declining West;
Whatever dies, was not mixed equally;
If our two loves be one, or thou and I
Love so alike that none do slacken, none can die.

Poems, 1633 (written *c*.1600)

Going to Bed

Come, Madam, come, all rest my powers defy;
Until I labour, I in labour lie,
The foe oft-times having the foe in sight,
Is tired with standing, though he never fight.
Off with that girdle, like heaven's zone glittering,
But a far fairer world encompassing.
Unpin that spangled breast-plate, which you wear
That th'eyes of busy fools may be stopped there.
Unlace yourself, for that harmonious chime
Tells me from you that now it is bed-time.
Off with that happy busk, which I envy,
That still can be, and still can stand so nigh.
Your gown, going off, such beauteous state reveals,
As when through flowery meads th'hill's shadow steals.
Off with that wiry coronet, and show
The hairy diadem which on you doth grow.
Now off with those shoes; and then softly tread
In this, love's hallow'd temple, this soft bed,
In such white robes heaven's angels used to be
Revealed to men; thou, angel, bring'st with thee
A heaven like Mahomet's paradise; and though
Ill spirits walk in white, we easily know
By this these angels from an evil sprite;
Those set our hairs, but these our flesh, upright.
　　Licence my roving hands, and let them go
Before, behind, between, above, below.
Oh, my America, my new-found-land!
My kingdom, safest when with one man manned!
My mine of precious stones! My empery!
How blest am I in thus discovering thee!
To enter in these bonds is to be free;
Then, where my hand is set, my seal shall be.
　　Full nakedness! All joys are due to thee;
As souls unbodied, bodies unclothed must be,
To taste whole joys. Gems which you women use

Are like Atlanta's ball cast in men's views;
That, when a fool's eye lighteth on a gem,
His earthly soul may covet that, not them.
Like pictures, or like books' gay coverings made
For laymen, are all women thus arrayed.
Themselves are mystic books, which only we
(Whom their imputed grace will dignify)
Must see revealed. Then, since that I may know,
As liberally as to thy midwife show
Thyself; cast all, yea, this white linen hence;
There is no penance due to innocence.
    To teach thee, I am naked first; why than,
What needst thou have more covering than a man?

                    Poems, 1669 (written *c*.1600)

Love's Growth

I scarce believe my love to be so pure
    As I had thought it was,
Because it doth endure
    Vicissitude, and season, as the grass;
Methinks I lied all winter, when I swore
My love was infinite, if spring make it more.

But if this medicine, love, which cures all sorrow
    With more, not only be no quintessence,
    But mixed of all stuffs, paining soul, or sense,
And of the sun his working vigour borrow,
    Love's not so pure and abstract as they use
    To say, which have no mistress but their Muse,
But, as all else, being elemented too,
Love sometimes would contemplate, sometimes do.

And yet no greater, but more eminent,
    Love by the spring is grown;
As, in the firmament,
    Stars by the sun are not enlarged, but shown.
Gentle love deeds, as blossoms on a bough,
From love's awakened root do bud out now.

If, as in water stirred more circles be
    Produced by one, love such additions take,
    Those, like so many spheres, but one heaven make,
For they are all concentric unto thee;
    And though each spring do add to love new heat,
    As princes do in times of action get
New taxes, and remit them not in peace,
No winter shall abate the spring's increase.

Poems, 1633 (written *c*. 1600)

Love's Infiniteness

If yet I have not all thy love,
    Dear, I shall never have it all,
I cannot breathe one other sigh, to move,
    Nor can entreat one other tear to fall.
And all my treasure, which should purchase thee,
    Sighs, tears, and oaths, and letters I have spent,
Yet no more can be due to me
    Than at the bargain made was meant:
If then thy gift of love were partial,
That some to me, some should to others fall,
Dear, I shall never have thee all.

Or if then thou gavest me all,
    All was but all, which thou hadst then;
But if in thy heart, since, there be or shall
    New love created be, by other men,

Which have their stocks entire, and can in tears,
  In sighs, in oaths, and letters outbid me,
This new love may beget new fears,
  For this love was not vowed by thee.
And yet it was, thy gift being general,
The ground, thy heart is mine, whatever shall
Grow there, dear, I should have it all.

Yet I would not have all yet;
  He that hath all can have no more;
And since my love doth every day admit
  New growth, thou shouldst have new rewards in store:
Thou canst not every day give me thy heart;
  If thou canst give it, then thou never gavest it.
Love's riddles are that though thy heart depart
  It stays at home, and thou, with losing, savest it:
But we will have a way more liberal
Than changing hearts – to join them; so we shall
Be one, and one another's all.

Poems, 1633 (written c. 1601)

Henry Chettle

Damelus' Song to his Diaphenia

Diaphenia, like the daffadown-dilly,
White as the sun, fair as the lily,
  Heigh-ho, how I do love thee!
I do love thee as my lambs
Are belovëd of their dams:
  How blessed were I if thou wouldst prove me!

Diaphenia, like the spreading roses,
That in thy sweets all sweets encloses,
  Fair sweet, how I do love thee!
I do love thee as each flower
Loves the sun's life-giving power,
  For, dead, thy breath to life might move me.

Diaphenia, like to all things blessëd,
When all thy praises are expressëd,
   Dear joy, how I do love thee!
As the birds do love the Spring,
Or the bees their careful king,
   Then in requite, sweet virgin, love me!

In *Englands Helicon*, 1600

Anonymous

Clear or cloudy, sweet as April showering,
   Smooth or frowning, so is her face to me.
Pleased or smiling, like mild May all flowering,
   When skies blue silk, and meadows carpets be,
Her speeches, notes of that night bird that singeth,
Who, thought all sweet, yet jarring notes out-ringeth.

Her grace, like June, when earth and trees be trimmed
   In best attire of complete beauty's height.
Her love again like summer's days be-dimmed
   With little clouds of doubtful constant faith.
Her trust, her doubt, like rain and heat in skies
Gently thundering, she lightning to mine eyes.

Sweet summer-spring, that breatheth life and growing
   In weeds as into herbs and flowers,
And sees of service divers sorts in sowing,
   Some haply seeming, and some being, yours;
Rain on your herbs and flowers that truly serve,
And let your weeds lack dew, and duly starve.

In John Dowland's *Second Booke of Songes or Ayres*, 1600

Anonymous

I saw my lady weep,
  And sorrow proud to be advancèd so
In those fair eyes where all perfections keep.
  Her face was full of woe,
But such a woe (believe me) as wins more hearts
Than mirth can do, with her enticing parts.

Sorrow was there made fair,
  And passion wise, tears a delightful thing,
Silence beyond all speech a wisdom rare.
  She made her sighs to sing,
And all things with so sweet a sadness move,
As made my heart at once both grieve and love.

O fairer than aught else
  The world can show! Leave off in time to grieve.
Enough, enough! Your joyful looks excels:
  Tears kill the heart, believe.
O strive not to be excellent in woe,
Which only breeds your beauty's overthrow.

In John Dowland's *Second Booke of Songes or Ayres*, 1600

Thomas Campion

My love bound me with a kiss,
  That I should no longer stay:
When I felt so sweet a bliss,
  I had less power to part away.
Alas, that women doth not know
Kisses make men loath to go.

Yes, she knows it but too well,
  For I heard when Venus' dove
In her ear did softly tell
  That kisses were the seals of love.

Oh muse not then, though it be so:
Kisses make men loath to go.

Wherefore did she thus inflame
  My desires, heat my blood,
Instantly to quench the same,
  And starve whom she had given food?
I the common sense can show:
Kisses make men loath to go.

Had she bid me go at first,
  It would ne'er have grieved my heart;
Hope delayed had been the worst:
  But ah! to kiss and then to part!
How deep it struck, speak, Gods, you know:
Kisses make men loath to go.

> In Robert Jones's *Second Booke of Songs and Ayres*, 1601.
> (The first stanza in Sidney's *Astrophel and Stella*, 1591)

And would you see my mistress' face?
It is a flowery garden place
Where knots of beauties have such grace
That all is work and nowhere space.

It is a sweet delicious morn
Where day is breeding, never born.
It is a meadow yet unshorn
Whom thousand flowers do adorn.

It is the heavens' bright reflex,
Weak eyes to dazzle and to vex;
It is th' Idea of her sex,
Envy of whom doth world perplex.

It is a face of death that smiles,
Pleasing though it kills the whiles,
Where death and love in pretty wiles
Each other mutually beguiles.

It is fair beauty's freshest youth,
It is the feigned Elysium's truth,
The Spring that wintered hearts reneweth;
And this is that my soul pursueth.

In Philip Rosseter's Booke of Ayres, 1601

When to her lute Corinna sings,
Her voice revives the leaden strings,
And doth in highest notes appear
As any challenged echo clear.
But when she doth of mourning speak,
E'en with her sighs the strings do break.

And as her lute doth live or die,
Led by her passion, so must I.
For when of pleasure she doth sing,
My thoughts enjoy a sudden spring;
But if she doth of sorrow speak,
E'en from my heart the strings do break.

In Philip Rosseter's Booke of Ayres, 1601

Follow your saint, follow with accents sweet!
Haste you, sad notes, fall at her flying feet!
There, wrapped in cloud of sorrow, pity move,
And tell the ravisher of my soul I perish for her love:
But, if she scorns my never ceasing pain,
Then burst with sighing in her sight and ne'er return again.

All that I sung still to her praise did tend,
Still she was first, still she my songs did end;
Yet she my love and music both doth fly,
The music that her echo is and beauty's sympathy.
Then let my notes pursue her scornful flight:
It shall suffice that they were breathed and died for her delight.

In Philip Rosseter's Booke of Ayres, 1601

Anonymous

Love winged my hopes and taught me how to fly
Far from base earth, but not to mount too high:
  For true pleasure
  Lives in measure,
Which, if men forsake,
Blinded they into folly run, and grief for pleasure take.

But my vain hopes, proud of their new-taught flight,
Enamoured, sought to woo the sun's fair light,
  Whose rich brightness
  Moved their lightness
To aspire so high,
That, all scorched and consumed with fire, now drowned in
  woe they lie.

And none but Love their woeful hap did rue;
For Love did know that their desires were true:
  Though fate frowned
  And now drowned
They in sorrow dwell,
It was the purest light of heaven for whose fair love they fell.

In Robert Jones's Second Booke of Songs and Ayres, 1601

Anonymous

Only, sweet Love, afford me but thy heart,
  Then close thine eyes within their ivory covers,
That they to me no beam of light impart,
  Although they shine on all thy other lovers.

As for thy lip of ruby, cheeks of rose,
    Though I have kissed them oft with sweet content,
I am content that sweet content to lose:
    If thy sweet will will bar me, I assent.
Let me not touch thy hand but through thy glove,
    Nor let it be the pledge of kindness more;
Keep all thy beauties to thyself, sweet Love,
    I ask not such bold favours as before.
        I beg but this, afford me but thy heart,
        For then, I know, thou wilt the rest impart.

In *A Poetical Rapsody*, 1602

Charles Best

A Sonnet of the Moon

Look how the pale Queen of the silent night
    Doth cause the ocean to attend upon her,
And he, as long as she is in his sight,
    With his full tide is ready her to honour:
But when the silver wagon of the moon
    Is mounted up so high he cannot follow,
The sea calls home his crystal waves to moan,
    And with low ebb doth manifest his sorrow.
So you, that are the sovereign of my heart,
    Have all my joys attending on your will:
My joys low ebbing when you do depart,
    When you return, their tide my heart doth fill.
        So as you come, and as you do depart,
        Joys ebb and flow within my tender heart.

In *A Poetical Rapsody*, 1602

Francis Davison

He Compares Himself to a Candle-fly

Like to the silly fly
To the dear light I fly
Of your disdainful eyes:
But in a diverse wise
She with the flame doth play
By night alone; and I both night and day.
She to a candle runs;
I to a light far brighter than the sun's:
She near at hand is fired,
I both near hand, and far away retired;
She fondly thinks, nor dead nor burnt to be;
But I my burning and my death foresee.

In *A Poetical Rapsody*, 1602

Anonymous

My Love in her attire doth show her wit,
    It doth so well become her;
For every season she hath dressings fit,
    For Winter, Spring and Summer.
No beauty she doth miss
    When all her robes are on:
But Beauty's self she is
    When all her robes are gone.

In *A Poetical Rapsody*, 1602

I.S.

Were I as base as is the lowly plain,
    And you (my Love) as high as heaven above,
Yet should the thoughts of me, your humble swain,
    Ascend to Heaven in honour of my love.

Were I as high as Heaven above the plain,
  And you (my Love) as humble and as low
As are the deepest bottoms of the main,
  Wheresoe'er you were, with you my love should go.
Were you the Earth (dear Love) and I the skies,
  My love should shine on you like to the sun,
And look upon you with ten thousand eyes,
  Till Heaven waxed blind, and till the world were done.
    Wheresoe'er I am, below, or else above you,
    Wheresoe'er you are, my heart shall truly love you.

In A Poetical Rapsody, 1602

A.W.

Petition to Have Her Leave to Die

When will the fountain of my tears be dry?
  When will my sighs be spent?
When will desire agree to let me die?
  When will thy heart relent?
It is not for my life I plead,
Since death the way to rest doth lead;
    But stay for thy consent,
    Lest thou be discontent.

For if myself without thy leave I kill,
  My ghost will never rest;
So hath it sworn to work thine only will,
  And holds that ever best;
For since it only lives by thee,
Good reason thou the ruler be.
    Then give me leave to die,
    And show thy power thereby.

In A Poetical Rapsody, 1602

Smooth are thy looks, so is the deepest stream;
   Soft are thy lips, so is the swallowing sand;
Fair is thy sight, but like unto a dream;
   Sweet is thy promise, but it will not stand.
Smooth, soft, fair, sweet, to them that lightly touch;
Rough, hard, foul, sour, to them that take too much.

Thy looks so smooth have drawn away my sight:
   Who would have thought that hooks could so be hid?
Thy lips so soft have fretted my delight,
   Before I once suspected what they did.
Thy face so fair hath burnt me with desire;
Thy words so sweet were bellows for the fire.

And yet I love the looks that made me blind,
   And like to kiss the lips that fret my life;
In heat of fire an ease of heat I find,
   And greatest peace in midst of greatest strife:
That if my choice were now to make again,
I would not have this joy without this pain.

                In *A Poetical Rapsody*, 1602

Where His Lady Keeps His Heart

Sweet Love, mine only treasure,
   For service long unfeigned,
   Wherein I nought have gained,
Vouchsafe this little pleasure,
   To tell me in what part
   My lady keeps my heart.

If in her hair so slender,
   Like golden nets untwined,
   Which fire and art have fined,
Her thrall my heart I render,
   For ever to abide
   With locks so dainty tied.

If in her eyes she bind it,
    Wherein that fire was framed,
    By which it is inflamed,
I dare not look to find it:
    I only wish it sight,
    To see that pleasant light.

But if her breast have deigned
    With kindness to receive it,
    I am content to leave it,
Though death thereby were gained:
    Then, lady, take your own,
    That lives for you alone.

            In *A Poetical Rapsody*, 1602

To Her Eyes

Fain would I learn of thee, thou murdering eye,
    Whether thy glance be fire, or else a dart:
For with thy look in flames thou mak'st me fry,
    And with the same thou strik'st me to the heart.
      Pierced with thy looks I burn in fire,
      And yet those looks I still desire.

The fly that buzzeth round about the flame
    Knows not (poor soul) she gets her death thereby;
I see my death, and seeing, seek the same,
    And seeking, find, and finding, choose to die;
      That when thy looks my life hath slain,
      Thy looks may give me life again.

Turn then to me those sparkling eyes of thine,
    And with their fiery glances pierce my heart:
Quench not my light, lest I in darkness pine;
    Strike deep and spare not, pleasant is the smart:
      So by thy looks my life be spilt,
      Kill me as often as thou wilt.

            In *A Poetical Rapsody*, 1602

Anonymous

Weep you no more, sad fountains;
   What need you flow so fast?
Look how the snowy mountains
   Heaven's sun doth gently waste.
But my sun's heavenly eyes
    View not your weeping,
    That now lies sleeping
Softly, now softly lies
    Sleeping.

Sleep is a reconciling,
   A rest that peace begets:
Doth not the sun rise smiling
   When fair at even he sets?
Rest you then, rest, sad eyes,
    Melt not in weeping,
    While she lies sleeping
Softly, now softly lies
    Sleeping.

In John Dowland's Third and Last Booke
of Songs or Ayres, 1603

Jacobeans
and Cavaliers

Anonymous

Whither so fast? See how the kindly flowers
   Perfume the air, and all to make thee stay
The climbing woodbind, clipping all these bowers,
   Clips thee likewise for fear thou pass away.
   Fortune, our friend, our foe will not gainsay.
Stay but awhile, Phoebe no tell-tale is:
She her Endymion, I'll my Phoebe kiss.

Fear not, the ground seeks but to kiss thy feet.
   Hark, hark how Philomela sweetly sings,
Whilst water-wanton fishes, as they meet,
   Strike crochet time amidst these crystal springs,
   And Zephyrus 'mongst the leaves sweet murmur rings.
Stay but awhile, Phoebe no tell-tale is;
She her Endymion, I'll my Phoebe kiss.

See how the heliotrope, herb of the sun,
   Though he himself long since be gone to bed,
Is not of force thine eyes' bright beams to shun,
   But with their warmth his goldy leaves unspread,
   And on my knee invites thee rest thy head.
Stay but awhile, Phoebe no tell-tale is;
She her Endymion, I'll my Phoebe kiss.

In Francis Pilkington's *First Booke of Songs or Ayres*, 1605

Ben Jonson

Come, my Celia, let us prove
While we can, the sports of love,
Time will not be ours for ever,
He, at length, our good will sever;
Spend not then his gifts in vain.
Suns that set may rise again;

But if once we lose this light,
'Tis with us perpetual night.
Why should we defer our joys?
Fame and rumour are but toys.
Cannot we delude the eyes
Of a few poor household spies?
Or his easier ears beguile,
Thus removèd by our wile?
'Tis no sin love's fruits to steal;
But the sweet thefts to reveal:
To be taken, to be seen,
These have crimes accounted been.

Volpone, or The Fox, 1607

To Celia

Drink to me only with thine eyes,
    And I will pledge with mine;
Or leave a kiss but in the cup,
    And I'll not look for wine.
The thirst, that from the soul doth rise,
    Doth ask a drink divine:
But might I of Jove's nectar sup,
    I would not change for thine.

I sent thee, late, a rosy wreath,
    Not so much honouring thee,
As giving it a hope, that there
    It could not withered be.
But thou thereon did'st only breathe,
    And sent'st it back to me:
Since when it grows, and smells, I swear,
    Not of itself, but thee.

The Forrest, 1616

Do but look on her eyes, they do light
  All that Love's world compriseth.
Do but look on her hair, it is bright
  As Love's star when it riseth.
Do but mark, her forehead's smoother
  Than words that soothe her.
And from her arched brows such a grace
  Sheds itself through the face,
As alone there triumphs to the life
All the gain, all the good of the elements' strife.

Have you seen but a bright lily grow
  Before rude hands have touched it?
Have you marked but the fall of the snow
  Before the soil hath smutched it?
Have you felt the wool o' the beaver
  Or swan's down ever?
Or have smelt o' the bud o' the brier,
  Or the nard i' the fire?
Or have tasted the bag o' the bee?
O, so white, O, so soft, O, so sweet is she.

The Devil Is an Ass, 1616

It was a beauty that I saw
    So pure, so perfect, as the frame
    Of all the universe was lame,
To that one figure, could I draw,
Or give least line of it a law!

A skein of silk without a knot,
  A fair march made without a halt,
  A curious form without a fault,
A printed book without a blot,
All beauty, and without a spot!

The New Inn, 1631 (acted 1629)

Thomas Heywood

Ye little birds that sit and sing
Amidst the shady valleys,
And see how Phyllis sweetly walks
Within her garden alleys;
Go, pretty birds, about her bower,
Sing pretty birds; she may not lour –
Ah me! methinks, I see her frown;
    Ye pretty wantons, warble.

Go, tell her through your chirping bills,
As you by me are bidden,
To her is only known my love,
Which from the world is hidden:
Go, pretty birds, and tell her so,
See that your notes strain not too low,
For still, methinks, I see her frown,
    Ye pretty wantons, warble.

Go, tune your voices' harmony,
And sing I am her lover:
Strain loud and sweet that every note
With sweet content may move her;
And she that hath the sweetest voice,
Tell her I will not change my choice –
Yet still, methinks, I see her frown,
    Ye pretty wantons, warble.

O fly, make haste! see, see, she falls
Into a pretty slumber:
Sing round about her rosy bed,
That waking she may wonder:
Say to her 'tis her lover true
That sendeth love to you, to you;
And when you hear her kind reply,
    Return with pleasant warblings.

The Fair Maid of the Exchange, 1607

Pack, clouds, away, and welcome day!
  With night we banish sorrow;
Sweet air, blow soft; mount, lark, aloft
  To give my Love good-morrow.
Wings from the wind, to please her mind,
  Notes from the lark I'll borrow:
Bird, prune thy wing; nightingale, sing,
  To give my Love good-morrow.
  To give my Love good-morrow
  Notes from them all I'll borrow.

Wake from thy nest, robin red-breast!
  Sing, birds, in every furrow;
And from each bill let music shrill
  Give my fair Love good-morrow.
Blackbird and thrush, in every bush,
  Stare,* linnet and cocksparrow,
You pretty elves, among yourselves,
  Sing my fair Love good-morrow.
  To give my Love good-morrow
  Sing, birds in every furrow.

*stare] starling   *The Rape of Lucrece*, 1608

Hence with passion, sighs and tears,
Disasters, sorrows, cares and fears!
See, my Love, my Love, appears,
  That thought himself exiled!
Whence might all these loud joys grow,
Whence might mirth and banquets flow,
But that he's come, he's come, I know?
  Fair Fortune, thou hast smiled.

Give to these blind windows eyes,
Daze the stars and mock the skies,
And let us two, us two, devise
   To lavish our best treasures;
Crown our wishes with content,
Meet our souls in sweet consent,
And let this night, this night, be spent
   In all abundant pleasures.

A Maidenhead Well Lost, 1634

Anonymous

And is it night? Are they thine eyes that shine?
   Are we alone and here? and here alone?
May I come near? May I touch thy shrine?
   Is jealousy asleep or is he gone?
O gods! no more silence my lips with thine,
Lips, kisses, joys, hap – blessings most divine.

Oh come, my dear, our griefs are turned to night,
   And night to joys: night blinds pale envy's eyes:
Silence and sleep prepare us our delight:
   Oh cease we then our woes, our griefs, our cries:
Oh vanish words! words do but passions move:
O dearest life, joy's sweet, O sweetest love!

In Robert Jones's A Musicall Dreame, 1609

Anonymous

The fountains smoke, and yet no flames they show;
   Stars shine all night, though undiscerned by day;
And trees do spring, yet are not seen to grow;
   And shadows move, although they seem to stay.
In Winter's woe is buried Summer's bliss,
And Love loves most when Love most secret is.

The stillest streams descry the greatest deep;
   The clearest sky is subject to a shower;
Conceit's most sweet whenas it seems to sleep;
   And fairest days do in the morning lour.
The silent groves sweet nymphs they cannot miss,
For Love loves most where Love most secret is.

The rarest jewels hidden virtue yield;
   The sweet of traffic is a secret gain;
The year once old doth show a barren field;
   And plants seem dead, and yet they spring again:
Cupid is blind: the reason why is this:
Love loveth most when Love most secret is.

In Robert Jones's *The Muse's Gardin for Delights*, 1610

Anonymous

Once did my thoughts both ebb and flow,
   As passion did them move;
Once did I hope, straight fear again –
   And then I was in love.

Once did I waking spend the night,
   And told how many minutes move;
Once did I wishing waste the day –
   And then I was in love.

Once, by my carving true love's knot,
   The weeping trees did prove
That wounds and tears were both our lot –
   And then I was in love.

Once did I breathe another's breath
   And in my mistress move;
Once was I not mine own at all –
   And then I was in love.

Once wore I bracelets made of hair,
   And collars did approve,
Once were my clothes made out of wax,
   And then I was in love.

Once did I sonnet to my saint,
   My soul in numbers moved,
Once did I tell a thousand lies –
   And then in truth I loved.

Once in my ear did dangling hang
   A little turtle-dove,
Once, in a word, I was a fool –
   And then I was in love.

In Robert Jones's *The Muse's Gardin for Delights*, 1610

Lord Herbert of Cherbury

Elegy over a Tomb

Must I then see, alas, eternal night
   Sitting upon those fairest eyes,
And closing all those beams, which once did rise
   So radiant and bright,
That light and heat in them to us did prove
Knowledge and Love?

Oh, if you did delight no more to stay
   Upon this low and earthly stage,
But rather chose an endless heritage,
   Tell us at least, we pray,
Where all the beauties that those ashes owed
Are now bestowed?

Doth the sun now his light with yours renew?
   Have waves the curling of your hair?
Did you restore unto the sky and air,
   The red, and white, and blue?
Have you vouchsafed to flowers since your death,
That sweetest breath?

Had not Heaven's lights else in their houses slept,
  Or to some private life retired?
Must not the sky and air have else conspired,
  And in their regions wept?
Must not each flower else the earth could breed
Have been a weed?

But thus enriched, may we not yield some cause
  Why they themselves lament no more?
That must have changed the course they held before,
  And broke their proper laws,
Had not your beauties given this second birth
To Heaven and earth?

Tell us (for oracles must still ascend,
  For those that crave them at your tomb),
Tell us, where are those beauties now become,
  And what they now intend?
Tell us, alas, that cannot tell our grief,
Or hope relief.

Occasional Verses, 1665 (written in 1617)

Kissing

Come hither, womankind and all their worth,
Give me thy kisses as I call them forth.
Give me the billing kiss, that of the dove,
  A kiss of love;
The melting kiss, a kiss that doth consume
  To a perfume;
The extract kiss, of every sweet a part,
  A kiss of art;
The kiss which ever stirs some new delight,
  A kiss of might;
The twaching smacking kiss, and when you cease,
  A kiss of peace;

The music kiss, crochet-and-quaver time;
  The kiss of rhyme;
The kiss of eloquence, which doth belong
  Unto the tongue;
The kiss of all the sciences in one,
  The Kiss alone.
So, 'tis enough.

Occasional Verses, 1665 (written *c*.1620)

Nathaniel Field

Rise, lady mistress, rise!
  The night hath tedious been;
No sleep hath fallen into my eyes,
  Nor slumbers made me sin.
Is not she a saint, then, say,
Thought of whom keeps sin away?

Rise, madam, rise and give me light,
  Whom darkness still will cover,
And ignorance, darker than night,
  Till thou smile on thy lover.
All want day till thy beauty rise
For the grey morn breaks from thine eyes.

Amends for Ladies, 1618

George Wither

Now gentle sleep hath closëd up those eyes
  Which, waking, kept my boldest thoughts in awe;
And free access unto that sweet lip lies,
  From whence I long the rosy breath to draw.

Methinks no wrong it were, if I should steal
   From those two melting rubies one poor kiss;
None sees the theft that would the thief reveal,
   Nor rob I her of aught which she can miss;
Nay, should I twenty kisses take away,
   There would be little sign I had done so;
Why then should I this robbery delay?
   Oh! she may wake, and therewith angry grow.
     Well, if she do, I'll back restore that one,
     And twenty hundred thousand more for loan.

Fair Virtue, the Mistress of Phil'arete, 1622

Henry King

Tell me no more how fair she is,
   I have no mind to hear
The story of that distant bliss
   I never shall come near:
By sad experience I have found
That her perfection is my wound.

And tell me not how fond I am
   To tempt a daring fate,
From whence no triumph ever came,
   But to repent too late:
There is some hope ere long I may
In silence dote myself away.

I ask no pity, Love, from thee
   Nor will thy justice blame,
So that thou wilt not envy me
   The glory of my flame:
Which crowns my heart whene'er it dies,
In that it falls her sacrifice.

Poems, 1657 (written before 1624)

117

From *The Exequy*

So close the ground, and 'bout her shade
Black curtains draw; my Bride is laid.

Sleep on, my Love, in thy cold bed,
Never to be disquieted!
My last good night! Thou wilt not wake,
Till I thy fate shall overtake;
Till age, or grief, or sickness must
Marry my body to that dust
It so much loves; and fill the room
My heart keeps empty in thy tomb.
Stay for me there: I will not fail
To meet thee in that hollow vale:
And think not much of my delay;
I am already on the way,
And follow thee with all the speed
Desire can make, or sorrows breed.
Each minute is a short degree,
And every hour a step towards thee.
At night, when I betake to rest,
Next morn I rise nearer my West
Of life, almost by eight hours' sail,
Than when sleep breathed his drowsy gale.

Thus from the sun my bottom steers,
And my day's compass downward bears;
Nor labour I to stem the tide,
Through which to thee I swiftly glide.

'Tis true, with shame and grief I yield,
Thou, like the van, first took'st the field,
And gotten hast the victory,
In thus adventuring to die
Before me, whose more years might crave
A just precedence in the grave.
But hark! My pulse, like a soft drum,
Beats my approach, tells thee I come;

And slow howe'er my marches be,
I shall at last sit down by thee.

The thought of this bids me go on,
And wait my dissolution
With hope and comfort. Dear (forgive
The crime), I am content to live
Divided, with but half a heart,
Till we shall meet and never part.

Poems, 1657 (written *c*.1624)

William Bosworth

See'st not, my Love, with what a grace
The Spring resembles thy sweet face?
Here let us sit, and in these bowers
Receive the odours of the flowers,
For Flora, by thy beauty wooed, conspires thy good.

See how she sends her fragrant sweet,
And doth this homage to thy feet,
Bending so low her stooping head
To kiss the ground where thou dost tread,
And all her flowers proudly meet, to kiss thy feet.

Then let us walk, my dearest Love,
And on this carpet strictly prove
Each other's vow; from thy request
No other love invades my breast:
For how can I contemn that fire which gods admire?

To crop that rose why dost thou seek,
When there's a purer in thy cheek?
Like coral held in thy fair hands,
Or blood and milk that mingled stands:
To whom the powers all grace have given, a type of Heaven.

119

Yon lily, stooping t'wards this place,
Is a pale shadow for thy face,
Under which veil doth seem to rush
Modest Endymion's ruddy blush:
A blush, indeed, more pure and fair than lilies are.

Glance on those flowers thy radiant eyes,
Through which clear beams they'll sympathise
Reflective love, to make them far
More glorious than the Hesperian star,
For every swain amazèd lies, and gazing dies.

See how these silly flowers twine
With sweet embracings, and combine,
Striving with curious looms to set
Their pale and red into a net,
To show how pure desire doth rest for ever blessed.

Why wilt thou then unconstant be
To infringe the laws of amity,
And so much disrespect my heart
To derogate from what thou art,
When in harmonious love there is Elysian bliss?

The Chaste and Lost Lovers, 1651 (written *c*.1626)

Francis Andrewes

Come, be my valentine!
I'll gather eglantine,
Cowslips and sops-in-wine,
    With fragrant roses;
Down by thy Phyllis sit,
She will white lilies get,
And daffadillies fit
    To make thee posies.

I have a milk-white lamb
New taken from the dam,
It comes where'er I am
    When I call 'Willie.'
I have a wanton kid
Under mine apron hid,
A colt that ne'er was rid,
    A pretty filly.

I bear, in sign of love,
A sparrow in my glove,
And in my breast a dove,
    These shall be all thine;
Besides, of sheep a flock
Which yieldeth many a lock,
And that shall be thy stock –
    Come, be my valentine!

B.M. Harl. MS. 4955 (written *c*.1629)

Peter Hausted

Have you a desire to see
The glorious heaven's epitome?
Or an abstract of the Spring?
Adonis' garden? or a thing
    Fuller of wonder, Nature's shop displayed
    Hung with the choicest pieces she has made?
    Here behold it open laid.

Or else, would you bless your eyes
With a type of paradise?
Or behold how poets feign
Jove to site amidst his train?
    Or see (what made Actaeon rue)
    Diana 'mongst her virgin crew?
    Lift up your eyes and view.

The Rival Friends, 1632

William Strode

On Chloris Walking in the Snow

I saw fair Chloris walk alone,
Whilst feathered rain came softly down,
And Jove descended from his tower
To court her in a silver shower.
The wanton snow flew on her breast
Like little birds unto their nest;
But overcome with whiteness there,
For grief it thawed into a tear;
Thence falling on her garment's hem,
To deck her, froze into a gem.

In Walter Porter's *Madrigales and Ayres*, 1632

James Shirley

To His Mistress Confined

Think not, my Phoebe, 'cause a cloud
Doth now thy heavenly beauty shroud,
    My wandering eye
Can stoop to common beauties of the sky.
    Be thou but kind, and this eclipse
    Shall neither hinder eyes nor lips;
        For we will meet
Within our hearts, and kiss, when none shall see't.

Nor canst thou in thy prison be
Without some loving signs of me:
    When thou dost spy
A sunbeam peep into thy room, 'tis I,
    For I am hid within that flame,
    And thus unto thy chamber came
        To let thee see
In what a martyrdom I burn for thee.

There's no sad picture that doth dwell
Upon thy arras wall, but well
    Resembles me.
No matter though our years do not agree,
  Love can make old, as well as time,
  And he that doth but twenty climb,
    If he will prove
As true as I, shows fourscore years in love.

Poems, etc., 1646 (written before 1639)

Thomas Carew

Celia Singing

You that think Love can convey
    No other way
But through the eyes, into the heart,
    His fatal dart,
Close up those casements, and but hear
    This siren sing;
    And on the wing
Of her sweet voice, it shall appear
That Love can enter at the ear.

Then unveil your eyes; behold
    The curious mould
Where that voice dwells, and as we know,
    When the cocks crow,
And Sol is mounted on his way,
    We freely may
    Gaze on the day;
So may you, when the music's done,
Awake, and see the rising sun.

Poems, 1640 (written before 1639)

Mediocrity in Love Rejected

Give me more love, or more disdain;
  The torrid or the frozen zone
Bring equal ease unto my pain;
  The temperate affords me none:
Either extreme, of love or hate,
Is sweeter than a calm estate.

Give me a storm; if it be love,
  Like Danae in that golden shower,
I swim in pleasure; if it prove
  Disdain, that torrent will devour
My vulture hopes; and he's possessed
Of heaven, that's but from hell released.
  Then crown my joys, or cure my pain;
  Give me more love, or more disdain.

Poems, 1640 (written before 1639)

Ask me no more where Jove bestows,
When June is past, the fading rose;
For in your beauty's orient deep
These flowers, as in their causes, sleep.

Ask me no more whither do stray
The golden atoms of the day;
For in pure love heaven did prepare
Those powders to enrich your hair.

Ask me no more whither doth haste
The nightingale, when May is past;
For in your sweet dividing throat
She winters, and keeps warm her note.

Ask me no more where those stars light
That downwards fall in dead of night;
For in your eyes they sit, and there
Fixëd become, as in their sphere.

Ask me no more if East or West
The phoenix builds her spicy nest;
For unto you at last she flies,
And in your fragrant bosom dies.

Poems, 1640 (written before 1639)
(text from the edition of 1651)

A Rapture

I will enjoy thee now, my Celia, come
And fly with me to Love's Elysium:
The giant, Honour, that keeps cowards out,
Is but a masquer, and the servile rout
Of baser subjects only bend in vain
To the vast idol, whilst the nobler train
Of valiant soldiers daily sail between
The huge Colossus' legs, and pass unseen
Unto the blissful shore. Be bold and wise,
And we shall enter: the grim Swiss denies
Only tame fools a passage, that not know
He is but form, and only frights in show
The duller eyes that look from far; draw near,
And thou shalt scorn what we were wont to fear.
We shall see how the stalking pageant goes
With borrowed legs, a heavy load to those
That made and bear him; not as we once thought
The seed of gods, but a weak model wrought
By greedy men that seek t' enclose the common
And within private arms impale free woman.
Come, then, and mounted on the wings of Love
We'll cut the flitting air, and soar above

The monster's head, and in the noblest seats
Of those blest shades quench and renew our heats.
There shall the Queen of Love, and Innocence,
Beauty, and Nature, banish all offence
From our close ivy-twines; there I'll behold
Thy barèd snow and thy unbraided gold;
There my enfranchised hand on every side
Shall o'er thy naked polished ivory slide.
No curtain there, though of transparent lawn,
Shall be before thy virgin-treasure drawn;
But the rich mine, to the enquiring eye
Exposed, shall ready still for mintage lie,
And we will coin young Cupids. There a bed
Of roses and fresh myrtles shall be spread
Under the cooler shade of cypress groves,
Our pillows of the down of Venus' doves,
Whereon our panting limbs we'll gently lay
In the faint respites of our active play,
That so our slumbers may in dreams have leisure
To tell the nimble fancy our past pleasure;
And so our souls, that cannot be embraced,
Shall the embraces of our bodies taste.
Meanwhile the bubbling stream shall court the shore;
Th' enamoured chirping wood-choir shall adore
In varied tunes the deity of Love;
The gentle blasts of western winds shall move
The trembling leaves, and through their close boughs breathe
Still music, whilst we rest ourselves beneath
Their dancing shade; till a soft murmur, sent
From souls entranced in amorous languishment,
Rouse us, and shoot into our veins fresh fire,
Till we in their sweet ecstasy expire.
    Then, as the empty bee, that lately bore
Into the common treasure all her store,
Flies 'bout the painted field with nimble wing,
Deflowering the fresh virgins of the spring,

So will I rifle all the sweets that dwell
In my delicious paradise, and swell
My bag with honey, drawn forth by the power
Of fervent kisses, from each spicy flower.
I'll seize the rose-buds in their perfumed bed,
The violet knots, like curious mazes spread
O'er all the garden, taste the ripened cherry,
The warm firm apple, tipped with coral berry;
Then will I visit, with a wandering kiss,
The vale of lilies and the bower of bliss;
And, where the beauteous region doth divide
Into two milky ways, my lips shall slide
Down those smooth alleys, wearing as I go
A tract for lovers on the printed snow;
Thence climbing o'er the swelling Apennine
Retire into thy grove of eglantine,
Where I will all those ravished sweets distil
Through love's alembic, and with chemic skill
From the mixed mass one sovereign balm derive,
Then bring that great elixir to thy hive.
  Now in more subtle wreaths I will entwine
My sinewy thighs, my legs and arms, with thine;
Thou like a sea of milk shalt lie displayed,
Whilst I the smooth, calm ocëan invade
With such a tempest as when Jove of old
Fell down on Danae in a storm of gold:
Yet my tall pine shall in the Cyprian strait
Ride safe at anchor, and unlade her freight;
My rudder with thy bold hand, like a tried
And skilful pilot, thou shalt steer, and guide
My bark into love's channel, where it shall
Dance, as the bounding waves do rise or fall.
Then shall thy circling arms embrace and clip
My willing body, and thy balmy lip
Bathe me in juice of kisses, whose perfume
Like a religious incense shall consume,

And send up holy vapours to those powers
That bless our loves and crown our sportful hours
That with such halcyon calmness fix our souls
In steadfast peace as no affright controls.
There no rude sounds shake us with sudden starts;
No jealous ears, when we unrip our hearts,
Suck our discourse in; no observing spies
This blush, that glance, traduce; no envious eyes
Watch our close meetings; nor are we betrayed
To rivals by the bribèd chambermaid.
No wedlock bonds unwreathe our twisted loves;
We seek no midnight arbour, no dark groves,
To hide our kisses; there the hated name
Of husband, wife, lust, modest, chaste, or shame,
Are vain and empty words, whose very sound
Was never heard in the Elysian ground.
All things are lawful there that may delight
Nature or unrestrainèd appetite;
Like and enjoy, to will and act, is one:
We only sin when Love's rites are not done.
   The Roman Lucrece there reads the divine
Lectures of love's great master, Aretine,
And knows as well as Lais how to move
Her pliant body in the act of love.
To quench the burning ravisher, she hurls
Her limbs into a thousand winding curls,
And studies artful postures, such as be
Carved on the bark of every neighbouring tree
By learned hands that so adorned the rind
Of those fair plants, which as they lay entwined
Have fanned their glowing fires. The Grecian Dame,
That in her endless web toiled for a name
As fruitless as her work, doth there display
Herself before the Youth of Ithaca,
And th' amorous sport of gamesome nights prefer
Before dull dreams of the lost Traveller.

Daphne hath broke her bark, and that swift foot
Which th' angry gods had fastened with a foot
To the fixed earth doth now unfettered run
To meet th' embraces of the youthful Sun:
She hangs upon him like his Delphic lyre;
Her kisses blow the old and breathe new fire;
Full of her god, she sings inspirëd lays,
Sweet odes of love, such as deserve the bays,
Which she herself was. Next her, Laura lies
In Petrarch's learned arms, drying those eyes
That did in such sweet smooth-paced numbers flow
As made the world enamoured of his woe.
These, and ten thousand beauties more, that died
Slave to the tyrant, now enlarged deride
His cancelled laws, and for their time mis-spent
Pay into Love's exchequer double rent.
   Come then, my Celia, we'll no more forbear
To taste our joys, struck with a Panic fear,
But will depose from his imperious sway
This proud usurper and walk free as they,
With necks unyoked; nor is it just that he
Should fetter your soft sex with chastity,
Which Nature made unapt for abstinence;
When yet this false impostor can dispense
With human justice, and with sacred right
And maugre both their laws command me fight
With rivals, or with em'lous loves, that dare
Equal with thine their mistress' eyes or hair:
If thou complain of wrong, and call my sword
To carve out thy revenge, upon that word
He bids me fight and kill, or else he brands
With marks of infamy my coward hands;
And yet Religion bids from bloodshed fly,
And damns me for that act. Then tell me why
   This goblin Honour, which the world adores,
   Should make men atheists, and not women whores.

              Poems, 1640 (written before 1639)

Henry Glapthorne

Unclose those eyelids, and out-shine
   The brightness of the breaking day;
The light they cover is divine,
   Why should it fade so soon away?
Stars vanish so, and day appears,
The sun's so drowned i' the morning's tears.

Oh! let not sadness cloud this beauty,
   Which if you lose, you'll ne'er recover;
It is not love's, but sorrow's duty
   To die so soon for a dead lover.
Banish, oh! banish grief, and then
Our joys will bring our hopes again.

Poems, 1639

James Mabbe

Whilst I behold thy glittering golden hairs
Dishevelled thus, waving about thy ears,
And see those locks thus loosëd and undone
For their more pomp to sport them in the sun,
Love takes those threads and weaves them with that art
He knits a thousand knots about my heart,
And with such skill and cunning he them sets,
My soul lies taken in those lovely nets,
Making me cry, 'Fair prison, that dost hold
My heart in fetters wrought of burnished gold.'

Exemplary Novels, 1640

Anonymous

Give me a kiss from those sweet lips of thine
And make it double by enjoining mine,

Another yet, nay yet and yet another,
And let the first kiss be the second's brother.
Give me a thousand kisses and yet more;
And then repeat those that have gone before;
Let us begin while daylight springs in heaven,
And kiss till Night descends into the even,
And when that modest secretary, Night,
Discolours all but thy heaven beaming bright,
We will begin revels of hidden love
In that sweet orb where silent pleasures move.
In high new strains, unspeakable delight,
We'll vent the dull hours of the silent Night:
Were the bright Day no more to visit us,
Oh, then for ever would I hold thee thus,
Naked, enchained, empty of idle fear,
As the first lovers in the garden were.
I'll die betwixt thy breasts that are so white,
For, to die there, would do a man delight.
Embrace me still, for time runs on before,
And being dead we shall embrace no more.
Let us kiss faster than the hours do fly,
Long live each kiss and never know to die.
Yet if that fade and fly away too fast,
Impress another and renew the last;
Let us vie kisses, till our eyelids cover,
And if I sleep, count me an idle lover;
Admit I sleep, I'll still pursue the theme,
And eagerly I'll kiss thee in a dream.
Oh, give me way: grant love to me thy friend!
Did hundred thousand suitors all contend
For thy virginity, there's none shall woo
With heart so firm as mine; none better do
Than I with your sweet sweetness; if you doubt,
Pierce with your eyes my heart, or pluck it out.

Wit's Recreations, 1641

131

Lady Catherine Dyer

My dearest dust, could not thy hasty day
Afford thy drowsy patience leave to stay
One hour longer: so that we might either
Sat up, or gone to bed together?
But since thy finished labour hath possessed
Thy weary limbs with early rest,
Enjoy it sweetly: and thy widow bride
Shall soon repose her by thy slumbering side.
Whose business, now, is only to prepare
My nightly dress, and call to prayer:
Mine eyes wax heavy and the day grows old.
The dew falls thick, my belov'd grows cold.
Draw, draw the closëd curtains: and make room:
My dear, my dearest dust; I come, I come.

Epitaph on the monument to Sir William Dyer
in the parish church of Colmworth in Bedfordshire, 1641

Sir John Suckling

Out upon it, I have loved
   Three whole days together;
And am like to love three more,
   If it prove fair weather.

Time shall moult away his wings
   Ere he shall discover
In the whole wide world again
   Such a constant lover.

But the spite on 't is, no praise
   Is due at all to me:
Love with me had made no stays,
   Had it any been but she.

Had it been but she,
   And that very face,
There had been at least ere this
   A dozen dozen in her place.

The Last Remains, 1659 (written before 1642)

Attributed to

Sir John Suckling

I prithee send me back my heart,
   Since I can not have thine:
For if from yours you will not part,
   Why then shouldst thou have mine?

Yet now I think on't, let it lie:
   To find it were in vain,
For th' hast a thief in either eye
   Would steal it back again.

Why should two hearts in one breast lie,
   And yet not lodge together?
O love, where is thy sympathy,
   If thus our breasts thou sever?

But love is such a mystery,
   I cannot find it out:
For when I think I'm best resolved,
   I then am in most doubt.

Then farewell care, and farewell woe,
   I will no longer pine:
For I'll believe I have her heart
   As much as she has mine.

In J. Playford's Select Musical Airs, 1653

133

Sidney Godolphin

Or love me less, or love me more,
    And play not with my liberty,
Either take all, or all restore,
    Bind me at least, or set me free;
Let me some nobler torture find
Than of a doubtful wavering mind,
Take all my peace, but you betray
Mine honour too this cruel way.

'Tis true that I have nursed before
    That hope of which I now complain,
And, having little, sought no more,
    Fearing to meet with your disdain:
The sparks of favour you did give
I gently blow to make them live:
And yet have gained by all this care
No rest in hope, nor in despair.

I see you wear that pitying smile
    Which you have still vouchsafed my smart,
Content thus cheaply to beguile
    And entertain a harmless heart:
But I no longer can give way
To hope, which doth so little pay;
And yet I dare no freedom owe
Whilst you are kind, though but in show.

Then give me more or give me less,
    Do not disdain a mutual sense,
Or your unpitying beauties dress
    In their own free indifference.
But show not a severer eye
Sooner to give me liberty,
For I shall love the very scorn
Which for my sake you do put on.

Bodleian MS. Malone 13 (written before 1643)

Edmund Waller

Go, lovely rose,
  Tell her that wastes her time and me,
That now she knows,
  When I resemble her to thee,
  How sweet and fair she seems to be.

Tell her that's young,
  And shuns to have her graces spied,
That hadst thou sprung
  In deserts where no men abide,
  Thou must have uncommended died.

Small is the worth
  Of beauty from the light retired:
Bid her come forth,
  Suffer herself to be desired,
  And not blush so to be admired.

Then die – that she
  The common fate of all things rare
May read in thee;
  How small a part of time they share
  That are so wondrous sweet and fair!

Poems, 1645

On a Girdle

That which her slender waist confined
Shall now my joyful temples bind;
No monarch but would give his crown
His arms might do what this has done.

It was my Heaven's extremest sphere,
The pale which held that lovely Dear,
My joy, my grief, my hope, my love,
Did all within this circle move.

A narrow compass! and yet there
Dwelt all that's good, and all that's fair!
Give me but what this ribbon bound,
Take all the rest the sun goes round.

Poems, 1645 (text from edition of 1686)

William Cavendish, Duke of Newcastle
Love's Vision

Dear, let us two each other spy:
How curious! In each other's eye
We're drawn to life and thus we see
Ourselves at once, both thee and me,
Distinctly two, yet not alone,
Incorporated, that's but one.

My picture in your eyes you bear:
I yours, as much as mine you wear.
'Tis not our spreties * can not pass,
Or shining makes a looking-glass,
Nor picture; really we lie
Contracted each in other's eye.

When that our milk-white purer lawn,
Our eyelid curtains, when they're drawn,
Soft sleep, made with sweet vapour's rain,
To cool us shrinks into each brain,
Rejoicing with love's running streams,
Which grosser lovers call but dreams.

Because we two must never part,
We move down to each other's heart,
And there, all passions turned to joy,
Our loving hearts feel no annoy
Delated, lest our souls outskips
With joy, kiss quickly! stop our lips!

* spreties] spirits *The Phanseys*, *c*.1645 (*B.M. Add. MS.* 32,497)

The Ravishing Voice

Your voice, that's ravishing, so rare,
It moves the Cerean panting air,
    And makes the woods to walk;
Hard-hearted rocks are moved to tears,
And earth doth stretch her porous ears,
    Rivers leave murmuring talk.

The sun so ravished in his ear
As will not leave thy hemisphere;
    The fixëd stars now move,
And all the planets have no choice
But now are fixëd by thy voice:
    Thus all is turned to love.

Hard minerals now liquid flow,
Swelled hills fall into valleys low,
    Amazed where you do come;
The wilder beasts tame, void of fears,
And all man's senses turned to ears,
    The twatling echo dumb.

                The Phanseys, *c*.1645 (*B.M. Add. MS.* 32,497)

The Too Serious Love

    Sweet, let us love enjoy,
    And play and tick and toy,

And all our cares will drown;
Smile, laugh, and sometimes frown,
Make love's parenthesis
With a sweet, melting kiss.

Then whisper in each ear,
Love's pretty tales to hear;
If wanton, cry, 'Oh, man!'
And strike me with your fan;
If offer thee to dandle,
Then rap me with the handle.

For all this, I'll not miss
Thy lips, but steal a kiss;
'Cause it is stolen, then
I'll give it you again,
Play with your little hand,
And kiss it as I stand.

Then, though you think it much,
We'll one another touch,
As carelessly, not knowing
How love is now a-growing,
As if you did not mind it –
Yet both of us will find it.

And speak, too, all the while,
But in a lover's style:
Short-breathed with love's omissions,
Nonsense in repetitions.
If dare I am a villain,
Take notice you are willing.

Then flatter, kiss, collogue,
You say, 'Away, you rogue!'
When your cheek's red I'll pull thee,
And gently then will cull thee:
You say, 'Away!' So so,
Too serious you do grow.

The Phanseys, c.1645 (B.M. Add. MS. 32,497)

Love's Matrimony

There is no happy life
But in a wife;
The comforts are so sweet
When they do meet:
'Tis plenty, peace, a calm
Like dropping balm:
Love's weather is so fair,
Perfumëd air,
Each word such pleasure brings
Like soft-touched strings;
Love's passion moves the heart
On either part.
Such harmony together,
So pleased in either,
No discords, concords still,
Sealed with one will.

By love, God man made one,
Yet not alone:
Like stamps of king and queen
It may be seen,
Two figures but one coin;
So they do join,
Only they not embrace,
We, face to face.

The Phanseys, c.1645 (B.M. Add. MS. 32,497)

Unto a feast I will invite thee,
Where various dishes shall delight thee;
The steaming vapours drawn up hot
From earth, that Nature's porridge-pot,
Shall be our broth; we'll drink, my dear,
The thinner air for our small beer;

139

And if thou lik'st it not I'll call aloud,
And make our butler broach a cloud;
Of paler planets, for thy sake,
White-pots and trembling custards make;
The twinkling stars shall to our wish
Make a grand salad in a dish;
Snow for our sugar shall not fail,
Fine candied ice, comfits of hail;
For oranges, gilt clouds we'll squeeze,
The Milky Way we'll turn to cheese;
Sunbeams we'll catch shall stand in place
Of hotter ginger, nutmegs, mace;
Sunsetting clouds for roses sweet,
And violet skies strewed for our feet;
The spheres shall for our music play,
While spirits dance the time away;
When we drink healths Jove shall be proud,
The old cannoneer, to fire a cloud,
That all the Gods may know our mirth,
And trembling mortals, too, on earth;
And when our feasting shall be done
I'll lead thee uphill to the sun,
And place thee there that thy eyes may
Add greater lustre to the day.

The Humorous Lovers, 1677

John Fletcher

Come hither, you that love, and hear me sing
    Of joys still growing,
Green, fresh, and lusty as the pride of spring,
    And ever blowing.
Come hither, youths that blush, and dare not know
    What is desire:

And old men, worse than you, that cannot blow
  One spark of fire;
And with the power of my enchanting song,
Boys shall be able men, and old men young.

Come hither, you that hope, and you that cry;
  Leave off complaining;
Youth, strength, and beauty, that shall never die,
  Are here remaining.
Come hither, fools, and blush you stay so long
  From being blest;
And mad men, worse than you, that suffer wrong,
  Yet seek no rest;
And in an hour, with my enchanting song,
You shall be ever pleased, and young maids long.

The Captain, in *Comedies and Tragedies*, 1647

Abraham Cowley

The Thief

Thou robb'st my days of business and delights,
Of sleep thou robb'st my nights:
  Ah, lovely thief, what wilt thou do?
  What? rob me of heaven too?
  Thou even my prayers dost steal from me:
  And I, with wild idolatry,
  Begin, to God, and end them all, to thee.

Is it a sin to love, that it should thus
Like an ill conscience torture us?
  Whate'er I do, where'er I go
  (None guiltless e'er was haunted so)
  Still, still, methinks, thy face I view,
  And still thy shape does me pursue,
  As if, not you me, but I had murthered you.

From books I strive some remedy to take,
But thy name all the letters make:
   Whate'er 'tis writ, I find that there,
   Like points and commas everywhere.
   Me blessed for this let no man hold;
   For I, as Midas did of old,
   Perish by turning everything to gold.

What do I seek, alas, or why do I
Attempt in vain from thee to fly?
   For, making thee my deity,
   I gave thee then ubiquity.
   My pains resemble hell in this:
   The divine presence there too is,
   But to torment men, not to give them bliss.

The Mistress, 1647 (text from *Miscellanies*, 1656)

The Spring

Though you be absent here, I needs must say
The trees as beauteous are, and flowers as gay,
   As ever they were wont to be;
     Nay the birds' rural music too
   Is as melodious and free,
     As if they sung to pleasure you:
I saw a rose-bud ope this morn; I'll swear
The blushing morning opened not more fair.

How could it be so fair, and you away?
How could the trees be beauteous, flowers so gay?
   Could they remember but last year,
     How you did them, they you delight,
   The sprouting leaves which saw you here,
     And called their fellows to the sight,
Would, looking round for the same sight in vain,
Creep back into their silent barks again.

Where e'er you walked, trees were as reverend made,
As when of old gods dwelt in every shade.
   Is't possible they should not know,
     What loss of honour they sustain,
   That thus they smile and flourish now,
     And still their former pride retain?
Dull creatures! 'Tis not without cause that she,
Who fled the god of Wit, was made a tree.

In ancient times sure they much wiser were,
When they rejoiced the Thracian verse to hear;
   In vain did Nature bid them stay,
     When Orpheus had his song begun,
   They called their wondering roots away,
     And bade them silent to him run.
How would those learnëd trees have followed you?
You would have drawn them, and their poet too.

But who can blame them now? For, since you're gone,
They're here the only fair, and shine alone.
   You did their natural rights invade;
     Wherever you did walk or sit,
   The thickest boughs could make no shade,
     Although the sun had granted it:
The fairest flowers could please no more, near you,
Than painted flowers, set next to them, could do.

When e'er then you come hither, that shall be
The time, which this to others is, to me.
   The little joys which here are now,
     The name of punishments do bear;
   When by their sight they let us know
     How we deprived of greater are.
'Tis you the best of seasons with you bring;
This is for beasts, and that for men, the Spring.

The Mistress, 1647

The Change

Love in her sunny eyes does basking play,
Love walks the pleasant mazes of her hair,
Love does on both her lips for ever stray,
And sows and reaps a thousand kisses there.
  In all her outward parts Love's always seen;
  But, oh, he never went within.

Within, Love's foes, his greatest foes abide,
Malice, inconstancy, and pride.
So the earth's face, trees, herbs, and flowers do dress,
With other beauties numberless:
  But at the centre, darkness is, and hell;
  There wicked spirits, and there the damnëd dwell.

With me, alas, quite contrary it fares;
Darkness and Death lies in my weeping eyes;
Despair and paleness in my face appears,
And grief and fear, Love's greatest enemies;
  But, like the Persian tyrant, Love within
  Keeps his proud court, and ne'er is seen.

Oh, take my heart, and by that means you'll prove
Within too stor'd enough of Love:
Give me but yours, I'll by that change so thrive,
That Love in all my parts shall live.
  So powerful is this change, it render can,
  My outside Woman, and your inside Man.

The Mistress, 1647

Thomas Stanley

When I lie burning in thine eye,
  Or freezing in thy breast,
What martyrs, in wished flames that die,
  Are half so pleased or blest?

When thy soft accents, through mine ear,
   Into my soul do fly,
What angel would not quit his sphere
   To hear such harmony?

Or when the kiss thou gav'st me last
   My soul stole, in its breath,
What life would sooner be embraced
   Than so desired a death?

When I commanded am by thee,
   Or by thine eye or hand,
What monarch would not prouder be
   To serve than to command?

Then think not freedom I desire,
   Or would my fetters leave,
Since, Phoenix-like, I from this fire
   Both life and youth receive.

Poems and Translations, 1647

Jasper Mayne

   Time is a feathered thing,
And, whilst I praise
The sparklings of thy looks and call them rays,
   Takes wing,
Leaving behind him as he flies
An unperceivëd dimness in thine eyes.
His minutes, whilst they're told,
Do make us old;
And every sand of his fleet glass,
Increasing age as it doth pass,
Insensibly sows wrinkles there
Where flowers and roses do appear.

Whilst we do speak, our fire
Doth into ice expire,
  Flames turn to frost;
And ere we can
Know how our crow turns swan,
Or how a silver snow
Springs there where jet did grow,
  Our fading spring is in dull winter lost.

  Since, then, the Night hath hurled
Darkness, love's shade,
Over its enemy the Day, and made
  The world
Just such a blind and shapeless thing
As 'twas before light did from darkness spring,
Let us employ its treasure
And make shade pleasure:
Let's number out the hours by blisses,
And count the minutes by our kisses;
Let the heavens new motions feel
And by our embraces wheel;
And, whilst we try the way
By which love doth convey
  Soul into soul,
And mingling so
Making them such raptures know
As makes them entrancèd lie
In mutual ecstasy,
  Let the harmonious spheres in music roll!

The Amorous War, 1648

Robert Herrick

The Night-Piece, to Julia

Her eyes the glow-worm lend thee,
The shooting stars attend thee;
   And the elves also,
   Whose little eyes glow
Like the sparks of fire, befriend thee.

No will-o'-the-wisp mislight thee;
Nor snake or slow-worm bite thee:
   But on, on thy way
   Not making a stay,
Since ghost there's none to affright thee.

Let not the dark thee cumber;
What though the moon does slumber?
   The stars of the night
   Will lend thee their light,
Like tapers clear without number.

Then Julia, let me woo thee,
Thus, thus to come unto me:
   And when I shall meet
   Thy silvery feet,
My soul I'll pour into thee.

Hesperides, 1648

The Vine

I dreamed this mortal part of mine
Was metamorphosed to a vine,
Which, crawling one and every way,
Enthralled my dainty Lucia.

Methought her long, small legs and thighs ·
I with my tendrils did surprise;
Her belly, buttocks, and her waist
By my soft nervelets were embraced;
About her head I writhing hung,
And with rich clusters (hid among
The leaves) her temples I behung:
So that my Lucia seemed to me
Young Bacchus ravished by his tree.
My curls about her neck did crawl,
And arms and hands they did enthrall:
So that she could not freely stir
(All parts there made one prisoner).
But when I crept with leaves to hide
Those parts which maids keep unespied,
Such fleeting pleasures there I took
That with the fancy I awoke;
And found (ah me!) this flesh of mine
More like a stock than like a vine.

Hesperides, 1648

Upon the Nipples of Julia's Breast

Have ye beheld (with much delight)
A red rose peeping through a white?
Or else a cherry (double graced)
Within a lily's centre placed?
Or ever marked the pretty beam
A strawberry shows half-drowned in cream?
Or seen rich rubies blushing through
A pure smooth pearl, and orient, too?
So like to this, nay, all the rest,
Is each neat niplet of her breast.

Hesperides, 1648

To Anthea, Who May Command Him Any Thing

Bid me to live, and I will live
    Thy Protestant to be:
Or bid me love, and I will give
    A loving heart to thee.

A heart as soft, a heart as kind,
    A heart as sound and free
As in the whole world thou canst find,
    That heart I'll give to thee.

Bid that heart stay, and it will stay,
    To honour thy decree:
Or bid it languish quite away,
    And 't shall do so for thee.

Bid me to weep and I will weep
    While I have eyes to see:
And having none, yet I will keep
    A heart to weep for thee.

Bid me despair, and I'll despair,
    Under that cypress tree:
Or bid me die, and I will dare
    E'en death, to die for thee.

Thou art my life, my love, my heart,
    The very eyes of me,
And hast command of every part,
    To live and die for thee.

Hesperides, 1648

To the Virgins, to Make Much of Time

Gather ye rose-buds while ye may,
    Old Time is still a-flying:
And this same flower that smiles to-day,
    To-morrow will be dying.

The glorious lamp of heaven, the sun,
  The higher he's a-getting,
The sooner will his race be run,
  And nearer he's to setting.

That age is best which is the first,
  When youth and blood are warmer;
But being spent, the worse, and worst
  Times still succeed the former.

Then be not coy, but use your time;
  And while ye may, go marry:
For having lost but once your prime,
  You may for ever tarry.

Hesperides, 1648

Richard Lovelace

The Rose

Sweet, serene, sky-like flower,
Haste to adorn her bower,
From thy long cloudy bed
Shoot forth thy damask head.

New startled blush of Flora,
The grief of pale Aurora,
Who will contest no more,
Haste, haste to strow her floor.

Vermilion ball that's given
From lip to lip in heaven,
Love's couch's coverled,
Haste, haste to make her bed.

Dear offspring of pleased Venus
And jolly plump Silenus,
Haste, haste to deck the hair
Of the only sweetly fair.

See! rosy is her bower,
Her floor is all this flower,
Her bed a rosy nest
By a bed of roses pressed.

But early as she dresses,
Why fly you her bright tresses?
Ah! I have found I fear,
Because her cheeks are near.

Lucasta, 1649

To Lucasta, Going beyond the Seas

If to be absent were to be
Away from thee;
Or that when I am gone
You or I were alone;
Then, my Lucasta, might I crave
Pity from blustering wind, or swallowing wave.

But I'll not sigh one blast or gale
To swell my sail,
Or pay a tear to swage
The foaming blue god's rage;
For whether he will let me pass
Or no, I'm still as happy as I was.

Though seas and land be 'twixt us both,
Our faith and troth,
Like separated souls,
All time and space controls:
Above the highest sphere we meet
Unseen, unknown, and greet as angels greet.

So then we do anticipate
Our after-fate,
And are alive i' the skies,
If thus our lips and eyes
Can speak like spirits unconfined
In Heaven, their earthy bodies left behind.

Lucasta, 1649

To Lucasta, Going to the Wars

Tell me not, Sweet, I am unkind
  That from the nunnery
Of thy chaste breasts, and quiet mind,
  To war and arms I fly.

True, a new mistress now I chase,
  The first foe in the field;
And with a stronger faith embrace
  A sword, a horse, a shield.

Yet this inconstancy is such
  As you too shall adore;
I could not love thee, Dear, so much,
  Loved I not honour more.

Lucasta, 1649

To Althea, from Prison

When Love with unconfinëd wings
   Hovers within my gates,
And my divine Althea brings
   To whisper at the grates;
When I lie tangled in her hair
   And fettered to her eye,
The birds, that wanton in the air,
   Know no such liberty.

When flowing cups run swiftly round
   With no allaying Thames,
Our careless heads with roses bound,
   Our hearts with loyal flames;
When thirsty grief in wine we steep,
   When healths and draughts go free,
Fishes, that tipple in the deep,
   Know no such liberty.

When, like committed linnets, I
   With shriller throat shall sing
The sweetness, mercy, majesty
   And glories of my King;
When I shall voice aloud, how good
   He is, how great should be,
Enlargëd winds, that curl the flood,
   Know no such liberty.

Stone walls do not a prison make,
   Nor iron bars a cage;
Minds innocent and quiet take
   That for an hermitage:
If I have freedom in my love,
   And in my soul am free,
Angels alone, that soar above,
   Enjoy such liberty.

Lucasta, 1649

John Reynolds

Say, crimson rose and dainty daffodil,
    With violet blue,
Since you have seen the beauty of my saint,
    And eke her view,
Did not her sight (fair sight!) you lovely fill
    With sweet delight
Of goddess' grace and angel's sacred taint
    In fine, most bright?

Say, golden primrose, sanguine cowslip fair,
    With pink most fine,
Since you beheld the visage of my dear,
    And eyes divine,
Did not her globy front and glistering hair,
    With cheeks most sweet,
So gloriously like damask flowers appear,
    The gods to greet?

Say, snow-white lily, speckled gillyflower,
    With daisy gay,
Since you have viewed the queen of my desire
    In brave array,
Did not her ivory paps, fair Venus' bower,
    With heavenly glee,
Of Juno's grace, conjure you to require
    Her face to see?

Say rose, say daffodil, and violet blue,
    With primrose fair,
Since you have seen my nymph's sweet dainty face
    And gesture rare,
Did not (bright cowslip, bloomy pink) her view
    (White lily) shine
(Ah, gillyflowers and daisy!) with a grace
    Like stars divine?

The Flower of Fidelitie, 1650

Andrew Marvell

The Mower to the Glow-worms

Ye living lamps, by whose dear light
   The nightingale does sit so late,
And, studying all the summer night,
   Her matchless songs does meditate;

Ye country comets that portend
   No war, nor prince's funeral,
Shining unto no higher end
   Than to presage the grass's fall;

Ye glow-worms, whose officious flame
   To wandering mowers shows the way,
That in the night have lost their aim,
   And after foolish fires do stray;

Your courteous lights in vain you waste,
   Since Juliana here is come,
For she my mind hath so displaced
   That I shall never find my home.

Miscellaneous Poems, 1681 (written about 1650)

To His Coy Mistress

Had we but world enough, and time,
This coyness, lady, were no crime.
We would sit down, and think which way
To walk, and pass our long love's day.
Thou by the Indian Ganges' side
Shouldst rubies find: I by the tide
Of Humber would complain. I would
Love you ten years before the Flood,
And you should, if you please, refuse
Till the Conversion of the Jews;

My vegetable love should grow
Vaster than empires and more slow;
An hundred years should go to praise
Thine eyes, and on thy forehead gaze;
Two hundred to adore each breast,
But thirty thousand to the rest;
An age at least to every part,
And the last age should show your heart.
For, lady, you deserve this state,
Nor would I love at lower rate,
   But at my back I always hear
Time's wingèd chariot hurrying near,
And yonder, all before us lie
Deserts of vast eternity.
Thy beauty shall no more be found,
Nor, in thy marble vault, shall sound
My echoing song; then worms shall try
That long-preserved virginity,
And your quaint honour turn to dust,
And into ashes all my lust:
The grave's a fine and private place,
But none, I think, do there embrace.
   Now, therefore, while the youthful hue
Sits on thy skin like morning dew,
And while thy willing soul transpires
At every pore with instant fires,
Now let us sport us while we may,
And now, like amorous birds of prey,
Rather at once our time devour,
Than languish in his slow-chapt power.
Let us roll all our strength and all
Our sweetness up into one ball,
And tear our pleasures with rough strife,
Thorough the iron gates of life;
Thus, though we cannot make our sun
Stand still, yet we will make him run.

Miscellaneous Poems, 1684 (written before 1653)

The Definition of Love

My love is of a birth as rare
   As 'tis for object strange and high:
It was begotten by Despair
   Upon Impossibility.

Magnanimous Despair alone
   Could show me so divine a thing,
Where feeble Hope could ne'er have flown
   But vainly flapped its tinsel wing.

And yet I quickly might arrive
   Where my extended soul is fixed;
But Fate does iron wedges drive,
   And always crowds itself betwixt.

For Fate with jealous eye doth see
   Two perfect loves; nor lets them close:
Their union would her ruin be
   And her tyrannic power depose.

And therefore her decrees of steel
   Us as the distant poles have placed,
(Though Love's whole world on us doth wheel)
   Not by themselves to be embraced:

Unless the giddy heaven fall,
   And earth some new convulsion tear,
And, us to join, the world should all
   Be cramped into a planisphere.

As lines, so loves oblique may well
   Themselves in every angle greet:
But ours, so truly parallel,
   Though infinite, can never meet.

Therefore the love which us doth bind,
   But Fate so enviously debars,
Is the conjunction of the mind,
   And opposition of the stars.

Miscellaneous. Poems, 1681 (written before 1653)

Anonymous

Tell me, you wandering spirits of the air,
Did you not see a nymph more bright, more fair
Than Beauty's darling, or of parts more sweet
Than stol'n content? If such a one you meet,
Wait on her hourly wheresoe'er she flies,
And cry, and cry, 'Amyntas for her absence dies'.

Go search the valleys; pluck up every rose,
You'll find a scent, a blush of her in those;
Fish, fish for pearl or coral, there you'll see
How oriental all her colours be;
Go, call the echoes to your aid, and cry
'Chloris! Chloris!' for that's her name for whom I die.

But stay a while; I have informed you ill,
Were she on earth, she had been with me still:
Go, fly to heaven, examine every sphere;
And try what star hath lately lighted there:
If any brighter than the sun you see,
Fall down, fall down and worship it, for that is she.

In J. Playford's *Select Musical Airs*, 1652

Henry Noel
Beauty's Excellency

Gaze not on swans, in whose soft breast
A full-hatched beauty seems to nest;
Nor snow, which falling from the sky
Hovers in its virginity.

Gaze not on roses, though new blown,
Graced with a fresh complexion;
Nor lilies, which no subtle bee
Hath robbed by kissing chymistry.

158

Gaze not on that pure Milky Way,
Where Night vies splendour with the Day;
Nor pearl, whose silver walls confine
The riches of an Indian mine.

For if my Emperess appears,
Swans moulting die, snow melts to tears,
Roses do blush and hang their heads,
Pale lilies shrink into their beds:

The Milky Way rides post to shroud
Its baffled glory in a cloud;
And pearls do climb into her ear,
To hang themselves for envy there.

So have I seen stars big with light
Prove lanthorns to the moon-eyed Night,
Which, when Sol's rays were once displayed,
Sunk in their sockets, and decayed.

In Henry Lawes' Airs and Dialogues, 1653

Nicholas Hookes

To Amanda Walking in the Garden

And now what monarch would not gardener be,
My fair Amanda's stately gait to see?
How her feet tempt! how soft and light she treads,
Fearing to wake the flowers from their beds!
Yet from their sweet green pillows everywhere
They start and gaze about to see my Fair.
Look at yon flower yonder, how it grows,
Sensibly! how it opes its leaves and blows,
Puts its best Easter clothes on, neat and gay:

Amanda's presence makes it holiday!
Look how on tiptoe that fair lily stands
To look on thee, and court thy whiter hands
To gather it! I saw in yonder crowd—
That tulip bed of which Dame Flora's proud—
A short dwarf flower did enlarge its stalk,
And shoot an inch to see Amanda walk.
Nay, look, my Fairest! look how fast they grow
Into a scaffold-method spring, as though,
Riding to Parliament, were to be seen
In pomp and state some royal amorous Queen!
The gravelled walks, though even as a die,
Lest some loose pebble should offensive lie,
Quilt themselves o'er with downy moss for thee;
The walls are hanged with blossomed tapestry
To hide their nakedness when looked upon;
The maiden fig tree puts Eve's apron on;
The broad-leaved sycamore, and every tree,
Shakes like the trembling asp, and bends to thee,
And each leaf proudly strives, with fresher air
To fan the curlëd tresses of thy hair.
Nay, and the bee too, with his wealthy thigh,
Mistakes his hive, and to thy lips doth fly,
Willing to treasure up his honey there,
Where honey-combs so sweet and plenty are.
Look how that pretty modest columbine
Hangs down its head, to view those feet of thine!
See the fond motion of the strawberry,
Creeping on th' earth, to go along with thee!
The lovely violet makes after too,
Unwilling yet, my Dear, to part with you;
The knot-grass and the daisies catch thy toes,
To kiss my fair one's feet before she goes;
All court and wish me lay Amanda down,
And give my Dear a new green-flowered gown.
  Come, let me kiss thee falling, kiss at rise,
  Thou in the garden, I in Paradise.

Amanda, 1653

Sir William Davenant

The lark now leaves his watery nest
  And, climbing, shakes his dewy wings;
He takes this window for the East,
  And to implore your light, he sings,
Awake! Awake! The morn will never rise,
Till she can dress her beauty at your eyes.

The merchant bows unto the seaman's star,
  The ploughman from the sun his season takes;
But still the lover wonders what they are,
  Who look for day before his mistress wakes.
Awake! Awake! Break through your veils of lawn!
Then draw your curtains, and begin the dawn.

Works, 1673 (written before 1656)

Under the willow shades they were
  Free from the eye-sight of the sun,
For no intruding beam could there
    Peep through to spy what things were done:
      Thus sheltered, they unseen did lie,
      Surfeiting on each other's eye;
Defended by the willow shades alone,
The sun's heat they defied, and cooled their own.

Whilst they did embrace unspied,
  The conscious willows seemed to smile,
That they with privacy supplied,
    Holding the door, as 'twere, the while,
      And, when their dalliances were o'er,
      The willows, to oblige 'em more,
Bowing, did seem to say, as they withdrew,
'We can supply you with a cradle, too.'

The Rivals, 1668

161

John Milton

Methought I saw my late espousëd Saint
  Brought to me like Alcestis from the grave,
  Whom Jove's great son to her glad husband gave,
Rescued from death by force though pale and faint.
Mine, as whom washed from spot of child-bed taint,
  Purification in the old law did save,
  And such, as yet once more I trust to have
Full sight of her in Heaven without restraint,
Came vested all in white, pure as her mind:
  Her face was veiled, yet to my fancied sight,
Love, sweetness, goodness, in her person shined
  So clear, as in no face with more delight.
But oh as to embrace me she inclined
  I waked, she fled, and day brought back my night.

Poems, &c., upon Several Occasions, 1673 (written in 1658)

Charles Cotton

Laura Sleeping

Winds, whisper gently whilst she sleeps,
  And fan her with your cooling wings;
Whilst she her drops of beauty weeps
  From pure and yet-unrivalled springs.

Glide over beauty's field, her face,
  To kiss her lip and cheek be bold,
But with a calm and stealing pace,
  Neither too rude, nor yet too cold.

Play in her beams, and crisp her hair,
  With such a gale as wings soft love,
And with so sweet, so rich an air,
  As breathes from the Arabian grove,

A breath as hushed as lover's sigh,
　　Or that unfolds the morning door;
Sweet as the winds that gently fly
　　To sweep the Spring's enamelled floor.

Murmur soft music to her dreams,
　　That pure and unpolluted run,
Like to the new-born crystal streams
　　Under the bright enamoured sun.

But when she waking shall display
　　Her light, retire within your bar:
Her breath is life, her eyes are day,
　　And all mankind her creatures are.

Poems, 1689 (written *c*.1660)

The
Restoration
Wits

Pathericke Jenkyn
On the Death of His Mistress

Ask me not why the rose doth fade,
   Lilies look pale, and flowers die;
Question not why the myrtle shade
   Her wonted shadows doth deny.

Seek not to know from whence begun
   The sadness of the nightingale,
Nor why the heliotrope and sun
   Their constant amity do fail.

The turtle's grief look not upon,
   Nor why the palm-tree doth mourn,
When widow-like they're left alone,
   Nor phoenix, why her self doth burn.

For she is dead which life did give
   Unto those things that here I name;
They fade, change, wither, cease to live,
   Pine, and consume into a flame.

Amorea, 1661

John Dryden

I feed a flame within, which so torments me
That it both pains my heart, and yet contents me:
'Tis such a pleasing smart, and I so love it,
That I had rather die than once remove it.

Yet he for whom I grieve shall never know it;
My tongue does not betray, nor my eyes show it.
Not a sign, nor a tear, my pain discloses,
But they fall silently, like dew on roses.

Thus, to prevent my Love from being cruel,
My heart's the sacrifice, as 'tis the fuel;
And while I suffer this to give him quiet,
My faith rewards my Love, though he deny it.

On his eyes will I gaze, and there delight me;
While I conceal my love no frown can fright me.
To be more happy I dare not aspire,
Nor can I fall more low, mounting no higher.

Secret-Love, or The Maiden-Queen, 1668

Ah, how sweet it is to love!
    Ah, how gay is young desire!
And what pleasing pains we prove
    When we first approach love's fire!
        Pains of love be sweeter far
        Than all other pleasures are.

Sighs which are from lovers blown
    Do but gently heave the heart:
Even the tears they shed alone
    Cure, like trickling balm, their smart.
        Lovers, when they lose their breath,
        Bleed away in easy death.

Love and time with reverence use,
    Treat 'em like a parting friend:
Nor the golden gifts refuse,
    Which in youth sincere they send:
        For each year their price is more,
        And they less simple than before.

Love, like spring-tides full and high,
    Swells in every youthful vein;
But each tide does less supply,
    Till they quite shrink in again;
        If a flow in age appear,
        'Tis but rain, and runs not clear.

Tyrannick Love, or, The Royal Martyr, 1670

After the pangs of a desperate lover,
    When day and night I have sighed all in vain,
Ah what a pleasure it is to discover
    In her eyes pity, who causes my pain!

When with unkindness our love at a stand is,
    And both have punished ourselves with the pain,
Ah what a pleasure the touch of her hand is!
    Ah what a pleasure to press it again!

When the denial comes fainter and fainter,
    And her eyes give what her tongue does deny,
Ah what a trembling I feel when I venture!
    Ah what a trembling does usher my joy!

When, with a sigh, she accords me the blessing,
    And her eyes twinkle 'twixt pleasure and pain,
Ah what a joy 'tis, beyond all expressing!
    Ah what a joy to hear, *Shall we again?*

An Evening's Love, or, The Mock Astrologer, 1671

Farewell, ungrateful traitor,
    Farewell, my perjured swain;
Let never injured creature
    Believe a man again.
The pleasure of possessing
Surpasses all expressing,
But 'tis too short a blessing,
    And love too long a pain.

'Tis easy to deceive us
    In pity of your pain,
But when we love you leave us
    To rail at you in vain.
Before we have descried it,
There is no bliss beside it,
But she that once has tried it
    Will never love again.

169

The passion you pretended
　　Was only to obtain;
But when the charm is ended
　　The charmer you disdain.
Your love by ours we measure,
Till we have lost our treasure;
But dying is a pleasure
　　When living is a pain.

The Spanish Fryar, or, The Double Discovery, 1681

No, no, poor suffering heart, no change endeavour;
Choose to sustain the smart, rather than leave her.
My ravished eyes behold such charms about her,
I can die with her, but not live without her.
One tender sigh of hers, to see me languish,
Will more than pay the price of my past anguish.
Beware, O cruel Fair, how you smile on me!
'Twas a kind look of yours that has undone me.

Love has in store for me one happy minute,
And she will end my pain who did begin it;
Then, no day void of bliss or pleasure leaving,
Ages shall slide away without perceiving:
Cupid shall guard the door, the more to please us,
And keep out Time and Death, when they would seize us:
Time and Death shall depart, and say, in flying,
Love has found out a way to live by dying.

Cleomenes, 1692

Sir Charles Sedley

Ah Cloris! that I now could sit
  As unconcerned as when
Your infant beauty could beget
  No pleasure nor no pain.

When I the dawn used to admire,
  And praised the coming day,
I little thought the growing fire
  Must take my rest away.

Your charms in harmless childhood lay
  Like metals in the mine;
Age from no face took more away
  Than youth concealed in thine.

But, as your charms insensibly
  To their perfection pressed,
Fond love as unperceived did fly,
  And in my bosom rest.

My passion with your beauty grew,
  And Cupid at my heart,
Still as his mother favoured you,
  Threw a new flaming dart.

Each gloried in their wanton part;
  To make a lover he
Employed the utmost of his art,
  To make a beauty, she.

Though now I slowly bend to love,
  Uncertain of my fate,
If your fair self my chains approve,
  I shall my freedom hate.

Lovers, like dying men, may well
  At first disordered be,
Since none alive can truly tell
  What fortune they must see.

The Mulberry-Garden, 1668

Get you gone, you will undo me,
If you love me don't pursue me;
Let that inclination perish
Which I dare no longer cherish.
With harmless thoughts I did begin,
But in the crowd Love entered in;
I knew him not, he was so gay,
So innocent and full of play.
At every hour, in every place,
I either saw or formed your face.
All that in plays was finely writ
Fancy for you and me did fit;
My dreams at night were all of you,
Such as till then I never knew.
I sported thus with young desire,
Never intending to go higher;
But now his teeth and claws are grown,
Let me the fatal lion shun.
You found me harmless; leave me so;
For, were I not, you'd leave me too.

In A Collection of Poems . . . by Several Persons, 1672
(text from Sedley's *Miscellaneous Works*, 1702)

Phillis, let's shun the common fate,
And let our love ne'er turn to hate.
I'll dote no longer than I can,
Without being called a faithless man.
When we begin to want discourse,
And kindness seems to taste of force,
As freely as we met we'll part,
Each one possessed of their own heart.
Thus, whilst rash fools themselves undo,
We'll game, and give off savers too.
So equally the match we'll make,
Both shall be glad to draw the stake.

A smile of thine shall make my bliss;
I will enjoy thee in a kiss.
If from this height our kindness fall,
We'll bravely scorn to love at all.
If thy affection first decay,
I will the blame on Nature lay.
Alas, what cordial can remove
The hasty fate of dying love?
Thus we will all the world excel
In loving and in parting well.

In *A Collection of Poems* . . . *by Several Persons*, 1672
(text from Sedley's *Miscellaneous Works*, 1702)

Love still has something of the sea,
    From whence his mother rose;
No time his slaves from doubt can free,
    Nor give their thoughts repose.

They are becalmed in clearest days,
    And in rough weather tossed;
They wither under cold delays,
    Or are in tempests lost.

One while they seem to touch the port,
    Then straight into the main
Some angry wind in cruel sport
    The vessel drives again.

At first disdain and pride they fear,
    Which, if they chance to 'scape,
Rivals and falsehood soon appear,
    In a more dreadful shape.

By such degrees to joy they come,
    And are so long withstood,
So slowly they receive the sum,
    It hardly does them good.

173

'Tis cruel to prolong a pain,
   And to defer a joy,
Believe me, gentle Celemene
   Offends the wingëd boy.

An hundred thousand oaths your fears
   Perhaps would not remove;
And, if I gazed a thousand years,
   I could no deeper love.

In A Collection of Poems . . . by Several Persons, 1672
(text from Sedley's Miscellaneous Works, 1702)

Not, Celia, that I juster am
   Or better than the rest;
For I would change each hour, like them,
   Were not my heart at rest.

But I am tied to very thee
   By every thought I have;
They face I only care to see,
   Thy heart I only crave.

All that in woman is adored
   In thy dear self I find;
For the whole sex can but afford
   The handsome and the kind.

Why then should I seek further store,
   And still make love anew?
When change itself can give no more,
   'Tis easy to be true.

In A Collection of Poems . . . by Several Persons, 1672
(text from Sedley's Miscellaneous Works, 1702)

Attributed to
King Charles II
The First Song in the Ball at Court

I pass all my hours in a shady old grove,
And I live not the day that I see not my Love.
I survey every walk now my Phillis is gone,
And sigh when I think we were there all alone.
    Oh, then 'tis! oh, then, I think there's no such hell
    Like loving, like loving too well!

But each shade and each conscious bower that I find,
Where I once have been happy and she has been kind,
And I see the print left of her shape in the green,
And imagine the pleasure may yet come again;
    Oh, then 'tis! oh, then, I think no joy's above
    The pleasures, the pleasures of love!

While alone to myself I repeat all her charms
She I love may be locked in another man's arms:
She may laugh at my cares, and so false she may be
To say all the kind things she before said to me;
    Oh, then 'tis! oh, then, I think there's no such hell
    Like loving, like loving too well!

But when I consider the truth of her heart,
Such an innocent passion, so kind, without art,
I fear I have wronged her, and hope she may be
So full of true love to be jealous of me.
    Oh, then 'tis! oh, then, I think no joy's above
    The pleasures, the pleasures of love!

In Westminster Drollery, 1671

Charles Sackville, Earl of Dorset

Phyllis, for shame, let us improve,
  A thousand several ways,
These few short minutes stol'n by love
  From many tedious days.

Whilst you want courage to despise
  The censure of the grave,
For all the tyrants in your eyes,
  Your heart is but a slave.

My love is full of noble pride,
  And never will submit
To let that fop Discretion ride
  In triumph over Wit.

False friends I have, as well as you,
  That daily counsel me
Vain frivolous trifles to pursue,
  And leave off loving thee.

When I the least belief bestow
  On what such fools advise,
May I be dull enough to grow
  Most miserably wise.

  In *Westminster Drollery*, 1671, and *Windsor Drollery*, 1671

May the ambitious pleasure find
  In crowds and empty noise,
While gentle love does fill my mind
  With silent real joys.

Let knave and fool grow rich and cruel,
  And the world think 'em wise,
While I lie dying at her feet,
  And all that world despise.

Let conquering kings new trophies raise,
   And melt in Court delights;
Her eyes can give me brighter days,
   Her arms much softer nights.

In Choice Ayres and Songs, 1684

The fire of love in youthful blood,
Like what is kindled in brushwood,
   But for a moment burns;
Yet in that moment makes a mighty noise,
It crackles, and to vapour turns,
   And soon itself destroys.

But, when crept into aged veins,
It slowly burns, and long remains,
   And, with a sullen heat,
Like fire in logs, it glows and warms 'em long,
And, though the flame be not so great,
   Yet is the heat as strong.

In The Amorous Bigotte, by Thomas Shadwell, 1690

Aphra Behn

Amyntas led me to a grove
   Where all the trees did shade us:
The sun itself, though it had strove,
   Yet could not have betrayed us.
The place, secure from human eyes,
   No other fear allows,
But when the winds that gently rise
   Do kiss the yielding boughs.

Down there we sat upon the moss,
   And did begin to play
A thousand amorous tricks, to pass
   The heat of all the day.

A many kisses he did give,
　　And I returned the same,
Which made me willing to receive
　　That which I dare not name.

His charming eyes no aid required,
　　To tell their softening tale;
On her that was already fired
　　'Twas easy to prevail.
He did but kiss and clasp me round,
　　Whilst those his thoughts expressed,
And laid me gently on the ground;
　　Ah, who can guess the rest?

In *Covent Garden Drolery*, 1672
(text from *Poems upon Several Occasions*, 1684)

Love in fantastic triumph sat,
　　Whilst bleeding hearts around him flowed,
For whom fresh pains he did create
　　And strange tyrannic power he showed:
From thy bright eyes he took his fires,
　　Which round about in sport he hurled,
But 'twas from mine he took desires
　　Enough t' undo the amorous world.

From me he took his sighs and tears,
　　From thee his pride and cruelty;
From me his languishment and fears,
　　And every killing dart from thee:
Thus thou and I the God have armed,
　　And set him up a deity;
But my poor heart alone is harmed,
　　Whilst thine the victor is, and free.

Abdelazer, or, The Moor's Revenge, 1677
(also in *The Last and Best Edition of New Songs*, 1677)

Anonymous

Oh! the time that is past,
When she held me so fast,
And declared that her honour no longer could last:
No light but her languishing eyes did appear,
To prevent all excuses of blushing and fear.

When she sighed and unlaced
With such trembling and haste,
As if she had longed to be closer embraced!
My lips the sweet pleasure of kisses enjoyed,
While my hands were in search of hid treasure employed.

With my heart all on fire
In the flames of desire,
I boldly pursued what she seemed to require:
She cried: 'Oh, for pity's sake! change your ill mind:
Pray, Amyntas, be civil, or I'll be unkind.

'All your bliss you destroy,
Like a naked young boy,
Who fears the kind river he came to enjoy . . .'
'Let's in, my dear Cloris! I'll save thee from harm,
And make the cold element pleasant and warm.'

'Dear Amyntas!' she cries;
Then she casts down her eyes,
And with kisses consents what she faintly denies:
Too sure of my conquest, I purpose to stay
Till her freer consent did more sweeten the prey.

But too late I begun;
For her passion was done:
'Now, Amyntas,' she cries, 'I will never be won:
Thy tears and thy courtship no pity can move;
Thou hast slighted the critical minute of love.'

In *New Court-Songs, and Poems*, 1672

Sir George Etherege

The Fair but Cruel Girl

The nymph that undoes me is fair and unkind,
No less than a wonder by nature designed;
She's the grief of my heart, but joy of my eye,
The cause of my flame, that never can die.

Her lips, from whence wit obligingly flows,
Have the colour of cherries and smell of the rose;
Love and destiny both attend on her will;
She saves with a smile, with a frown she can kill.

The desperate lover can hope no redress,
Where beauty and rigour are both in excess;
In Caelia they meet, so unhappy am I;
Who sees her must love; who loves her must die.

In *Westminster Drollery*, II, 1672

Ye happy swains, whose hearts are free
    From Love's imperial chain,
Take warning, and be taught by me
    To avoid the enchanting pain:
Fatal the wolves to trembling flocks,
    Fierce winds to blossoms prove;
To careless seamen, hidden rocks,
    To human quiet, Love.

Fly the fair sex if bliss you prize;
    The snake's beneath the flower:
Who ever gazed on beauteous eyes
    That tasted quiet more?
How faithless is the lovers' joy!
    How constant is their care!
The kind with falsehood do destroy;
    The cruel, with despair.

In Aphra Behn's *Miscellany*, 1685

180

Anonymous

Ah! cruel eyes, that first inflamed
  My poor resistless heart,
That when I would my thoughts have blamed
  They still increase the smart.
    What power above
    Creates such love,
  To languish with desire?
    May some disdain
    Increase my pain
  Or may the flame expire!

And yet I die to think how soon
  My wishes may return:
If slighted, and my hope once gone,
  I must in silence mourn.
    Then, tyranness,
    Do but express
  The mystery of your power;
    'Tis as soon said,
    You'll love and wed,
  As studying for't an hour.

I yield to Fate, though your fair eyes
  Have made the power your own;
'Twas they did first my heart surprise;
  Dear nymph! 'twas they alone.
    For honour's sake,
    Your heart awake,
  And let your pity move,
    Lest in despair
    Of one so fair
  I bid adieu to love.

In *Methinks the Poor Town* . . . , 1673

Richard Leigh

Sleeping on Her Couch

Thus lovely, sleep did first appear,
    Ere yet it was with death allied,
When the first fair one, like her here,
    Lay down, and for a little died.

Ere happy souls knew how to die,
    And trod the rougher paths to bliss,
Transported in an ecstasy,
    They breathed out such smooth ways as this.

Her hand bears gently up her head,
    And, like a pillow, raised does keep,
But softer than her couch is spread,
    Though that be softer than her sleep.

Alas! that death-like sleep, or night,
    Should power have to close those eyes,
Which once vied with the fairest light
    Or what gay colours thence did rise.

Ah! that lost beams thus long have shined
    To them with darkness over-spread,
Unseen, as day breaks, to the blind,
    Or the sun rises, to the dead.

That sun, in all his eastern pride,
    Did never see a shape so rare
Nor night within its black arms hide
    A silent beauty half so fair.

Poems, upon Several Occasions, 1675

Gathering Peaches

Behold, wherever she does pass,
　How all the amorous trees contend
Whose loaded arms should her embrace,
　While with their fruit tow'rds her they bend,
　　As if the willing branches meant
　　To her their bounty to present.

The upper boughs, all bending low,
　Her raisëd arm seem to prevent;
While those that level with her grow
　To meet her easy hand consent:
　　To court her thus, Lo! every peach
　　Submits itself, within her reach.

These she prefers, refusing those,
　Unhappy, in their ripening last;
Persuaded by her eye to choose,
　As that the coloured fruit does taste;
　　Which her desire does gently move
　　To what her sense did first approve.

Fair as this golden fruit here seems,
　The sun, with kind salutes, thus streaks,
And, gilding them with amorous beams,
　Prints purple kisses on their cheeks –
　　Kisses soft as that tender down
　　Which their young blushing cheeks does crown.

Ah, could the Fair, who this does see,
　Be by this great example won,
And learn but thus to smile on me
　As *they* smile on the kissing sun!
　　Bright as their cheeks with kisses shine,
　　Hers brighter should appear with mine.

Poems, upon Several Occasions, 1675

Bathing Her Self

Happy this wandering stream!
Which gently proud does seem,
As it had ne'er before
So rich a burden bore.

Swelled with her body now,
It does with joy o'erflow.
The exulting waves forget
The limits to them set;
With joy now swelling more
Than e'er with rage before,
Her breast yet lightly raise
To measure its smooth ways,
While her soft arms divide
The current on each side,
Which, in new circles broke
By every bending stroke,
Thus troubled, does appear
As struck with sunbeams clear.

From out of water ne'er
Did rise a shape so fair;
Nor could it e'er to sight
Reflect a form so bright:
Such sweetness, nor such grace,
Shined not in Venus' face,
When froth did it enclose,
As 'bove the waves it rose,
And in white circles crowned
The whiter goddess round:
Less pleasing she did show
Her naked glories new,
Though all the deep then smiled
To see the sea-born child.

No undisturbëd brook,
In which th' heavens choose to look,
Sees such a beauty move
As this reflects above;
No deeps such treasures know,
As what this hides below.

Poems, upon Several Occasions, 1675

Fanning Her Self

See how the charming Fair
Does break the yielding air,
Which, by her troubled so,
More pure, more smooth, does flow.
Winds without murmurs rise,
Complaining in sad sighs,
Though they dare not repine,
How loath they're to resign
Their interest in the Fair
To new succeeding air.
How silently they grieve,
Their snatched embrace to leave
To new winds, who their place
Supply, and their embrace,
Courting their longer bliss
At every parting kiss,
While, with a gentle gale,
They swell her painted sail.
Then, trembling, they give way,
Fearing to disobey,
Though fain they her would bear
With every moving air.

In vain, alas! they prove
Unkindness to remove;
In vain to win the field;
Air may, she cannot, yield.
Her hand a thousand ways
New favourites does raise,
Which, to salute her proud,
Do round about her crowd,
And rival-like pursue
Th' old, thrust out by the new.

Well may they boast they can
Move false trees, in her fan,
And with their tremblings make
Their trunks, though rooted, shake.
With oaks they may contend,
But she can never bend.
She, should even storms engage
Her with their roughest rage,
And all their utmost prove,
Too stubborn is, to move.

Poems, upon Several Occasions, 1675

John Wilmot, Earl of Rochester

Love and Life

All my past life is mine no more;
  The flying hours are gone:
Like transitory dreams given o'er,
Whose images are kept in store
  By memory alone.

Whatever is to come, is not;
　　How can it then be mine?
The present moment's all my lot;
And that, as fast as it is got,
　　Phillis, is wholly thine.

Then talk not of inconstancy,
　　False hearts, and broken vows;
If I, by miracle, can be
This livelong minute true to thee,
　　'Tis all that Heaven allows.

> In *Songs . . . Composed by Henry Bowman*, [1677]
> (text from Rochester's *Poems on Several Occasions*, 1680)

I cannot change, as others do,
　　Though you unjustly scorn:
Since that poor swain that sighs for you
　　For you alone was born.
No, Phillis, no, your heart to move
　　A surer way I'll try:
And, to revenge my slighted love,
Will still love on, will still love on, and die.

When, killed with grief, Amyntas lies,
　　And you to mind shall call
The sighs that now unpitied rise,
　　The tears that vainly fall;
That welcome hour that ends this smart,
　　Will then begin your pain;
For such a faithful tender heart
Can never break, can never break in vain.

> In *Choice Ayres and Songs . . . The Second Book*, 1679
> (text from Rochester's *Poems on Several Occasions*, 1680)

My dear mistress has a heart
  Soft as those kind looks she gave me;
When, with love's resistless art,
  And her eyes, she did enslave me.
But her constancy's so weak,
  She's so wild, and apt to wander,
That my jealous heart would break,
  Should we live one day asunder.

Melting joys about her move,
  Killing pleasures, wounding blisses;
She can dress her eyes in love,
  And her lips can arm with kisses.
Angels listen when she speaks,
  She's my delight, all mankind's wonder:
But my jealous heart would break,
  Should we live one day asunder.

In Aphra Behn's *Miscellany*, 1685

I promised Sylvia to be true;
  Nay, out of zeal, I swore it too:
And, that she might believe me more,
  Gave her in writing what I swore:
Not vows, not oaths, can lovers bind;
  So long as blessed, so long they're kind:
'Twas in a leaf; the wind but blew:
Away both leaf and promise flew.

In *Thesaurus Musicus . . . Book V*, 1696 (written before 1680)

The Mistress

An age in her embraces passed
  Would seem a winter's day,
Where life and light with envious haste
  Are torn and snatched away.

But, oh! how slowly minutes roll,
   When absent from her eyes,
That fed my love, which is my soul;
   It languishes and dies.

For then, no more a soul but shade,
   It mournfully does move,
And haunts my breast, by absence made
   The living tomb of love.

You wiser men, despise me not,
   Whose love-sick fancy raves
On shades of souls, and heaven knows what;
   Short ages live in graves.

Whene'er those wounding eyes, so full
   Of sweetness, you did see,
Had you not been profoundly dull,
   You had gone mad like me.

Nor censure us, you who perceive
   My best beloved and me,
Sigh and lament, complain and grieve;
   You think we disagree.

Alas! 'tis sacred jealousy,
   Love raised to an extreme;
The only proof 'twixt them and me
   We love, and do not dream.

Fantastic fancies fondly move,
   And in frail joys believe,
Taking false pleasure for true love;
   But pain can ne'er deceive.

Kind jealous doubts, tormenting fears,
   And anxious cares, when past,
Prove our heart's treasure fixed and dear,
   And make us blessed at last.

Poems on Several Occasions, 1691 (written before 1680)

Absent from thee, I languish still;
   Then ask me not, When I return?
The straying fool 'twill plainly kill
   To wish all day, all night to mourn.

Dear, from thine arms then let me fly,
   That my fantastic mind may prove
The torments it deserves to try,
   That tears my fixed heart from my Love.

When, wearied with a world of woe,
   To thy safe bosom I retire,
Where love and peace and truth does flow,
   May I contented there expire.

Lest, once more wandering from that heaven,
   I fall on some base heart unblessed;
Faithless to thee, false, unforgiven,
   And lose my everlasting rest.

Poems on Several Occasions, 1691 (written before 1680)

'Ephelia'

To one that asked me why I loved J.G.

Why do I love? Go, ask the glorious sun
Why every day it round the world doth run;
Ask Thames and Tiber why they ebb and flow;
Ask damask roses why in June they blow;
Ask ice and hail the reason why they're cold;
Decaying beauties, why they will grow old.
They'll tell thee Fate, that every thing doth move,
Enforces them to this, and me to love.
There is no reason for our love or hate;
'Tis irresistible, as death or fate.

'Tis not his face; I've sense enough to see
That is not good, though doated on by me;
Nor is't his tongue that has this conquest won,
For that at least is equalled by my own:
His carriage can to none obliging be;
'Tis rude, affected, full of vanity,
Strangely ill-natured, peevish and unkind,
Unconstant, false, to jealousy inclined:
His temper could not have so great a power;
'Tis mutable, and changes every hour:
Those vigorous years that women so adore
Are past in him; he's twice my age, and more.
And yet I love this false, this worthless man
With all the passion that a woman can;
Doat on his imperfections; though I spy
Nothing to love, I love, and know not why:
Since 'tis decreed in the dark book of fate
That I should love and he should be ingrate.

Female Poems on Several Occasions, 1679

Richard Duke

See what a conquest love has made!
Beneath the myrtle's amorous shade
  The charming fair Corinna lies,
All melting in desire,
  Quenching in tears those flaming eyes
That set the world on fire.

What cannot tears and beauty do!
The youth, by chance, stood by and knew
  For whom those crystal streams did flow;
And, though he ne'er before
  To her eyes' brightest rays did bow,
Weeps too, and does adore.

So, when the heavens serene and clear,
Gilded with gaudy light appear,
   Each craggy rock and every stone
Their native rigour keep;
   But when in rain the clouds fall down
The hardest marbles weep.

In J. Playford's Choice Ayres and Songs, IV, 1683

After the fiercest pangs of hot desire,
   Between Panthea's rising breasts
   His bending head Philander rests,
Though vanquished, yet unknowing to retire,
   Close hugs the charmer, and, ashamed to yield,
   Though he has lost the day, still keeps the field.

When, with a sigh, the fair Panthea said,
   'What pity 'tis, ye gods, that all
   The bravest warriors soonest fall!'
Then, with a kiss, she gently raised his head,
   Armed him again for fight, for nobly she
   More loved the combat than the victory.

Then, more enraged for being beat before,
   With all his strength he does prepare
   More fiercely to renew the war;
Nor ceases till that noble prize he bore;
   Even her such wondrous courage did surprise;
   She hugs the dart that wounded her, and dies.

In The Newest Collection of the Choicest Songs, 1683

Thomas D'Urfey

To Cynthia

Enamoured angels leave the sky
   To hear the music of her tongue:
Fond Cupids round about her fly,
   To kiss her as she walks along:

The trees all bow their verdant heads,
  Like humble lovers, when she talks;
And blushing flowers deck the meads,
  As proud they may adorn her walks.

She has such beauty as were fit
  To bless the greatest monarch's side,
A mine of rich obliging wit
  Without the least alloy of pride:
Tell me no more of joys above,
  With which immortal souls are crowned;
There is a rapture in her love
  Which zealous bigots never found.

Choice New Songs, 1684

Born with the vices of my kind,
  I should inconstant be,
Dear Celia, could I rambling find
  More beauty than in thee:
The rolling surges of my blood,
  By virtue now grown low,
Should a new shower increase the flood,
  Too soon would overflow:
But frailty (when thy face I see)
  Does modestly retire;
Uncommon must her graces be
  Whose look can bound desire:
Not to my virtue but thy power
  This constancy is due:
When change itself can give no more,
  'Tis easy to be true.

In The Banquet of Musick, 1689

Philip Ayres

Love's Contrariety

I make no war, and yet no peace have found;
  With heat I melt, when starved to death with cold:
I soar to heaven, while grovelling on the ground,
  Embrace the world, yet nothing do I hold.

I'm not confined, yet cannot I depart,
  Nor loose the chain, though not a captive led;
Love kills me not, yet wounds me to the heart,
  Will neither have m'alive, nor have me dead.

Being blind, I see; not having voice, I cry;
  I wish for death, while I of life make choice;
I hate myself, yet love you tenderly;
  Do feed of tears, and in my grief rejoice.

Thus, Cynthia, all my health is but disease;
Both life and death do equally displease.

Lyric Poems, 1687

The Restless Lover

The birds to wanton in the air desire;
The salamander sports himself in fire;
The fish in water plays; and of the earth
Man ever takes possession at his birth:
Only unhappy I, who, born to grieve,
In all these elements at once do live:
Grief does with air of sighs my mouth supply;
My wretched body on cold earth does lie;
The streams which from mine eyes flow, night and day,
Cannot the fire which burns my heart allay.

Lyric Poems, 1687

The Request. To Love

O Love, who in my breast's most noble part
  Did'st that fair image lodge, that form divine,
  In whom the sum of heavenly graces shine,
And there engrav'dst it with thy golden dart:

Now, mighty workman, help me by thy art
  (Since my dull pen trembles to strike a line)
  That I on paper copy the design,
By thee expressed so lively in my heart.

Lend me, when I this great attempt do try,
  A feather from thy wings, that, whilst to write
My hand's employed, my thoughts may soar on high;
  Thy torch, which fires our hearts and burns so bright,
My darker fancy let its flame supply,
  And through my numbers dart celestial light.

Lyric Poems, 1687

Cynthia Sporting

Along the river's side did Cynthia stray,
More like a goddess than a nymph at play;
The flood stopped to behold her; pleased to see't,
She to its kisses yields her naked feet.

Brisk air saluted her, ne'er stayed to woo;
The very boughs reached to be toying, too;
The little birds came thronging to admire,
And for her entertainment made a choir.

The meadows smile, and joy surrounds the place,
As if all things were influenced by her face;
The grass and leaves take freshness from her eyes,
And, as of lesser force, Sol's beams despise.

195

No herb, pressed by her foot, but blossoms straight;
Flowers, for her touch to ripen them, do wait;
They, from her hand, new fragrancy do yield;
Her presence fills with perfumes all the field.

Lyric Poems, 1687

John, Lord Cutts

Only tell her that I love;
   Leave the rest to her and Fate;
Some kind planet from above
May perhaps her pity move:
   Lovers on their stars must wait;
Only tell her that I love.

Why, oh why, should I despair?
   Mercy's pictured in her eye;
If she once vouchsafe to hear,
Welcome hope, and farewell fear:
   She's too good to let me die;
Why, oh why, should I despair?

Poetical Exercises, Written upon Several Occasions, 1687

John Sheffield, Duke of Buckingham

Come, Cælia, let's agree at last
   To love and live in quiet;
And tie the knot so very fast
   That time shall ne'er untie it.

Love's purest joys they never prove
   Who free from quarrels live;
'Tis sure the tend'rest part of love
   Each other to forgive.

When first I seemed concerned I took
   No pleasure nor no rest;
And, when I showed an angry look,
   Alas! I loved you best.

Say but the same to me, you'll find
   How happy is our fate.
Ah! to be grateful, to be kind,
   It never is too late.

Comes Amoris, Book I, 1687

From all uneasy passions free,
Revenge, ambition, jealousy,
Contented, I had been too blessed,
If love and you would let me rest:
   Yet that dull life I now despise;
   Safe from your eyes,
I feared no griefs, but Oh! I found no joys.

Amidst a thousand soft desires,
Which beauty moves and love inspires,
I feel such pangs of jealous fear,
No heart so kind as mine can bear:
   Yet I'll defy the worst of harms;
   Such are those charms,
'Tis worth a life to die within your arms.

In *A Collection of Poems by Several Hands*, 1693

Thomas Cheeke

Love's a dream of mighty treasure,
   Which in fancy we possess;
In the folly lies the pleasure,
   Wisdom ever makes it less.

When we think, by passion heated,
   We a goddess have in chase,
Ixion-like we all are cheated,
   And a gaudy cloud embrace.

Only happy is the lover,
   Whom his mistress well deceives;
Seeking nothing to discover,
   He contented lives at ease.
But the wretch that will be knowing
   What the fair one would disguise,
Labours for his own undoing,
   Changing happy, to be wise.

In *Vinculum Societatis, or The Tie of Good Company*, II, 1688

Thomas Betterton

What shall I do to show how much I love her?
   How many millions of sighs can suffice?
That which wins other hearts never can move her,
   Those common methods of love she'll despise.

I will love more than man e'er loved before me,
   Gaze on her all the day, melt all the night,
Till for her own sake at last she'll implore me
   To love her less to preserve our delight.

Since gods themselves could not ever be loving,
   Men must have breathing recruits for new joys;
I wish my love could be always improving,
   Though eager love, more than sorrow, destroys.

In fair Aurelia's arms leave me expiring
   To be embalmed by the sweets of her breath,
To the last moment I'll still be desiring:
   Never had hero so glorious a death.

The Prophetess, 1690

Anonymous

Fair Sylvia, cease to blame my youth
    For having loved before;
So men, till they have learnt the truth,
    Strange deities adore:
My heart, 'tis true, has often ranged
    Like bees o'er gaudy flowers,
And many thousand loves has changed,
    Till it was fixed on yours.

But, Sylvia, when I saw those eyes,
    'Twas soon determined there;
Stars might as well forsake the skies,
    And vanish in despair:
When I from this great rule do err,
    New beauties to implore,
May I again turn wanderer,
    And never settle more.

In *The Banquet of Musick*, Book IV, 1690

John Crowne

I once had virtue, wealth and fame;
    Now I'm a ruined sinner:
I lost 'em all at love's sweet game,
    Yet think myself a winner.

Since that dear lovely youth to gain
    My heart was long pursuing,
I'm rich enough, nor shall complain
    Of such a sweet undoing.

I'll laugh at cruel fortune's spite,
    While I have any feature
To keep his love, for that's delight
    Enough for mortal creature.

The sport's so pleasant, you will own,
    When once you have been in it,
You'd gladly be an age undone,
    For one such charming minute.

The English Frier; or, The Town Sparks, 1690

Thomas Heyrick
Dorinda Weeping

Stay, pretty prodigal, oh stay:
Throw not those pearly drops away;
Each little shining gem might be
Price for a captive prince's liberty:
See down her cheeks the shining jewels slide,
Brighter than meteors that from heaven do glide.

Sorrow n'er looked before so fair,
Nor ever had so sweet an air:
All-conquering rays her woes do dart,
And unknown passions to the soul impart:
More fair she looks, while grief her face doth shroud,
Than the sun peeping through a watery cloud.

Oh, turn away those killing eyes!
Venus from such a sea did rise:
Love doth in tears triumphant ride;
Such mighty charms can never be denied:
That at one sight such different passions move,
Relenting pity, and commanding love.

Come, curious artist, as they fall,
Gather the shining jewels all;
Harden the gems, and each will be
More valued than the Indies' treasury:
But, if the secret doth exceed thy art,
It is but borrowing hardness from her heart.

Miscellany Poems, 1691

George Granville, Lord Lansdowne
Cloe

Cloe's the wonder of her sex;
    'Tis well her heart is tender:
How might such killing eyes perplex,
    With virtue to defend her!

But nature, graciously inclined,
    With liberal hand to please us,
Has to her boundless beauty joined
    A boundless bent to ease us.

In *The History of Adolphus*, 1691
(text from *The Genuine Works*, 1732)

Song to Mira

Why, cruel creature, why so bent
    To vex a tender heart?
To gold and title you relent;
    Love throws in vain his dart.

Let glittering fools in Courts be great;
    For pay, let armies move;
Beauty should have no other bait
    But gentle vows and love.

If on those endless charms you lay
    The value that's their due,
Kings are themselves too poor to pay,
    A thousand worlds too few.

But, if a passion without vice,
    Without disguise or art,
Ah Mira! if true love's your price,
    Behold it in my heart.

In *The History of Adolphus*, 1691
(text from *The Genuine Works*, 1732)

To Mira

Thoughtful nights, and restless waking,
  Oh, the pains that we endure!
Broken faith, unkind forsaking,
  Ever doubting, never sure.

Hopes deceiving, vain endeavours,
  What a race has love to run!
False protesting, fleeting favours,
  Every, every way undone.

Still complaining and defending,
  Both to love, yet not agree,
Fears tormenting, passion rending,
  O the pangs of jealousy!

From such painful ways of living,
  Ah! how sweet, could love be free;
Still presenting, still receiving,
  Fierce, immortal ecstasy.

The British Enchanters, 1706
(written *c*.1691: text from *The Genuine Works*, 1732)

Song to Mira

Why should a heart so tender break?
  O Mira! give its anguish ease;
The use of beauty you mistake,
  Not meant to vex, but please.

Those lips for smiling were designed;
  That bosom to be pressed;
Your eyes to languish and look kind;
  For amorous arms, your waist.

Each thing has its appointed right,
  Established by the powers above;
The sun to give us warmth and light,
  Mira to kindle love.

Poems upon Several Occasions, 1712
(written *c*.1691: text from *The Genuine Works*, 1732)

Love

Love is begot by fancy, bred
By ignorance, by expectation fed,
Destroyed by knowledge, and, at best,
Lost in the moment 'tis possessed.

Poems upon Several Occasions, 1712
(written *c*. 1691: text from *The Genuine Works*, 1732)

The happiest mortals once were we;
I loved Mira, Mira me:
  Each desirous of the blessing,
  Nothing wanting but possessing,
I loved Mira, Mira me;
The happiest mortals once were we.

But since cruel fates dissever,
Torn from love, and torn for ever,
  Tortures end me,
  Death befriend me!
Of all pains the greatest pain
Is to love, and love in vain.

The British Enchanters, 1706
(written *c*.1691: text from *The Genuine Works*, 1732)

Bacchus Disarmed
To Mrs Laura Dillon, now Lady Falkland

Bacchus, to arms! the enemy's at hand;
Laura appears; stand to your glasses, stand!
The God of Love the God of Wine defies:
Behold him in full march in Laura's eyes.
Bacchus, to arms! and to resist the dart,
Each with a faithful brimmer guard his heart!

Fly, Bacchus, fly! there's treason in the cup,
For Love comes pouring in with every drop:
I feel him in my heart, my blood, my brain:
Fly, Bacchus, fly! resistance is in vain:
Or, craving quarter, crown a friendly bowl
To Laura's health, and give up all thy soul.

The Genuine Works, 1732

William Walsh

To His Mistress: Against Marriage

Yes, all the world must sure agree,
He who's secured of having thee
   Will be entirely blessed:
But 'twere in me too great a wrong
To make one who have been so long
   My Queen, my slave at last.

Nor ought those things to be confined,
That were for public good designed;
   Could we, in foolish pride,
Make the sun always with us stay,
'Twould burn our corn and grass away,
   To starve the world beside.

Let not the thoughts of parting fright
Two souls which passion does unite;
   For, while our love does last,
Neither will strive to go away;
And why the devil should we stay,
   When once that love is past?

Letters and Poems. Amorous and Gallant, 1692

Francis Atterbury, Bishop of Rochester

Written in the Leaves of a Fan

Flavia the least and slightest toy
Can with resistless art employ:
This fan, in meaner hands, would prove
An engine of small force in love;
Yet she, with graceful air and mien
(Not to be told, or safely seen),
Directs its wanton motions so
That it wounds more than Cupid's bow:
Gives coolness to the matchless dame,
To every other breast a flame.

In *The Gentleman's Journal*, 1692

William Congreve

Pious Celinda goes to prayers,
   If I but ask the favour;
And yet the tender fool's in tears
   When she believes I'll leave her.

Would I were free from this restraint,
   Or else had hopes to win her;
Would she could make of me a saint,
   Or I of her a sinner.

In *Deliciae Musicae*, 1695

205

Love's but the frailty of the mind,
When 'tis not with ambition joined;
A sickly flame, which if not fed expires,
And feeding, wastes in self-consuming fires.

'Tis not to wound a wanton boy
Or amorous youth, that gives the joy;
But 'tis the glory to have pierced a swain
For whom inferior beauties sighed in vain.

Then I alone the conquest prize,
When I insult a rival's eyes:
If there's delight in love, 'tis when I see
That heart, which others bleed for, bleed for me.

The Way of the World, 1700

See, see, she wakes, Sabina wakes!
And now the sun begins to rise:
Less glorious is the morn that breaks
From his bright beams, than her fair eyes.

With light united, day they give,
But different fates ere night fulfil:
How many by his warmth will live!
How many will her coldness kill!

In *Poetical Miscellanies: The Fifth Part*, 1704

John Oldmixon

Prithee, Cloe, not so fast:
Let's not run and wed in haste;
We've a thousand things to do;
You must fly, and I pursue,
You must frown, and I must sigh,
I entreat, and you deny.

Stay – If I am never crossed,
Half the pleasure will be lost;
Be, or seem to be, severe;
Give me reason to despair;
Fondness will my wishes cloy,
Make me careless of the joy.
Lovers may, of course, complain
Of their trouble and their pain;
But, if pain and trouble cease,
Love without it will not please.

Poems on Several Occasions, 1696

Fie, Cœlia, scorn the little arts
  Which meaner beauties use,
Who think they can't secure our hearts
  Unless they still refuse;
Are coy and shy, will seem to frown,
  To raise our passions higher;
But when the poor deceit is known,
  It quickly palls desire.

Come, let's not trifle time away,
  Or stop you know not why;
Your blushes and your eyes betray
  What death you mean to die:
Let all your maiden fears be gone,
  And love no more be crossed;
Ah, Cœlia, when the joys are known,
  You'll curse the minutes lost.

Poems on Several Occasions, 1696

I lately vowed, but 'twas in haste,
  That I no more would court
The joys which seem, when they are past,
  As dull as they are short.

I oft to hate my mistress swear,
　　But soon my weakness find;
I make my oaths when she's severe,
　　And break 'em when she's kind.

Twelve New Songs, 1699

Sir John Vanbrugh

Fly, fly, you happy shepherds, fly;
　　Avoid Philira's charms;
The rigour of her heart denies
　　The heaven that's in her arms:
Ne'er hope to gaze and then retire,
　　Nor yielding, to be blessed;
Nature, who formed her eyes of fire,
　　Of ice composed her breast.

Yet, lovely maid, this once believe
　　A slave whose zeal you move:
The gods, alas! your youth deceive;
　　Their heaven consists in love:
In spite of all the thanks you owe,
　　You may reproach 'em this,
That where they did their form bestow
　　They have denied their bliss.

The Provok'd Wife, 1697

Anonymous

I gently touched her hand: she gave
A look that did my soul enslave;
I pressed her rebel lips in vain:
They rose up to be pressed again.
　　Thus happy, I no farther meant
　　Than to be pleased and innocent.

On her soft breasts my hand I laid,
And a quick, light impression made;
They with a kindly warmth did glow
And swelled, and seemed to over-flow.
   Yet, trust me, I no farther meant,
   Than to be pleased and innocent.

On her eyes my eyes did stay:
O'er her smooth limbs my hand did stray;
Each sense was ravished with delight,
And my soul stood prepared for flight.
   Blame me not if at last I meant
   More to be pleased than innocent.

In *Mercurius Musicus*, 1699 (the last stanza occurs only
in *The Hive*, III, third edition, 1729, and in *The Cupid*, 1736)

George Farquhar

How blessed are lovers in disguise!
   Like gods they see,
   As I do thee,
Unseen by human eyes:
   Exposed to view,
   I'm hid from you;
I'm altered, yet the same:
   The dark conceals me;
   Love reveals me,
Love, which lights me by its flame.

Were you not false, you me would know;
   For, though your eyes
   Could not devise,
Your heart had told you so:
   Your heart would beat
   With eager heat,

And me by sympathy would find:
  True love might see
  One changed like me;
False love is only blind.

Love and a Bottle, 1699

Thomas Yalden

Advice to a Lover

For many unsuccessful years
  At Cynthia's feet I lay;
Battering them often with my tears,
  I sighed, but durst not pray.
No prostrate wretch before the shrine
  Of some loved saint above
E'er thought his goddess more divine
  Or paid more awful love.

Still the disdainful nymph looked down
  With coy insulting pride,
Received my passion with a frown,
  Or turned her head aside.
Then Cupid whispered in my ear:
  'Use more prevailing charms;
You modest whining fool, draw near,
  And clasp her in your arms.'

'With eager kisses tempt the maid;
  From Cynthia's feet depart;
The lips he briskly must invade
  That would possess the heart.'
With that I shook off all the slave,
  My better fortunes tried;
When Cynthia in a moment gave
  What she for years denied.

In *A New Collection of Poems on Several Occasions*, 1701

Elijah Fenton

The Rose

See, Sylvia, see this new-blown rose,
　The image of thy blush!
　Mark how it smiles upon the bush,
And triumphs as it grows.
'Oh pluck it not! we'll come anon;'
Thou say'st: Alas! 'twill then be gone.
　Now its purple beauty's spread,
Soon it will drop and fall,
And soon it will not be at all;
　No fine things draw a length of thread:
Then tell me, seems it not to say,
'Come on, and crop me whilst you may'?

In Oxford and Cambridge Miscellany Poems, 1708

Matthew Prior

Cupid Mistaken

As after noon one summer's day
　Venus stood bathing in a river,
Cupid a-shooting went that way,
　New strung his bow, new filled his quiver.

With skill he chose his sharpest dart,
　With all his might his bow he drew;
Aimed at his beauteous parent's heart,
　With certain speed the arrow flew.

'I faint! I die!' the goddess cried:
　'O cruel, could'st thou find none other
To wreck thy spleen on? Parricide!
　Like Nero thou hast slain thy mother.'

Poor Cupid, sobbing, scarce could speak:
  'Indeed, Mamma, I did not know ye.
Alas! how easy my mistake!
  I took you for your likeness, Cloe.'

Poems on Several Occasions, 1709

To Cloe, Weeping

See, whilst thou weep'st, fair Cloe, see
The world in sympathy with thee.
The cheerful birds no longer sing,
But drop the head, and hang the wing.
The clouds have bent their bosom lower,
And shed their sorrows in a shower.
The brooks beyond their limits flow,
And louder murmurs speak their woe.
The nymphs and swains adopt thy cares;
They heave thy sighs, and weep thy tears.
Fantastic nymph! that grief should move
The heart obdurate against love.
Strange tears! whose power can soften all
But that dear breast on which they fall.

Poems on Several Occasions, 1709

Thomas Otway

The Enjoyment

Clasped in the arms of her I love,
In vain, alas! for life I strove;
My fluttering spirits, wrapped in fire
    By love's mysterious art,
Born on the wings of fierce desire,
    Flew from my flaming heart.

Thus lying in a trance for dead,
Her swelling breasts bore up my head,
When, waking from a pleasing dream,
  I saw her killing eyes,
Which did in fiery glances seem
  To say, 'Now Cælia dies.'

Fainting, she pressed me in her arms,
And trembling lay, dissolved in charms,
When with a shivering voice she cried,
  'Must I alone then die?'
'No, no', I languishing replied,
  'I'll bear thee company.'

Melting our souls thus into one,
Swift joys our wishes did outrun;
Then, launched in rolling seas of bliss,
  We bid the world adieu,
Swearing by every charming kiss
  To be for ever true.

In *The Works of Rochester and Roscommon*, 1709

Anne Finch, Countess of Winchilsea
The Sigh

Gentlest air, the breath of lovers,
  Vapour from a secret fire,
Which by thee itself discovers,
  Ere yet daring to aspire.

Softest note of whispered anguish,
  Harmony's most subtle part,
Striking, while thou seem'st to languish,
  Full upon the listener's heart.

Safest messenger of passion,
　　Stealing through a crowd of spies,
Which constrain the outward fashion,
　　Close the lips, and guard the eyes.

Shapeless sigh! none ere can show thee,
　　Framed but to assault the ear:
Yet, ere to their cost they know thee,
　　Every nymph may read thee – here.

In *Poems on a Variety of Subjects*, 1710

John Smith

I saw Lucinda's bosom bare;
　　Transparent was the skin;
As through a crystal did appear
　　A beating heart within.

The beating heart transfixed I saw,
　　And yet the heart was stone;
I saw it bleed, and by the wound
　　I thought it was mine own.

But O! when I perceived it was
　　Enshrined within your breast,
I knew 'twas yours, for mine, alas!
　　Was never yet so blessed.

Poems upon Several Occasions, 1713

The Roses

Go, lovely pair of roses, go,
This clad in scarlet, that in snow.
Go, say to my ungentle fair,
　　(If on your forms she deigns to gaze)

You dare not hope to rival her,
   Or match the glories of her face;
But that you're humbly sent to prove
A youth undone by beauty and her love.

The sickly white in this pale rose
My wan and meagre looks disclose;
But that which shines so fiercely bright,
   Whose head in painted flames aspires,
And blushes so with purple light,
   It seems to send forth real fires,
Tell her that rose's ruddy fires impart
The flames her eyes have kindled in my heart.

Poems upon Several Occasions, 1713

Henry Carey

The Fashionable Lover

Love's the fever of the mind;
'Tis a grief that none can cure,
Till the nymph you love prove kind;
She can give you ease again;
She can best remove the pain
Which you for her endure.

Be not ever then repining,
Sighing, dying, canting, whining;
Spend not time in vain pursuing;
If she does not love you, make her;
When she loves you, then – forsake her;
'Tis the modish way of wooing.

Poems on Several Occasions, 1713

Love's a Riddle

The flame of love assuages
　　When once it is revealed;
But fiercer still it rages,
　　The more it is concealed.

Consenting makes it colder;
　　When met it will retreat:
Repulses make it bolder,
　　And dangers make it sweet.

Poems on Several Occasions, 1713

The
Georgians

Anonymous

On Some Snow That Melted on a Lady's Breast

Those envious flakes came down in haste,
   To prove her breast less fair:
Grieving to find themselves surpassed,
   Dissolved into a tear.

In Steele's Poetical Miscellanies, 1714

Thomas Parnell

My days have been so wondrous free,
   The little birds that fly
With careless ease from tree to tree
   Were but as blessed as I.

Ask gliding waters, if a tear
   Of mine increased their stream?
Or ask the flying gales, if e'er
   I lent a sigh to them?

But now my former days retire,
   And I'm by beauty caught,
The tender chains of sweet desire
   Are fixed upon my thought.

An eager hope within my breast
   Does every doubt control,
And charming Nancy stands confessed
   The favourite of my soul.

Ye nightingales, ye twisting pines,
   Ye swains that haunt the grove,
Ye gentle echoes, breezy winds,
   Ye close retreats of love;

With all of Nature, all of Art,
    Assist the dear design;
O teach a young unpractised heart
    To make her ever mine.

The very thought of change I hate,
    As much as of despair;
And hardly covet to be great,
    Unless it be for her.

'Tis true, the passion in my mind
    Is mixed with soft distress;
Yet while the Fair I love is kind,
    I cannot wish it less.

In Steele's Poetical Miscellanies, 1714

When thy beauty appears
  In its graces and airs,
All bright as an angel new dropped from the sky,
  At a distance I gaze, and am awed by my fears,
So strangely you dazzle my eye!

But when, without art,
  Your kind thoughts you impart,
When your love runs in blushes through every vein,
  When it darts from your eyes, when it pants in your heart
Then I know you're a woman again.

'There's a passion and pride
  In our sex' (she replied),
'And thus, might I gratify both, I would do:
  Still an angel appear to each lover beside,
But still be a woman to you.'

Poems on Several Occasions, 1722

William Tunstall

Eliza Playing upon the Spinet

Though fair Eliza, to conceal
  The charming beauties of her eyes,
Turns to her spinet, yet we feel
  The fair Eliza can surprise.

She can her laws on us impose,
  And triumph, when she does retreat,
As Parthians seem to fly their foes,
  The surer conquest to complete.

If in her blooming looks she appears,
  She through the eyes attacks the heart;
But when she plays she wounds the ears,
  And every finger turns a dart.

The listening captives round her stand,
  And, whilst each tuneful touch th' admire,
They own the conquest of her hand,
  And yield themselves to chains of wire.

But, if some hardy rebel's choice
  Bids a defiance to the strings,
Let but Eliza raise her voice;
  She gives no quarter when she sings.

Ballads and Some Occasional Poems, 1716

George Sewell

An Apology for Loving a Widow

Tell me not Celia once did bless
  Another mortal's arms;
That cannot make my passion less,
  Nor mitigate her charms.

221

Shall I refuse to quench my thirst,
    Depending life to save,
Because some droughty shepherd first
    Has kissed the smiling wave?

No, no; methinks 'tis wondrous great,
    And suits a noble blood,
To have in love, as well as state,
    A taster to our food.

Poems on Several Occasions, 1719

Matthew Concanen

The Picture

So numerous Flavia's charms appear,
    As may her form display,
In all the dresses of the year,
    And beauties of the day.

Calm and serene, like Spring, her air;
    Like Autumn, plump her mould;
Her face, like Summer, blooming fair;
    Her heart, like Winter, cold.

Her bosom, Cynthia's full-orbed light;
    Her cheeks Noon's rays adorn;
Her tresses show the falling Night;
    Her eyes the rising Morn.

Poems upon Several Occasions, 1722

The Theft

Why are those charms by frowns disgraced,
    Too lovely, and too coy!
Since from your lips, with timorous haste,
    I snatched transporting joy?

Too well I rue the hapless theft!
  Too fatal your disdain!
I lost – Ah, no! my life is left;
  I feel it by the pain.

Sure, might I taste another such,
  So warm with keen desire,
My soul, exulting at the touch,
  Would, through my lips, expire.

Then, Julia, take my parting breath,
  In such another kiss;
Glut your revenge, and let my death
  Atone the ravished bliss.

In Richard Savage's *Miscellaneous Poems*
and Translations by Several Hands, 1726

Ambrose Philips

Why we love, and why we hate,
  Is not granted us to know;
Random chance, or wilful fate,
  Guides the shaft from Cupid's bow.

If on me Zelinda frown,
  Madness 'tis in me to grieve:
Since her will is not her own,
  Why should I uneasy live?

If I for Zelinda die,
  Deaf to poor Mizella's cries,
Ask not me the reason why;
  Seek the riddle in the skies.

Pastorals, Epistles, Odes, and other Original Poems, 1748
(written before 1724)

Leonard Welsted

While in the bower, with beauty blest,
    The loved Amintor lies,
While sinking on Zelinda's breast,
    He fondly kissed her eyes,

A wakeful nightingale, who long
    Had mourned within the shade,
Sweetly renewed her plaintive song,
    And warbled thro' the glade.

'Melodious songstress,' cried the Swain,
    'To shades less happy go;
Or, if with us thou wilt remain,
    Forbear thy tuneful woe.

'While in Zelinda's arms I lie,
    To song I am not free;
On her soft bosom while I sigh,
    I discord find in thee.

'Zelinda gives me perfect joys:
    Then cease thy fond intrusion;
Be silent; music now is noise,
    Variety confusion.'

Epistles, Odes, &c., 1724

Barton Booth

Sweet are the charms of her I love,
    More fragrant than the damask rose;
Soft as the down of turtle dove,
    Gentle as wind when zephyr blows;
Refreshing as descending rains
To sun-burnt climes and thirsty plains.

True as the needle to the Pole,
    Or as the dial to the sun;

Constant as gliding waters roll,
  Whose swelling tides obey the moon;
From every other charmer free,
My life and love shall follow thee.

The lamb the flowery thyme devours,
  The dam the tender kid pursues;
Sweet Philomel, in shady bowers
  Of verdant Spring, her note renews:
All follow what they most admire,
As I pursue my soul's desire.

Nature must change her beauteous face,
  And vary as the seasons rise;
As Winter to the Spring gives place,
  Summer th' approach of Autumn flies:
No change in love the seasons bring,
Love only knows perpetual Spring.

Devouring Time, with stealing pace,
  Makes lofty oaks and cedars bow;
And marble towers and walls of brass
  In his rude march he levels low:
But Time, destroying far and wide,
Love from the Soul can ne'er divide.

Death only, with his cruel dart,
  The gentle Godhead can remove;
And drive him from the bleeding heart,
  To mingle with the blest above,
Where, known to all his kindred train,
He finds a lasting rest from pain.

Love and his sister fair, the Soul,
  Twin-born from Heaven together came;
Love will the universe control,
  When dying seasons lose their name;
Divine abodes shall own his power
When Time and Death shall be no more.

In *The Hive*, 1724

Anonymous

The Magnetic Mistress

Dorinda has such powerful arts,
   Such an attractive air,
None can resist her conquering darts,
But gladly yield their captive hearts
   To so divine a Fair.

Thus the mysterious loadstone's power
   Each wandering atom draws;
From Pole to Pole they take their course,
Confined by an intrinsic force,
   And circle in its laws.

Magnetic powers her charms attend;
   But then, here lies the riddle:
The loadstone does its force extend,
And strongest draws at either end;
   Dorinda – in the middle.

In *The Hive*, 1724

Anonymous

Thieving a Kiss

Belinda, see from yonder flowers
   The bee flies loaded to its cell;
Can you perceive what it devours?
   Are they impaired in show or smell?

So, though I robbed you of a kiss,
   Sweeter than their ambrosial dew,
Why are you angry at my bliss?
   Has it at all impoverished you?

'Tis by this cunning I contrive,
  In spite of your unkind reserve,
To keep my famished love alive,
  Which you inhumanly would starve.

In The Hive, 1724

Anonymous

Do not ask me, charming Phillis,
  Why I lead you here alone,
By this bank of pinks and lilies
  And of roses newly blown.

'Tis not to behold the beauty
  Of those flowers that crown the spring;
'Tis to – but I know my duty,
  And dare never name the thing.

('Tis, at worst, but her denying;
  Why should I thus fearful be?
Every minute, gently flying,
  Smiles and says, 'Make use of me.')

What the sun does to those roses,
  While the beams play sweetly in,
I would – but my fear opposes,
  And I dare not name the thing.

Yet I die, if I conceal it;
  Ask my eyes, or ask your own;
And if neither can reveal it,
  Think what lovers think alone.

On this bank of pinks and lilies,
  Might I speak what I would do;
I would with my lovely Phillis –
  I would; I would – Ah! would you?

In The Hive, 1724

Anonymous

Phillis has a gentle heart,
   Willing to the lover's courting,
Wanton nature, all love's art,
   To direct her in her sporting.

In the embrace, the look, the kiss,
   All is real inclination;
No false raptures in the bliss,
   No feigned sighing in the passion.

But oh! who the charms can speak,
   Who, the thousand ways of toying,
When she does the lover make
   All a god in her enjoying?

Who, the limbs that round him move
   And constrain him to the blisses?
Who, the eyes that swim in love,
   And the lips that suck in kisses?

Oh! the freaks when mad she grows,
   Raves all wild with the possessing!
Oh! the silent trance which shows
   The delight above expressing!

Every way she does engage,
   Idly talking, speechless lying,
She transports me with the rage,
   And she kills me in her dying.

In *The Hive*, II, 1724

Attributed to
Esther Johnson
Jealousy, by a Lady

Oh, shield me from his rage, celestial powers!
This tyrant that embitters all my hours.
Ah! Love, you've poorly played the monarch's part;
You conquered, but you can't defend my heart:
So blessed was I throughout thy happy reign,
I thought this monster banished from thy train;
But you would raise him to support your throne,
And now he claims your empire as his own:
Or tell me, tyrants, have you both agreed,
That where one reigns, the other shall succeed?

In Concanen's *Miscellaneous Poems* . . .
by Several Hands, 1724

Henry Baker
To Flora Dressed

Why art thou dressed, my lovely maid,
In gold, and gems, and rich brocade?
When gold, and gems, and rich brocade,
Conceal thy charms, my lovely maid!

Why spend'st thou all this time and care
To form thy shape, to fold thy hair?
Thy shape unbraced, thy flowing hair,
More beauteous are without thy care.

Would'st thou, indeed, be finely dressed?
Put by this robe which hides thy breast;
Unbind thy hair, and bare thy breast,
Thou art, my Charmer! finely dressed.

229

Remove these vestments all away,
Which like dark clouds obscure the day:
O! let them not obscure thy day:
Remove them all, my Fair! away.

Then shining forth adorned with charms,
Ah! let me fold thee in my arms!
Transported, fold thee in my arms!
And gaze and wonder at thy charms.

Original Poems, 1725

Anonymous

Upon Clarinda's panting breast
    The happy Strephon lay,
With love and beauty jointly pressed
    To pass the time away.
Fresh raptures of transporting love
    Have struck his senses dumb;
He envies not the powers above,
    Nor all the joys to come.

As painful bees abroad do rove,
    To fetch their treasures home,
So Strephon roved the fields of love,
    To fill her honeycomb:
Her ruby lips he kissed and pressed,
    From whence all joys derive;
Then, humming round her snowy breast,
    Straight crept into her hive.

In *The Hive* III, 1725

Anonymous

The Snow-ball

Julia, young wanton, flung the gathered snow,
Nor feared I burning from the watery blow:
'Tis cold, I cried; but ah! too soon I found,
Sent by that hand it dealt a scorching wound.
Resistless Fair! we fly thy power in vain,
Who turn'st to fiery darts the frozen rain.
Burn, Julia, burn like me, and that desire
With water which thou kindlest, quench with fire.

In David Lewis's *Miscellaneous Poems by Several Hands*, 1726

Anonymous

Translation from the Ancient British

Away, let nought to love displeasing,
  My Winifreda, move your care;
Let nought delay the heavenly blessing,
  Nor squeamish pride, nor gloomy fear.

What though no grants of royal donors
  With pompous titles grace our blood?
We'll shine in more substantial honours,
  And, to be noble, we'll be good.

Our name, while virtue thus we tender,
  Will sweetly sound where-e'er 'tis spoke:
And all the great ones, they shall wonder
  How they respect such little folk.

What though, from fortune's lavish bounty,
  No mighty treasures we possess?
We'll find, within our pittance, plenty,
  And be content without excess.

Still shall each kind returning Season
    Sufficient for our wishes give:
For we will live a life of Reason,
    And that's the only life to live.

Through youth and age, in love excelling,
    We'll hand in hand together tread;
Sweet-smiling peace shall crown our dwelling,
    And babes, sweet-smiling babes, our bed.

How should I love the pretty creatures,
    While round my knees they fondly clung,
To see them look their mother's features,
    To hear them lisp their mother's tongue!

And when with envy Time transported
    Shall think to rob us of our joys,
You'll, in your girls, again be courted,
    And I'll go wooing in my boys.

In David Lewis's *Miscellaneous Poems by Several Hands*, 1726

William Somervile

Presenting to a Lady a White Rose and a Red, on the Tenth of June

If this pale rose offend your sight
    It in your bosom wear;
'Twill blush to find itself less white,
    And turn Lancastrian there.

But, Celia, should the red be chose,
    With gay vermilion bright,
'Twould sicken at each blush that glows,
    And in despair turn white.

Let politicians idly prate,
    Their Babels build in vain;
As uncontrollable as Fate,
    Imperial Love shall reign.

Each haughty faction shall obey,
    And Whigs and Tories join,
Submit to your despotic sway,
    Confess your Right Divine.

Yet this (my gracious Monarch) own,
    They're tyrants that oppress;
'Tis mercy must support your throne,
    And 'tis like Heaven to bless.

Occasional Poems, Translations, Fables, Tales, &c., 1727

William Broome

The Rosebud: To a Young Lady

Queen of Fragrance, lovely Rose,
The beauties of thy leaves disclose!
The Winter's past, the tempests fly,
Soft gales breathe gently through the sky;
The lark sweet warbling on the wing
Salutes the gay return of Spring:
The silver dews, the vernal showers,
Call forth a bloomy waste of flowers;
The joyous fields, the shady woods,
Are clothed with green, or swell with buds;
Then haste thy beauties to disclose,
Queen of Fragrance, lovely Rose.

    Thou, beauteous flower, a welcome guest,
Shalt flourish on the fair one's breast,
Shalt grace her hand, or deck her hair,
The flower most sweet, the Nymph most fair;

Breathe soft, ye winds! be calm, ye skies!
Arise, ye flowery race, arise!
And haste thy beauties to disclose,
Queen of Fragrance, lovely Rose!

But thou, fair Nymph, thyself survey
In this sweet offspring of a day;
That miracle of face must fail,
Thy charms are sweet, but charms are frail:
Swift as the short-lived flower they fly,
At morn they bloom, at evening die:
Though sickness yet a while forbears,
Yet time destroys what sickness spares;
Now Helen lives alone in fame,
And Cleopatra's but a name;
Time must indent that heavenly brow,
And thou must be what Helen's now.

This moral to the Fair disclose,
Queen of Fragrance, lovely Rose.

Poems on Several Occasions, 1727

To Belinda
On Her Apron Embroidered with Arms and Flowers

The listening trees Amphion drew
To dance from hills where once they grew;
But you express a power more great:
The flowers you draw not, but create.

Behold your own creation rise,
And smile beneath your radiant eyes!
'Tis beauteous all, and yet receives
From you more graces than it gives.

But say, amid the softer charms
Of blooming flowers, what mean these arms?
So, round the fragrance of the rose,
The pointed thorn, to guard it, grows.

But cruel you, who thus employ
Both arms and beauty to destroy!
So Venus marches to the fray
In armour formidably gay.

It is a dreadful pleasing sight.
The flowers attract, the arms affright;
The flowers with lively beauty bloom,
The arms denounce an instant doom.

So, when the Britons in array
Their ensigns to the sun display,
In the same flag are lilies shown,
And angry lions sternly frown;
On high the glittering standard flies,
And conquers all things – like your eyes.

Poems on Several Occasions, 1727

Anonymous

The Rapture

Cried Strephon, panting in Cosmelia's arms,
   'I die, bright nymph, I die amidst your charms!'
'Cheer up, dear youth,' replied the maid,
   Dissolved in amorous pain,
'All men must die, bright boy, you know,
   E'er they can rise again.'

In *A Collection of Epigrams*, 1727

Anonymous

Can forms like yours want ornaments of dress?
Beauty, like truth, shines most in nakedness.
Dressing may screen deformities from view;
But e'en adornment does but shadow you.
Most but by what they wear are lovely made:
You, madam, lose, when'er you seek such aid.
While some but hide defects, and dress to arm,
You put off nothing but what veiled a charm.

In *A Collection of Epigrams*, 1727

Anonymous

To a Sempstress

Oh what bosom but must yield,
    When, like Pallas, you advance,
With a thimble for your shield,
    And a needle for your lance?

Fairest of the stitching train,
    Ease my passion by your art;
And, in pity to my pain,
    Mend the hole that's in my heart.

In *A Collection of Epigrams*, 1727

Anonymous

Belinda has such wondrous charms,
'Tis Heaven to lie within her arms:
And she's so charitably given,
She wishes all mankind in Heaven.

In *A Collection of Epigrams*, 1727

William Bedingfield
The Snake in the Grass: To a Lady of Pleasure

My heart inclines your chains to wear,
    But reason will not stoop;
I love that angel's face, but fear
    The serpent in your hoop.

Your eyes discharge the darts of love,
    But oh! what pains succeed,
When darts shall pins and needles prove
    And love a fire indeed!

The fly about the candle gay
    Dances with thoughtless hum;
But short, alas! his giddy play;
    His pleasure proves his doom.

The child, in such simplicity,
    About the bee-hive clings;
And with one drop of honey he
    Receives a hundred stings.

In *The Musical Miscellany*, IV, 1730
(a shorter version was printed in *A Collection of Epigrams*, 1727)

William Pattison
On His Mistress's Favours

Like Alexander, Coelia spreads her power,
Like him, she makes the vassal world adore;
But, ah! like him, to soothe a proud desire,
First conquers towns, then sets those towns on fire.

Poetical Works, 1728

237

John Gay

Youth's the season made for joys,
    Love is then our duty:
She alone who that employs
    Well deserves her beauty.
Let's be gay
While we may:
Beauty's a flower despised in decay.

Let us drink and sport today,
    Ours is not tomorrow.
Love with youth flies swift away:
    Age is nought but sorrow.
Dance and sing
Time's on the wing:
Life never knows the return of Spring.

The Beggar's Opera, 1728

My heart was so free,
    It roved like the bee,
Till Polly my passion requited;
    I sipped each flower
    I changed every hour,
But here every flower is united.

The Beggar's Opera, 1728

Love in her eyes sits playing,
    And sheds delicious death;
Love in her lips sits straying,
    And warbling in her breath.
Love on her breast sits panting,
    And swells with soft desire;
No grace, no charm is wanting,
    To set the heart on fire.

Acis and Galatea, 1732

Sir William Yonge

The Wheedler

In vain, dear Chloe, you suggest
That I, inconstant, have possessed
   Or loved a fairer she:
Would you with ease at once be cured
Of all the ills you've long endured,
   Consult your glass and me.

If then you think that I can find
A nymph more fair, or one more kind,
   You've reason for your fears:
But if impartial you will prove
To your own beauty and my love,
   How needless are your tears!

If, in my way, I should by chance
Receive, or give, a wanton glance,
   I like but while I view;
How slight the glance, how faint the kiss,
Compared to that substantial bliss
   Which I receive from you!

With wanton flight the curious bee
From flower to flower still wanders free,
   And, where each blossom blows,
Extracts the juice of all he meets,
But for his quintessence of sweets
   He ravishes the rose.

So my fond fancy to employ
On each variety of joy
   From nymph to nymph I roam;
Perhaps see fifty in a day;
Those are but visits which I pay –
   For Chloe is my home!

In James Ralph's *Miscellaneous Poems, by Several Hands*,1729

239

Joseph Thurston

The Scorner

Mistake me not, ungrateful Fair!
    Nor think you give the pain;
How great soe'er your falsehoods are,
    I'll meet them with disdain.

The fault, alas! was wholly mine,
    Nor to be charged on you;
How wild, how idle the design,
    To keep a woman true!

More easy would the project be
    (So well are you inclined)
To stop the motion of the sea,
    Or to confine the wind.

So zealously disposed to range
    Is every female heart,
They're still by nature prone to change,
    And constant but by art.

Then, Cynthia, let us both agree
    This method to pursue:
I'll follow every jilt I see,
    And every cully you.

Poems on Several Occasions, 1729

Phyllis, would you have me love you,
    Truce with that affected scorn!
Artless, if I fail to move you,
    I shall never learn to mourn.

Fops may ogle, sigh and languish
    Swear you life or death can give;
Though your rigour cause me anguish,
    Yet, believe me, I shall live.

You are but yourself disarming,
　While you give your lover pain;
Beauty ceases to be charming
　Once 'tis tainted with disdain.

Use me kindly, fairest creature,
　You shall ever find me true;
Yet, so stubborn is my nature,
　Slighted, I can bid adieu.

Poems on Several Occasions, 1729

Anonymous

An Epigram on Miss K. A—ls—n, by Mr H.

To heal the wound a bee had made
　Upon my Kitty's face,
Honey upon her cheek she laid,
　And bid me kiss the place.

Pleased, I obeyed, and from the wound
　Imbibed both sweet and smart,
The honey on my lips I found,
　The sting within my heart.

In *The Windsor Medley*, 1731

George, Lord Lyttelton

To Miss Lucy F—, with a New Watch

With me, while present, may thy lovely eyes
Be never turned upon this golden toy;
Think every pleasing hour too swiftly flies,
And measure time by joy succeeding joy.

241

But when the cares that interrupt our bliss
  To me not always will thy sight allow,
Then oft with kind impatience look on this,
  Then every minute count – as I do now.

In Dodsley's Collection of Poems, II, 1748 (written c.1732)

Philip Dormer Stanhope, Earl of Chesterfield

Verses Written in a Lady's Copy of 'Sherlock upon Death'

Mistaken Fair, lay Sherlock by,
  His doctrine is deceiving;
For whilst he teaches us to die,
  He cheats us of our living.

To die's a lesson we shall know
  Too soon, without a master;
Then let us only study now
  How we may live the faster.

To live's to love, to bless, be blessed
  With mutual inclination;
Share then my ardour in your breast,
  And kindly meet my passion.

But if thus blessed I may not live,
  And pity you deny,
To me, at least, your Sherlock give;
  'Tis I must learn to die.

In The Weekly Register, 12 May 1733

Whenever, Cloe, I begin
  Your heart, like mine, to move,
You tell me of the crying sin
  Of unchaste lawless love.

How can that passion be a sin,
    Which gave to Cloe birth?
How can those joys but be divine,
    Which make a Heaven on Earth?

To wed, mankind the priests trepanned,
    By some sly fallacy,
And disobeyed God's great command,
    Increase and multiply.

You say that love's a crime; content;
    Yet this allow you must:
More joy's in Heaven when one repent
    Than over ninety just.

Sin then, dear girl, for Heaven's sake,
    Repent, and be forgiven
Bless me, and by repentance make
    A holiday in Heaven.

In The Cupid, 1736

Anonymous

To a Lady, Presenting a Nosegay

Accept these flowers of different hue,
    The lily and the rose;
And let them, while the gift you view,
    The giver's pain disclose.

The lily shows the face he wears
    Who loving finds no rest;
Whilst the red rose expressive bears
    The flame within his breast.

In The Honey-Suckle, 1734

243

Soame Jenyns

When first I sought fair Celia's love,
 And every charm was new,
I swore by all the Gods above
 To be for ever true.

But long in vain did I adore,
 Long wept, and sighed in vain,
She still protested, vowed, and swore
 She ne'er would ease my pain.

At last o'ercome, she made me blessed,
 And yielded all her charms,
And I forsook her, when possessed,
 And fled to other's arms.

But let not this, dear Celia, now
 Thy breast to rage incline,
For why, since you forget your vow,
 Should I remember mine?

In The Cupid, 1736

Chloe Angling

On yon fair brook's enamelled side
 Behold my Chloe stands!
Her angle trembles o'er the tide,
 As conscious of her hands.

Calm as the gentle waves appear
 Her thoughts serenely flow,
Calm as the softly breathing air
 That curls the brook below.

Such charms her sparkling eyes disclose,
 With such soft power endued,
She seems a new-born Venus 'rose
 From the transparent flood.

From each green bank and mossy cave
   The scaly race repair;
They sport beneath the crystal wave,
   And kiss her image there.

Here the bright silver eel enrolled
   In shining volumes lies,
There basks the carp bedroopt with gold
   In the sunshine of her eyes.

With hungry pikes in wanton play
   The timorous trouts appear;
The hungry pikes forget to prey,
   The timorous trouts to fear.

With equal haste the thoughtless crew
   To the fair tempter fly;
Nor grieve they, whilst her eyes they view,
   That by her hand they die.

Thus I too viewed the Nymph of late;
   Ah! simple fish, beware!
Soon will you find my wretched fate,
   And struggle in the snare.

But, Fair-one, though these toils succeed,
   Of conquest be not vain;
Nor think o'er all the scaly breed
   Unpunished thus to reign.

Remember, in a watery glass
   His charms Narcissus spied,
When for his own bewitching face
   The youth despaired, and died.

No more, then, harmless fish ensnare,
   No more such wiles pursue,
Lest, whilst you baits for them prepare,
   Love finds out one for you.

Poems, 1752

Chloe Hunting

Whilst thousands court fair Chloe's love,
　　She fears the dangerous joy,
But, Cynthia-like, frequents the grove,
　　As lovely, and as coy.

With the same speed she seeks the hind,
　　Or hunts the flying hare,
She leaves pursuing swains behind,
　　To languish and despair.

Oh strange caprice in thy dear breast!
　　Whence first this whim began;
To follow thus each worthless beast,
　　And shun their sovereign, man!

Consider, Fair, what 'tis you do,
　　How thus they both must die,
Not surer they, when you pursue,
　　Than we, whene'er you fly.

Poems, 1752

To a Nosegay in Pancharilla's Breast

Must you alone then, happy flowers,
Ye short-lived sons of vernal showers,
Must you alone be still thus blessed,
And dwell in Pancharilla's breast?
Oh would the Gods but hear my prayer,
To change my form and place me there!
I should not sure so quickly die,
I should not so unactive lie;
But ever wandering, to and fro,
From this to that fair ball of snow,
Enjoy ten thousand thousand blisses,
And print on each ten thousand kisses.

Nor would I thus the task give o'er;
Curious new secrets to explore,
I'd never rest till I had found
Which globe was softest, which most round –
Which was most yielding, smooth and white,
Or the left bosom, or the right;
Which was the warmest, easiest bed,
And which was tipped with purest red.

Nor could I leave the beauteous scene,
Till I had traced the path between,
That Milky Way so smooth and even,
That promises to lead to Heaven:
Lower and lower I'd descend,
To find when it at last would end;
Till fully blessed I'd wandering rove
O'er all the fragrant Cyprian grove.

But ah! those wishes all are vain,
The fair one triumphs in my pain;
To flowers that know not to be blessed
The Nymph unveils her snowy breast,
While to her slave's desiring eyes
The heavenly prospect she denies;
Too cruel fate, too cruel Fair,
To place a senseless nosegay there,
And yet refuse my lips the bliss
To taste one dear transporting kiss.

Works, 1790

William Collins

When Phoebe formed a wanton smile,
  My soul! it reached not here.
Strange that thy peace, thou trembler, flies
  Before a rising tear!

From midst the drops, my love is born,
    That o'er those eyelids rove:
Thus issued from a teeming wave
    The fabled Queen of Love.

In The Gentleman's Magazine, 1739

Robert Dodsley

The Parting Kiss

One kind kiss before we part,
    Drop a tear, and bid adieu;
Though we sever, my fond heart
    Till we meet shall pant for you.

Yet, yet weep not so, my love,
    Let me kiss that falling tear;
Though my body must remove,
    All my soul will still be here.

All my soul, and all my heart,
    And every wish shall pant for you;
One kind kiss then e'er we part,
    Drop a tear, and bid adieu.

Colin's Kisses, 1742

James Drake

Can any transports equal those
    Which two fond lovers feel,
Who meet, that thought to meet no more,
    And their past woes reveal?

Their joys, too great to be expressed,
  So crowd the faltering tongue,
Fain would they breathe their soul in words,
  But passion strikes them dumb.

Yet do their eyes at the blest sight
  Enraptured glances dart;
By these and sighs their wishes paint,
  Which flutter round the heart.

Like statues fixed, amazed they stand,
  Survey their mutual charms;
Then, when the ecstasy gives leave,
  Fly to each other's arms.

The Humours of New Tunbridge Wells at Islington, 1742

Anonymous

The Resolution

Were I invited to a nectar feast
In Heaven, and Venus named me for her guest,
Though Mercury the messenger should prove,
Or her own son, the mighty God of Love;
At the same instant let but honest Tom
From Sylvia's dear terrestrial lodging come,
With look important, say — *desires at three* —
Alone — your company — to drink some tea —
Though Tom were mortal, Mercury divine,
Though Sylvia gave me water, Venus wine,
Though Heaven were here, and Bow Street lay as far
As the vast distance of the Polar Star,
With open arms to Sylvia would I fly;
Let who would meet the Beauty of the Sky.

In *A New Miscellany in Prose and Verse*, 1742

William Shenstone
The Landskip

How pleased within my native bowers
    Erewhile I passed the day!
Was ever scene so decked with flowers?
    Were ever flowers so gay?

How sweetly smiled the hill, the vale,
    And all the landskip round!
The river gliding down the dale!
    The hill with beeches crowned!

But now, when urged by tender woes
    I speed to meet my dear,
That hill and stream my zeal oppose,
    And check my fond career.

No more, since Daphne was my theme,
    Their wonted charms I see:
That verdant hill and silver stream
    Divide my love and me.

In Dodsley's *Collection of Poems by Several Hands*, V, 1758
(written before 1743)

Henry Fielding
The Price

Can there on earth, my Celia, be
A price I would not pay for thee?
Yes, one dear precious tear of thine
Should not be shed to make thee mine.

Miscellanies, II, 1743

Robert Nugent, Earl Nugent

My heart still hovering round about you,
I thought I could not live without you;
Now we have lived three months asunder,
How I lived with you is the wonder.

In Dodsley's *Collection of Poems by Several Hands*, II, 1748

Samuel Boyce

The Confession

Oh, Sephalissa! dearest maid!
　　So blooming, kind, and free,
The goddess of Cythera's shade
　　Is not so fair as thee!
Thy image always fills my mind,
　　The theme of every song;
I'm fixed to thee alone, I find,
　　But ask not for how long.
The fair in general I've admired;
　　Have oft been false and true;
And when the last my fancy tired,
　　It wandered round to you.
Then while I can I'll be sincere,
　　As turtles to their mates:
This moment's yours and mine, my dear!
　　The next, you know, is Fate's.

Poems on Several Occasions, 1757

251

Young Daphne was the prettiest maid
  The eyes of love could see;
And but one fault the charmer had –
  'Twas cruelty to me.
No Swain that e'er the Nymph adored
  Was fonder, or was younger;
Yet when her pity I implored,
  'Twas 'Stay a little longer.'

It chanced I met the blooming Fair
  One May morn in the grove;
When Cupid whispered in my ear,
  'Now, now's the time for love.'
I clasped the maid, it waked her pride,
  'What, did I mean to wrong her?'
'Not so, my gentle dear!' I cried,
  'But love will stay no longer.'

Then, kneeling at her feet, I swore
  How much I loved, how well,
And that my heart, which beat for her,
  With her should ever dwell.
Consent stood speaking in the eye
  Of all my care's prolonger;
Yet soft she uttered, with a sigh,
  'Oh, stay a little longer.'

The conflict in her soul I saw,
  'Twixt virtue and desire;
'Oh come,' I cried, 'Let Hymen's law
  Give sanction to love's fire.'
Ye lovers, guess how great my joys;
  Could rapture well prove stronger?
When virtue spoke, in Daphne's voice,
  'You now shall stay no longer.'

Poems on Several Occasions, 1757

William Woty

Occasioned by a Lady's Blushing as a
Gentleman Beheld Her through a Window

On Caelia's eyes with pleasure as I gazed,
And thence a thousand doubts and raptures raised,
A sudden change her blushing cheeks disclose;
The lily was contending with the rose.
The rival powers disputed empire there,
Ambitious each to grace and serve the Fair.
Quick was the combat, doubtful the success,
Each resolute, and each for conquest press.
At length the bloody rose, unused to yield,
Displayed his conquering ensigns through the field,
And, with triumphant rage and power possessed,
Thence hurled the panting lilies to her breast,
Where, doomed to endless exile, they remain,
Whilst in her cheeks the insulting victors reign.

The Shrubs of Parnassus, 1760

Francis Fawkes

A Nosegay for Laura

Come, ye fair ambrosial flowers,
Leave your beds and leave your bowers,
Blooming, beautiful, and rare,
Form a posy for my Fair;
Fair and bright and blooming be,
Meet for such a Nymph as she.
Let the young vermilion rose
A becoming blush disclose,
Such as Laura's cheeks display,
When she steals my heart away.

Add carnation's varied hue,
Moistened with the morning dew:
To the woodbine's fragrance join
Sprigs of snow-white jessamine.

Add no more; already I
Shall, alas! with envy die,
Thus to see my rival blessed,
Sweetly dying on her breast.

Original Poems and Translations, 1761

Myles Cooper
To Delia Singing

Yes, my Fair, to thee belong
All the noblest powers of song.
Trust me, for I scorn deceit,
Nought on earth is half so sweet
As the melting, dying note
Warbling through thy liquid throat,
Save the breath in which it flows,
Save the lips on which it grows.

Poems, 1761

Robert Lloyd
The Fan

For various purpose serves the fan,
    As thus – a decent blind,
Between the sticks to peep at man,
    Nor yet betray your mind.

Each action has a meaning plain:
Resentment's in the snap;
A flirt expresses strong disdain,
Consent a tiny tap.

All passions will the fan disclose,
All modes of female art;
And to advantage sweetly shows
The hand if not the heart.

'Tis Folly's sceptre, first designed
By Love's capricious boy,
Who knows how lightly all mankind
Are governed by a toy.

The Capricious Lovers, 1764

John Cunningham

Sent to Miss Bell H---, with a Pair of Buckles

Happy trifles, can ye bear
Sighs of fondness to the Fair?
If your pointed tongues can tell
How I love my charming Bell,
Fondly take a lover's part,
Plead the anguish of my heart.

Go, ye trifles, gladly fly
(Gracious in my fair one's eye),
Fly, your envied bliss to meet,
Fly, and kiss the charmer's feet.

Happy there, with waggish play,
Though you revel day by day,
Like the donor, every night
(Robbed of his supreme delight),
To subdue your wanton pride,
Useless, you'll be thrown aside.

Poems, Chiefly Pastoral, 1766

255

To a Young Widow

Let bashful virgins, nicely coy,
   Exalted rapture lose,
And, timid at untasted joy,
   Through fearfulness refuse.

Will you – the pleasing conflict tried –
   Though sure to conquer, fly?
In you – the sacred zone untied –
   'Tis peevish to deny.

But if, my Fair, the widow's name
   Hold gracious with you still,
The God of Love has formed a scheme
   Obsequious to your will.

Take, take me to thy twining arms
   (Oppressed with warm desire),
Where, conquered by such mighty charms,
   A monarch might expire.

Thou'lt be a widow every night
   (Thy wondrous power confessed!)
And, as I die in dear delight,
   My tomb shall be thy breast.

Poems, Chiefly Pastoral, 1766

Oliver Goldsmith

The Gift: to Iris

Say, cruel Iris, pretty rake,
   Dear mercenary beauty,
What annual offering shall I make,
   Expressive of my duty?

My heart, a victim to thine eyes,
    Should I at once deliver,
Say, would the angry fair one prize
    The gift, who slights the giver?

A bill, a jewel, watch or toy,
    My rivals give – and let them:
If gems, or gold, impart a joy,
    I'll give them – when I get them.

I'll give – but not the full-blown rose,
    Or rosebud more in fashion;
Such short-lived offerings but disclose
    A transitory passion.

I'll give thee something yet unpaid,
    Not less sincere than civil:
I'll give thee – Ah! too charming maid,
    I'll give thee – to the Devil.

In *A Collection of the Most Esteemed Pieces of Poetry*, 1767

Anonymous

One morning very early, one morning in the Spring,
I heard a maid in Bedlam who mournfully did sing,
Her chains she rattled on her hands while sweetly thus sung
    she,
I love my love, because I know my love loves me.

Oh cruel were his parents who sent my love to sea,
And cruel cruel was the ship that bore my love from me,
Yet I love his parents since they're his, although they've ruined
    me,
And I love my love, because I know my love loves me.

Oh should it please the pitying powers to call me to the sky,
I'd claim a guardian angel's charge around my love to fly;
To guard him from all dangers how happy should I be!
For I love my love, because I know my love loves me.

I'll make a strawy garland, I'll make it wondrous fine,
With roses, lilies, daisies, I'll mix the eglantine;
And I'll present it to my love when he returns from sea,
For I love my love, because I know my love loves me.

Oh if I were a little bird to build upon his breast,
Or if I were a nightingale to sing my love to rest!
To gaze upon his lovely eyes all my reward should be;
For I love my love, because I know my love loves me.

Oh if I were an eagle, to soar into the sky!
I'd gaze around with piercing eyes where I my love might spy;
But ah! unhappy maiden, that love you ne'er shall see,
Yet I love my love, because I know my love loves me.

In John Aikin's *Essays on Song-Writing
with a Collection of such English Songs*, 1774

Richard Brinsley Sheridan

I ne'er could any lustre see
In eyes that would not look on me;
I ne'er saw nectar on a lip,
But where my own did hope to sip.
Has the maid who seeks my heart
Cheeks of rose, untouched by art?
I will own the colour true
When yielding blushes add their hue.

Is her hand so soft and pure?
I must press it, to be sure;
Nor can I be certain then,
Till it, grateful, press again.
Must I, with attentive eye,
Watch her heaving bosom sigh?
I will do so, when I see
That heaving bosom sigh for me.

Songs, Duets, Trios, &c. in The Duenna, 1775

Dry be that tear, my gentlest love,
  Be hushed that struggling sigh;
Nor seasons, day, nor fate shall prove,
  More fixed, more true than I.
Hushed be that sigh, be dry that tear,
Cease boding doubt, cease anxious fear,
  Dry be that tear.

Ask'st thou how long my love will stay,
  When all that's new is past?
How long, ah Delia! can I say
  How long my life will last?
Dry be that tear, be hushed that sigh,
At least I'll love thee till I die.
  Hushed be that sigh.

And does that thought affect thee too,
  The thought of Sylvio's death,
That he who only breathed for you
  Must yield that faithful breath?
Hushed be that sigh, be dry that tear,
Nor let us lose our heaven here.
  Dry be that tear.

In *The European Magazine*, 1789 (text from *Memoirs*, 1825)

Richard Graves

The Setting Sun: To Lady —

When Phoebus glows with radiant gold
   In his meridian height,
What eye uninjured can behold
   Th' insufferable light?

But when, declining to the west,
   He shoots a feebler ray,
His charms in milder radiance dressed
   With pleasure we survey.

In height of bloom, thus Fulvia charmed,
   Thus tortured every heart;
Her dazzling eyes each breast alarmed,
   Each glance conveyed a dart.

Their lustre softened now by time,
   Less ardent is their fire:
Though amiable as in her prime –
   With safety we admire.

Euphrosyne: or, Amusements on the Road of Life, 1776

Anonymous

The fragrant Lily of the Vale,
   So elegantly fair,
Whose sweets perfume the fanning gale,
   To Chloe I compare.

What though on earth it lowly grows
   And strives its head to hide;
Its sweetness far out-vies the Rose,
   That flaunts with so much pride.

The costly Tulip owes its hue
　To many a gaudy stain;
In this, we view the virgin white
　Of innocence remain.

See how the curious Florist's hand
　Uprears its humble head;
And to preserve the charming flower,
　Transplants it to his bed.

There, while it sheds its sweets around,
　How shines each modest grace!
Enraptured how its owner stands,
　To view its lovely face!

But pray, my Chloe, now observe
　The inference of my tale;
May I the Florist be – and thou
　The Lily of the Vale.

In *The Bull-Finch*, *c*.1780

William Blake

How sweet I roamed from field to field
　And tasted all the summer's pride,
Till I the prince of love beheld
　Who in the sunny beams did glide.

He shewed me lilies for my hair,
　And blushing roses for my brow;
He led me through his gardens fair
　Where all his golden pleasures grow.

With sweet May dews my wings were wet
　And Phoebus fired my vocal range;
He caught me in his silken net,
　And shut me in his golden cage.

He loves to sit and hear me sing,
    Then, laughing, sports and plays with me;
Then stretches out my golden wing,
    And mocks my loss of liberty.

Poetical Sketches, 1783

I told my love, I told my love,
    I told her all my heart;
Trembling cold, in ghastly fears,
    Ah! she doth depart.

Soon as she was gone from me
    A traveller came by;
Silently, invisibly,
    O! was no deny.

Rossetti MS., *c*.1793

Are not the joys of morning sweeter
    Than the joys of night?
And are the vigorous joys of youth
    Ashamëd of the light?

Let age and sickness silent rob
    The vineyards in the night,
But those who burn with vigorous youth
    Pluck fruits before the light.

Rossetti MS., *c*.1793

Robert Burns

Ae fond kiss, and then we sever!
Ae fareweel, and then for ever!
Deep in heart-wrung tears I'll pledge thee,
Warring sighs and groans I'll wage thee.

Who shall say that Fortune grieves him
While the star of hope she leaves him?
Me, nae cheerfu' twinkle lights me,
Dark despair around benights me.

I'll ne'er blame my partial fancy,
Naething could resist my Nancy;
But to see her was to love her,
Love but her, and love for ever.
Had we never loved sae kindly,
Had we never loved sae blindly,
Never met – or never parted,
We had ne'er been broken-hearted.

Fare thee weel, thou first and fairest!
Fare thee weel, thou best and dearest!
Thine be ilka joy and treasure,
Peace, Enjoyment, Love, and Pleasure.
Ae fond kiss, and then we sever;
Ae fareweel, alas, for ever!
Deep in heart-wrung tears I'll pledge thee,
Warring sighs and groans I'll wage thee.

The Scots Musical Museum, iv, 1792

My love is like a red red rose
  That's newly sprung in June:
My love is like the melodie
  That's sweetly played in tune.

As fair art thou, my bonnie lass,
  So deep in love am I:
And I will love thee still, my dear,
  Till a' the seas gang dry.

Till a' the seas gang dry, my dear,
  And the rocks melt wi' the sun:
And I will love thee still, my dear,
  While the sands o' life shall run.

And fare thee weel, my only love,
And fare thee weel a while!
And I will come again, my love,
Tho' it were ten thousand mile.

In Selection of Scots Songs, ii, 1794

William Cowper

The twentieth year is well-nigh past,
Since first our sky was overcast;
Ah would that this might be the last!
    My Mary!

Thy spirits have a fainter flow,
I see thee daily weaker grow –
'Twas my distress that brought thee low,
    My Mary!

Thy needles, once a shining store,
For my sake restless heretofore,
Now rust disused, and shine no more,
    My Mary!

For though thou gladly would'st fulfil
The same kind office for me still,
Thy sight now seconds not thy will,
    My Mary!

But well thou played'st the housewife's part,
And all thy threads with magic art
Have wound themselves about this heart,
    My Mary!

Thy indistinct expressions seem
Like language uttered in a dream;
Yet me they charm, whate'er the theme,
    My Mary!

Thy silver locks, once auburn bright,
Are still more lovely in my sight
Than golden beams of orient light,
My Mary!

For, could I view nor them nor thee,
What sight worth seeing could I see?
The sun would rise in vain for me,
My Mary!

Partakers of thy sad decline,
Thy hands their little force resign;
Yet, gently pressed, press gently mine,
My Mary!

And then I feel that still I hold
A richer store ten thousandfold
Than misers fancy in their gold,
My Mary!

Such feebleness of limbs thou prov'st
That now at every step thou mov'st
Upheld by two; yet still thou lov'st,
My Mary!

And still to love, though pressed with ill,
In wintry age to feel no chill,
With me is to be lovely still,
My Mary!

But ah! by constant heed I know
How oft the sadness that I show
Transforms thy smiles to looks of woe,
My Mary!

And should my future lot be cast
With much resemblance of the past,
Thy worn-out heart will break at last,
My Mary!

Life and Letters, 1803 (written in 1793)

Samuel Bishop

To Mrs Bishop on the Anniversary of Her Wedding Day

'Thee, Mary, with this ring I wed,'
So, fourteen years ago, I said –
Behold another ring! – 'For what?'
'To wed thee o'er again – why not?'
With that first ring I married Youth,
Grace, Beauty, Innocence, and Truth;
Taste long admired, since long revered,
And all my Molly then appeared.
If she, by merit since disclosed,
Prove twice the woman I supposed,
I plead that double merit now,
To justify a double vow.
Here then, today (with faith as sure,
With ardour as intense, as pure,
As when, amidst the rites divine,
I took thy troth, and plighted mine),
To thee, sweet girl, my second ring
A token, and a pledge, I bring;
With this I wed, till death us part,
Thy riper virtues to my heart;
Those virtues, which, before untried,
The wife has added to the bride;
Those virtues, whose progressive claim
Endearing wedlock's very name,
My soul enjoys, my song approves,
For Conscience's sake, as well as Love's.
And why? – They show me every hour,
Honour's high thought, affection's power,
Discretion's deed, sound Judgement's sentence,
And teach me all things – but Repentance.

Poetical Works, 1796

Anonymous

Woman, doubtful theme, I sing,
Dear, delightful, dangerous thing!
Magic source of all our joy,
Tempting, trifling, tinselled toy:
Every faculty possessing
That constitute a curse or blessing:
Witty, empty, fond, capricious,
Pious sometimes, often vicious:
As angels handsome, devils proud,
Modest, pert, submissive, loud:
The most ambiguous work of Heaven,
To cheer us and torment us, given:
Without them, what, ye Gods, is life?
And with them – what but care and strife?

In *A Collection of English Songs*, 1796

William Wordsworth

She was a Phantom of delight
When first she gleamed upon my sight;
A lovely Apparition, sent
To be a moment's ornament;
Her eyes as stars of Twilight fair;
Like Twilight's, too, her dusky hair;
But all things else about her drawn
From May-time and the cheerful Dawn;
A dancing Shape, an Image gay,
To haunt, to startle, and way-lay.

I saw her upon nearer view,
A Spirit, yet a Woman too!
Her household motions light and free,
And steps of virgin-liberty;

267

A countenance in which did meet
Sweet records, promises as sweet;
A creature not too bright or good
For human nature's daily food;
For transient sorrows, simple wiles,
Praise, blame, love, kisses, tears, and smiles.

And now I see with eye serene
The very pulse of the machine;
A Being breathing thoughtful breath,
A Traveller between life and death;
The reason firm, the temperate will,
Endurance, foresight, strength, and skill;
A perfect Woman, nobly planned,
To warn, to comfort, and command;
And yet a Spirit still, and bright
With something of an angel-light.

Poems in Two Volumes, 1807 (written in 1804)

William Robert Spencer

To the Lady Anne Hamilton

Too late I stayed; forgive the crime;
    Unheeded flew the hours;
How noiseless falls the foot of Time
    That only treads on flowers!

What eye with clear account remarks
    The ebbing of his glass,
When all its sands are diamond sparks,
    That dazzle as they pass?

Ah! who to sober measurement
    Time's happy swiftness brings,
When birds of Paradise have lent
    Their plumage for his wings?

In *English Minstrelsy*, 1810 (text from *Poems*, 1811)

George Gordon, Lord Byron

From *To Ianthe, A Dedication*

Not in those climes where I have late been straying,
  Though Beauty long hath there been matchless deemed;
Not in those visions to the heart displaying
  Forms which it sighs but to have only dreamed,
Hath aught like thee in truth or fancy seemed:
  Nor, having seen thee, shall I vainly seek
To paint those charms which varied as they beamed –
  To such as see thee not my words were weak;
To those who gaze on thee what language could they speak?

Ah! may'st thou ever be what now thou art,
  Nor unbeseem the promise of thy Spring,
As fair in form, as warm yet pure in heart,
  Love's image upon earth without his wing,
And guileless beyond Hope's imagining!
  And surely she who now so fondly rears
Thy youth, in thee, thus hourly brightening,
  Beholds the rainbow of her future years,
Before whose heavenly hues all sorrow disappears . . .

Childe Harold's Pilgrimage, 1812

Stanzas to Lady Wilmot Horton

She walks in beauty, like the night
  Of cloudless climes and starry skies;
And all that's best of dark and bright
  Meet in her aspect and her eyes:
Thus mellowed to that tender light
  Which heaven to gaudy day denies.

One shade the more, one ray the less,
　　Had half impaired the nameless grace
Which waves in every raven tress,
　　Or softly lightens o'er her face;
Where thoughts serenely sweet express
　　How pure, how dear their dwelling-place.

And on that cheek, and o'er that brow,
　　So soft, so calm, yet eloquent,
The smiles that win, the tints that glow,
　　But tell of days in goodness spent,
A mind at peace with all below,
　　A heart whose love is innocent!

Hebrew Melodies, 1815

If I forsake thee, early be my tomb,
My bed untended, and unwept my doom;
Around my grave let no fresh verdure spring,
No plaintive bird within its precincts sing;
Let no fair flower adorn my turfy bed,
No violets spring, no roses lift their head;
But there let weeds, and noxious nightshade thrive;
There only what to life is fatal, live:
So shall mankind avoid the hated place,
Shunned and detested by the brutal race;
All but the shrieking owl, and bat obscene,
Shall fly the relics of a thing so mean.

But if, as Heaven is witness, such shall be,
Death only can divorce my heart from thee;
If this fond breast shall heave its parting sigh,
Loth only, as 'tis leaving thee, to die;
Then let affliction drop the pious tear,
The tribute sacred to the heart sincere:
Let not the gaudy pomps of seeming woe,
The paltry debt that pride to pride may owe –

Let, while surviving summers still are thine,
Let all thy thoughts, thy tenderest thoughts, be mine;
And when thy peaceful course fulfilled in this,
Thy fate shall call thee to the world of bliss,
In one sepulchral mansion let us rest,
By the same simple grassy tomb compressed;
Let mingling urns our mutual loves requite,
And death which parted once, once more unite.

In *The Gentleman's Pocket Magazine*, 1828
(written in 1818)

Percy Bysshe Shelley

From *Rosalind and Helen*

I know not how, but we were free:
And Lionel sate alone with me,
As the carriage drove thro' the streets apace;
And we looked upon each other's face;
And the blood in our fingers intertwined
Ran like the thoughts of a single mind,
As the swift emotions went and came
Thro' the veins of each united frame.
So thro' the long long streets we passed
Of the million-peopled City vast;
Which is that desert, where each one
Seeks his mate yet is alone,
Beloved and sought and mourned of none;
Until the clear blue sky was seen,
And the grassy meadows bright and green,
And then I sunk in his embrace,
Enclosing there a mighty space
Of love: and so we travelled on
By woods, and fields of yellow flowers,
And towns, and villages, and towers,
Day after day of happy hours.

271

It was the azure time of June,
When the skies are deep in the stainless noon,
And the warm and fitful breezes shake
The fresh green leaves of the hedgerow briar,
And there were odours then to make
The very breath we did respire
A liquid element, whereon
Our spirits, like delighted things
That walk the air on subtle wings,
Floated and mingled far away,
'Mid the warm winds of the sunny day.
And when the evening star came forth
Above the curve of the new bent moon,
And light and sound ebbed from the earth,
Like the tide of the full and weary sea
To the depths of its tranquillity,
Our natures to its own repose
Did the earth's breathless sleep attune:
Like flowers, which on each other close
Their languid leaves when daylight's gone,
We lay, till new emotions came,
Which seemed to make each mortal frame
One soul of interwoven flame,
A life in life, a second birth
In worlds diviner far than earth,
Which, like two strains of harmony
That mingle in the silent sky
Then slowly disunite, passed by
And left the tenderness of tears,
A soft oblivion of all fears,
A sweet sleep . . .

Rosalind and Helen, 1819

The
Victorians

Elizabeth Barrett Browning

Say over again, and yet once over again
  That thou dost love me. Though the word repeated
  Should seem 'a cuckoo song', as thou dost treat it,
Remember, never to the hill or plain,
Valley and wood, without her cuckoo-strain,
  Comes the fresh Spring in all her green completed.
  Beloved, I, amid the darkness greeted
By a doubtful spirit-voice, in that doubt's pain
  Cry, 'Speak once more . . . thou lovest!' Who can fear
Too many stars, though each in heaven shall roll,
  Too many flowers, though each shall crown the year?
Say thou dost love me, love me, love me – toll
  The silver iterance! – only minding, Dear,
To love me also in silence, with thy soul.

Sonnets from the Portuguese, 1830

When our two souls stand up erect and strong,
  Face to face, silent, drawing nigh and nigher,
  Until the lengthening wings break into fire
At either curvèd point, – what bitter wrong
Can the earth do us, that we should not long
  Be here contented? Think! In mounting higher,
  The angels would press on us and aspire
To drop some golden orb of perfect song
Into our deep, dear silence. Let us stay
  Rather on earth, Belovèd – where the unfit
Contrarious moods of men recoil away
  And isolate pure spirits, and permit
A place to stand and love in for a day,
  With darkness and the death-hour rounding it.

Sonnets from the Portuguese, 1830

275

Inclusions

Oh, wilt thou have my hand, Dear, to lie along in thine?
As a little stone in a running stream, it seems to lie and pine.
Now drop the poor pale hand, Dear, unfit to plight with thine.

Oh, wilt thou have my cheek, Dear, drawn closer to thine own?
My cheek is white, my cheek is worn, by many a tear run down.
Now leave a little space, Dear, lest it should wet thine own.

Oh, must thou have my soul, Dear, commingled with thy
    soul? –
Red grows the cheek, and warm the hand; the part is in the
    whole:
Nor hands nor cheeks keep separate, when soul is joined to
    soul.

Poems, 1844

Hartley Coleridge
To a Friend

When we were idlers with the loitering rills,
   The need of human love we little noted:
   Our love was nature; and the peace that floated
On the white mist, and dwelt upon the hills,
To sweet accord subdued our wayward wills:
   One soul was ours, one mind, one heart devoted,
   That, wisely doating, asked not why it doated,
And ours the unknown joy, which knowing kills.
   But now I find how dear thou wert to me;
That man is more than half of nature's treasure,
   Of that fair Beauty which no eye can see,
Of that sweet music which no ear can measure;
And now the streams may sing for others' pleasure,
   The hills sleep on in their eternity.

Poems, 1833

Alfred, Lord Tennyson

O Beauty, passing beauty! sweetest Sweet!
  How canst thou let me waste my youth in sighs?
I only ask to sit beside thy feet.
  Thou knowest I dare not look into thine eyes.
Might I but kiss thy hand! I dare not fold
  My arms about thee – scarcely dare to speak.
And nothing seems to me so wild and bold,
  As with one kiss to touch thy blessèd cheek.
Methinks if I should kiss thee, no control
  Within the thrilling brain could keep afloat,
    The subtle spirit. Even while I spoke,
The bare word KISS hath made my inner soul
  To tremble like a lutestring, ere the note
    Hath melted in the silence that it broke.

Poems, 1833

Fatima

O Love, Love, Love! O withering might!
O sun, that from thy noonday height
Shudderest when I strain my sight,
Throbbing through all thy heat and light,
  Lo, falling from my constant mind,
  Lo, parched and withered, deaf and blind,
  I whirl like leaves in roaring wind.

Last night I wasted hateful hours
Below the city's eastern towers:
I thirsted for the brooks, the showers:
I rolled among the tender flowers:
  I crushed them on my breast, my mouth:
  I looked athwart the burning drouth
  Of that long desert to the south.

277

Last night, when some one spoke his name,
From my swift blood that went and came
A thousand little shafts of flame
Were shivered in my narrow frame.
   O Love, O fire! once he drew
   With one long kiss my whole soul through
   My lips, as sunlight drinketh dew.

Before he mounts the hill, I know
He cometh quickly: from below
Sweet gales, as from deep gardens, blow
Before him, striking on my brow.
   In my dry brain my spirit soon,
   Down-deepening from swoon to swoon,
   Faints like a dazzled morning moon.

The wind sounds like a silver wire,
And from beyond the noon a fire
Is poured upon the hills, and nigher
The skies stoop down in their desire;
   And, isled in sudden seas of light,
   My heart, pierced through with fierce delight,
   Bursts into blossom in his sight.

My whole soul waiting silently,
All naked in a sultry sky,
Droops blinded with his shining eye:
I *will* possess him or will die.
   I will grow round him in his place,
   Grow, live, die looking on his face,
   Die, dying clasped in his embrace.

Poems, 1833

Now sleeps the crimson petal, now the white;
Nor waves the cypress in the palace walk;
Nor winks the gold fin in the porphyry font:
The firefly wakens: waken thou with me.

Now droops the milk-white peacock like a ghost,
And like a ghost she glimmers on to me.

Now lies the Earth all Danaë to the stars,
And all thy heart lies open unto me.

Now slides the silent meteor on, and leaves
A shining furrow, as thy thoughts in me.

Now folds the lily all her sweetness up,
And slips into the bosom of the lake:
So fold thyself, my dearest, thou, and slip
Into my bosom and be lost in me.

The Princess, 1847

From *In Memoriam*

Dark house, by which once more I stand
   Here in the long unlovely street,
   Doors, where my heart was used to beat
So quickly, waiting for a hand,

A hand that can be clasped no more –
   Behold me, for I cannot sleep,
   And like a guilty thing I creep
At earliest morning to the door.

He is not here; but far away
   The noise of life begins again,
   And ghastly through the drizzling rain
On the bald street breaks the blank day.

In Memoriam, 1850

279

From *Maud*

Come into the garden, Maud,
  For the black bat, night, has flown,
Come into the garden, Maud,
  I am here at the gate alone;
And the woodbine spices are wafted abroad,
  And the musk of the rose is blown.

For a breeze of morning moves,
  And the planet of Love is on high,
Beginning to faint in the light that she loves
  On a bed of daffodil sky,
To faint in the light of the sun she loves,
  To faint in his light, and to die.

All night have the roses heard
  The flute, violin, bassoon;
All night has the casement jessamine stirred
  To the dancers dancing in tune;
Till a silence fell with the waking bird,
  And a hush with the setting moon.

I said to the lily, 'There is but one
  With whom she has heart to be gay.
When will the dancers leave her alone?
  She is weary of dance and play.'
Now half to the setting moon are gone,
  And half to the rising day;
Low on the sand and loud on the stone
  The last wheel echoes away.

I said to the rose, 'The brief night goes
  In babble and revel and wine.
O young lord-lover, what sighs are those
  For one that will never be thine?
But mine, but mine,' so I sware to the rose,
  'For ever and ever, mine.'

And the soul of the rose went into my blood,
   As the music clashed in the hall;
And long by the garden lake I stood,
   For I heard your rivulet fall
From the lake to the meadow and on to the wood,
   Our wood, that is dearer than all;

From the meadow your walks have left so sweet
   That whenever a March-wind sighs
He sets the jewel-print of your feet
   In violets blue as your eyes,
To the woody hollows in which we meet
   And the valleys of Paradise.

The slender acacia would not shake
   One long milk-bloom on the tree;
The white lake-blossom fell into the lake,
   As the pimpernel dozed on the lea;
But the rose was awake all night for your sake,
   Knowing your promise to me;
The lilies and roses were all awake,
   They sighed for the dawn and thee.

Queen rose of the rosebud garden of girls,
   Come hither, the dances are done,
In gloss of satin and glimmer of pearls,
   Queen lily and rose in one;
Shine out, little head, sunning over with curls,
   To the flowers, and be their sun.

There has fallen a splendid tear
   From the passion-flower at the gate.
She is coming, my dove, my dear;
   She is coming, my life, my fate;
The red rose cries, 'She is near, she is near;'
   And the white rose weeps, 'She is late;'
The larkspur listens, 'I hear, I hear;'
   And the lily whispers, 'I wait.'

She is coming, my own, my sweet;
   Were it ever so airy a tread,
My heart would hear her and beat,
   Were it earth in an earthy bed;
My dust would hear her and beat,
   Had I lain for a century dead;
Would start and tremble under her feet,
   And blossom in purple and red.

Maud, and Other Poems, 1855

Edgar Allan Poe
To One in Paradise

Thou wast all that to me, love,
   For which my soul did pine –
A green isle in the sea, love,
   A fountain and a shrine,
All wreathed with fairy fruits and flowers,
   And all the flowers were mine.

Ah, dream too bright to last!
   Ah, starry Hope! that didst arise
But to be overcast!
   A voice from out the Future cries,
'On! On!' – but o'er the Past
   (Dim gulf!) my spirit hovering lies
Mute, motionless, aghast!

For, alas! alas! with me
   The light of Life is o'er!
No more – no more – no more –
   (Such language holds the solemn sea
   To the sands upon the shore)
Shall bloom the thunder-blasted tree
   Or the stricken eagle soar!

And all my days are trances,
   And all my nightly dreams
Are where thy grey eye glances,
   And where thy footstep gleams –
In what ethereal dances,
   By what eternal streams.

In *The Southern Literary Messenger*, July 1835

George Darley

Serenade of a Loyal Martyr

Sweet in her green cell the Flower of Beauty slumbers,
  Lulled by the faint breezes sighing through her hair;
Sleeps she, and hears not the melancholy numbers
  Breathed to my sad lute amid the lonely air.

Down from the high cliffs the rivulet is teeming
  To wind round the willow banks that lure him from above:
O that in tears from my rocky prison streaming,
  I too could glide to the bower of my Love!

Ah! where the woodbines with sleepy arms have wound her,
  Opes she her eyelids at the dream of my lay,
Listening, like the dove, while the fountains echo round her,
  To her lost mate's call in the forests far away?

Come then, my Bird! For the peace thou ever bearest,
  Still, heaven's messenger of comfort to me,
Come! – this fond bosom, my faithfullest! my fairest!
  Bleeds with its death-wound, but deeper yet for thee.

In *The Athenaeum*, 1836

283

It is not Beauty I demand,
   A crystal brow, the moon's despair,
Nor the snow's daughter, a white hand,
   Nor mermaid's yellow pride of hair.

Tell me not of your starry eyes,
   Your lips that seem on roses fed,
Your breasts where Cupid tumbling lies,
   Nor sleeps for kissing of his bed.

A bloomy pair of vermeil cheeks,
   Like Hebe's in her ruddiest hours,
A breath that softer music speaks
   Than summer winds a-wooing flowers:

These are but gauds: nay, what are lips?
   Coral beneath the ocean stream,
Whose brink when your adventurer sips
   Full oft he perisheth on them.

And what are cheeks but ensigns oft
   That wave hot youths to fields of blood?
Did Helen's breast, though ne'er so soft,
   Do Greece or Ilium any good?

Eyes can with baleful ardour burn;
   Poison can breathe that erst perfumed;
There's many a white hand holds an urn
   With lovers' hearts to dust consumed.

For crystal brows O there's naught within;
   They are but empty cells for pride;
He who the Siren's hair would win
   Is mostly strangled in the tide.

Give me, instead of beauty's bust,
   A tender heart, a loyal mind,
Which with temptation I could trust,
   Yet never linked with error find.

One in whose gentle bosom I
   Could pour my secret heart of woes,
Like the care-burthened honey-fly
   That hides his murmurs in the rose.

My earthly comforter! whose love
   So indefeasible might be,
That, when my spirit won above,
   Hers could not stay, for sympathy.

In Archbishop Trench's *Household Book of English Poetry*, 1868

Thomas Moore

Mute Courtship (from the Persian)

Love hath a language of his own –
   A voice that goes
From heart to heart – whose mystic tone
   Love only knows.

The lotus-flower, whose leaves I now
   Kiss silently,
Far more than words will tell thee how
   I worship thee.

The mirror, which to thee I hold, –
   Which, when impressed
With thy bright looks, I turn and fold
   To this fond breast –

Doth it not speak, beyond all spells
   Of poet's art,
How deep thy hidden image dwells
   In this hushed heart?

In *The Tribute*, 1837

285

Sara Coleridge

He came unlooked for, undesired,
    A sun-rise in the northern sky:
More than the brightest dawn admired,
    To shine and then for ever fly.

His love, conferred without a claim,
    Perchance was like the fitful blaze,
Which lives to light a steadier flame,
    And, while that strengthens, fast decays.

Glad fawn along the forest springing,
    Gay birds that breeze-like stir the leaves,
Why hither haste, no message bringing,
    To solace one that deeply grieves?

Thou star that dost the skies adorn
    So brightly heralding the day,
Bring one more welcome than the morn,
    Or still in night's dark prison stay.

Phantasmion, 1837

Emily Brontë

If grief for grief can touch thee,
    If answering woe for woe,
If any ruth can melt thee,
    Come to me now!

I cannot be more lonely,
    More drear I cannot be!
My worn heart throbs so wildly,
    'Twill break for thee.

And when the world despises,
    When heaven repels my prayer,
Will not mine angel comfort?
    Mine idol hear?

Yes, by the tears I've poured thee,
    By all my hours of pain,
O I shall surely win thee,
    Beloved, again!

Privately printed, New York, 1902 (written in May 1840)

Remembrance

Cold in the earth, and the deep snow piled above thee!
    Far, far removed, cold in the dreary grave!
Have I forgot, my only Love, to love thee,
    Severed at last by Time's all-wearing wave?

Now, when alone, do my thoughts no longer hover
    Over the mountains, on Angora's shore,
Resting their wings where heath and fern-leaves cover
    Thy noble heart for ever, ever more?

Cold in the earth, and fifteen wild Decembers
    From those brown hills have melted into Spring:
Faithful indeed is the spirit that remembers
    After such years of change and suffering!

Sweet Love of youth, forgive if I forget thee,
    While the World's tide is bearing me along;
Sterner desires and darker hopes beset me,
    Hopes which obscure, but cannot do thee wrong!

No other Sun has lightened up my heaven,
    No other Star has ever shone for me;
All my life's bliss from thy dear life was given,
    All my life's bliss is in the grave with thee.

But when the days of golden dreams have perished
  And even Despair was powerless to destroy;
Then did I learn how existence could be cherished,
  Strengthened and fed without the aid of joy.

Then did I check the tears of useless passion,
  Weaned my young soul from yearning after thine;
Sternly denied its burning wish to hasten
  Down to that tomb already more than mine!

And, even yet, I dare not let it languish,
  Dare not indulge in Memory's rapturous pain;
Once drinking deep of that divinest anguish,
  How could I seek the empty world again?

Poems by Currer, Ellis and Acton Bell, 1846 (text from BM. MS.)

Robert Browning

The Lost Mistress

All's over, then: does truth sound bitter
  As one at first believes?
Hark, 'tis the sparrows' good-night twitter
  About your cottage eaves!

And the leaf-buds on the vine are woolly,
  I noticed that, to-day;
One day more bursts them open fully
  – You know the red turns grey.

To-morrow we meet the same then, dearest?
  May I take your hand in mine?
Mere friends are we, – well, friends the merest
  Keep much that I'll resign:

For each glance of that eye so bright and black,
  Though I keep with heart's endeavour, –
Your voice, when you wish the snowdrops back,
  Though it stay in my soul for ever! –

Yet I will but say what mere friends say,
  Or only a thought stronger;
I will hold your hand but as long as all may,
  Or so very little longer!

Dramatic Lyrics, 1842

Two in the Campagna

I wonder do you feel to-day
  As I have felt since, hand in hand,
We sat down on the grass, to stray
  In spirit better through the land,
This morn of Rome and May?

For me, I touched a thought, I know,
  Has tantalized me many times,
(Like turns of thread the spiders throw
  Mocking across our path) for rhymes
To catch at and let go.

Help me to hold it! First it left
  The yellowing fennel, run to seed
There, branching from the brickwork's cleft,
  Some old tomb's ruin: yonder weed
Took up the floating weft,

Where one small orange cup amassed
  Five beetles, – blind and green they grope
Among the honey-meal: and last,
  Everywhere on the grassy slope
I traced it. Hold it fast!

The champaign with its endless fleece
  Of feathery grasses everywhere!
Silence and passion, joy and peace,
  An everlasting wash of air –
Rome's ghost since her decease.

Such life there, through such lengths of hours,
  Such miracles performed in play,
Such primal naked forms of flowers,
  Such letting Nature have her way
While Heaven looks from its towers!

How say you? Let us, O my dove,
  Let us be unashamed of soul,
As earth lies bare to heaven above!
  How is it under our control
To love or not to love?

I would that you were all to me,
  You that are just so much, no more.
Nor yours, nor mine, nor slave nor free!
  Where does the fault lie? What the core
Of the wound, since wound must be?

I would I could adopt your will,
  See with your eyes, and set my heart
Beating by yours, and drink my fill
  At your soul's springs, – your part, my part
In life, for good and ill.

No. I yearn upward, touch you close,
  Then stand away. I kiss your cheek,
Catch your soul's warmth, – I pluck the rose
  And love it more than tongue can speak –
Then the good minute goes.

Already how am I so far
  Out of that minute? Must I go
Still like the thistle-ball, no bar,
  Onward, whenever light winds blow,
Fixed by no friendly star?

Just when I seemed about to learn!
  Where is the thread now? Off again!
The old trick! Only I discern –
  Infinite passion, and the pain
Of finite hearts that yearn.

Dramatic Lyrics, 1842

From *In a Gondola*

The moth's kiss, first!
  Kiss me as if you made believe
  You were not sure, this eve,
How my face, your flower, had pursed
  Its petals up; so, here and there
  You brush it, till I grow aware
Who wants me, and wide open burst.

The bee's kiss, now!
  Kiss me as if you entered gay
  My heart at some noonday,
A bud that dares not disallow
  The claim, so all is rendered up,
  And passively its shattered cup
Over your head to sleep I bow.

Dramatic Romances, 1845

From *The Last Ride Together*

I said – Then, dearest, since 'tis so,
Since now at length my fate I know,
Since nothing all my love avails,
Since all my life seemed meant for fails,
  Since this was written and needs must be –
My whole heart rises up to bless
Your name in pride and thankfulness!
Take back the hope you gave – I claim
Only a memory of the same,
  – And this beside, if you will not blame;
  Your leave for one more last ride with me.

My mistress bent that brow of hers,
Those deep dark eyes where pride demurs

When pity would be softening through,
Fixed me a breathing-while or two
   With life or death in the balance: right!
The blood replenished me again;
My last thought was at least not vain:
I and my mistress, side by side
Shall be together, breathe and ride,
So one day more am I deified—
   Who knows but the world may end to-night?

Hush! if you saw some western cloud
All billowy-bosomed, over-bowed
By many benedictions – sun's
And moon's and evening-star's at once –
   And so, you, looking and loving best,
Conscious grew, your passion drew
Cloud, sunset, moonrise, star-shine too,
Down on you, near and yet more near,
Till flesh must fade for heaven was here! –
Thus leant she and lingered – joy and fear!
   Thus lay she a moment on my breast.

Then we began to ride. My soul
Smoothed itself out – a long-cramped scroll
Freshening and fluttering in the wind.
Past hopes already lay behind.
   What need to strive with a life awry?
Had I said that, had I done this,
So might I gain, so might I miss.
Might she have loved me? just as well
She might have hated, who can tell?
Where had I been now if the worst befell?
   And here we are riding, she and I. . .

What does it all mean, poet? Well,
Your brains beat into rhythm, you tell
What we felt only; you expressed
You hold things beautiful the best,

And pace them in rhyme so, side by side.
'Tis something, nay 'tis much – but then,
Have you yourself what's best for men?
Are you – poor, sick, old ere your time –
Nearer one whit your own sublime
Than we who never have turned a rhyme?
   Sing, riding's a joy! For me, I ride . . .

Dramatic Romances, 1845

John Clare

First Love

I ne'er was struck before that hour
   With love so sudden and so sweet.
Her face it bloomed like a sweet flower
   And stole my heart away complete.
My face turned pale as deadly pale,
   My legs refused to walk away,
And when she looked 'what could I ail?'
   My life and all seemed turned to clay.

And then my blood rushed to my face
   And took my sight away.
The trees and bushes round the place
   Seemed midnight at noonday.
I could not see a single thing,
   Words from my eyes did start;
They spoke as chords do from the string,
   And blood burnt round my heart.

Are flowers the winter's choice?
   Is love's bed always snow?
She seemed to hear my silent voice
   And love's appeal to know.

293

I never saw so sweet a face
As that I stood before:
My heart has left its dwelling-place
And can return no more.

Poems, 1920 (written 1842–64)

Love Lives beyond the Tomb

Love lives beyond
The tomb, the earth, which fades like dew!
I love the fond,
The faithful, and the true.

Love lives in sleep,
The happiness of healthy dreams:
Eve's dews may weep,
But love delightful seems.

'Tis seen in flowers,
And in the morning's pearly dew;
In earth's green hours,
And in the heaven's eternal blue.

'Tis heard in Spring
When light and sunbeams, warm and kind,
On angel's wing
Bring love and music to the mind.

And where is voice,
So young, so beautiful, and sweet
As Nature's choice,
Where Spring and lovers meet?

Love lives beyond
The tomb, the earth, the flowers, and dew.
I love the fond,
The faithful, young, and true.

Life and Remains, 1873 (written 1842–64)

Secret Love

I hid my love when young till I
Couldn't bear the buzzing of a fly;
I hid my love to my despite
Till I could not bear to look at light:
I dare not gaze upon her face
But left her memory in each place;
Where'er I saw a wild flower lie
I kissed and bade my love good-bye.

I met her in the greenest dells,
Where dewdrops pearl the wood bluebells;
The lost breeze kissed her bright blue eye,
The bee kissed and went singing by,
A sunbeam found a passage there,
A gold chain round her neck so fair;
As secret as the wild bee's song
She lay there all the summer long.

I hid my love in field and town
Till e'en the breeze would knock me down;
The bees seemed singing ballads o'er,
The fly's bass turned a lion's roar;
And even silence found a tongue,
To haunt me all the summer long;
The riddle nature could not prove
Was nothing else but secret love.

Poems, 1920 (written 1842–64)

Thomas Haynes Bayly
We Met

We met – 'twas in a crowd – and I thought he would shun me;
He came – I could not breathe, for his eye was upon me;
He spoke – his words were cold, and his smile was unaltered;
I knew how much he felt, for his deep-toned voice faltered.
I wore my bridal robe, and I rivalled its whiteness.
Bright gems were in my hair, how I hated their brightness;
He called me by my name, as the bride of another –
Oh, thou hast been the cause of this anguish, my mother!

And once again we met, and a fair girl was near him:
He smiled, and whispered low – as I once used to hear him.
She leant upon his arm – once 'twas mine, and mine only –
I wept, for I deserved to feel wretched and lonely.
And she will be his bride! at the altar he'll give her
The love that was too pure for a heartless deceiver.
The world may think me gay, for my feelings I smother;
O, thou hast been the cause of this anguish, my mother!

Songs, Ballads and Other Poems, 1844 (set to music by T. H. Severn)

I Cannot Dance Tonight

Oh! when they brought me hither, they wondered at my wild
    delight,
But would I were at home again, I cannot dance to-night!
How can they all look so cheerful? the dance seems strangely
    dull to me;
The music sounds so mournful, what can the reason be?
   Oh! when they brought me hither, they wondered at my wild delight,
   But would I were at home again, I cannot dance to-night!

Hark! Hark! at length he's coming; I'm not weary – let me stay!
I hear his laugh distinctly now; 'twill chase the gloom away.
Oh! would that I were near him, he sees me not amid the
    crowd,
He hears me not – ah! would I dared to breathe his name aloud.
   Oh! when they brought me hither, they wondered at my wild delight,
   But would I were at home again, I cannot dance to-night!

He leaves that group of triflers, and with the smile I love to see,
He seems to seek for some one – oh! is it not for me?
No, no! 'tis for that dark-eyed girl, I see her now return his
    glance,
He passes me, he takes her hand, he leads her to the dance!
   Oh! when they brought me hither, they wondered at my wild delight,
   But would I were at home again, I cannot dance tonight!

    Songs, Ballads and Other Poems, 1844 (set to music by the Author)

Thomas Lovell Beddoes

How many times do I love thee, dear?
  Tell me how many thoughts there be
    In the atmosphere
    Of a new-fallen year,
Whose white and sable hours appear
  The latest flake of Eternity:
So many times do I love thee, dear.

How many times do I love again?
  Tell me how many beads there are
    In a silver chain
    Of evening rain,
Unravelled from the tumbling main,
  And threading the eye of a yellow star:
So many times do I love again.

    Poems, Posthumous and Collected, 1851

Matthew Arnold
Absence

In this fair stranger's eyes of grey
    Thine eyes, my love! I see.
I shiver; for the passing day
    Had borne me far from thee.

This is the curse of life! that not
    A nobler, calmer train
Of wiser thoughts and feelings blot
    Our passions from our brain;

But each day brings its petty dust
    Our soon-choked souls to fill,
And we forget because we must
    And not because we will.

I struggle towards the light; and ye,
    Once-long'd-for storms of love!
If with the light ye cannot be,
    I bear that ye remove.

I struggle towards the light – but oh,
    While yet the night is chill,
Upon time's barren, stormy flow,
    Stay with me, Marguerite, still!

Empedocles on Etna, and Other Poems, 1852

Alexander Smith

Last night my cheek was wetted with warm tears,
    Each worth a world. They fell from eyes divine.
    Last night a loving lip was pressed to mine,
And at its touch fled all the barren years;

And softly couched upon a bosom white,
Which came and went beneath me like a sea,
   An emperor I lay in empire bright,
Lord of the beating heart, while tenderly
Love-words were glutting my love-greedy ears,
Kind Love, I thank thee for that happy night!
   Richer this cheek with those warm tears of thine
Than the vast midnight with its gleaming spheres.
   Leander toiling through the moonlight brine,
Kingdomless Anthony, were scarce my peers.

Poems, 1853

Coventry Patmore

Eros

Bright through the valley gallops the brooklet;
   Over the welkin travels the cloud;
Touched by the zephyr, dances the harebell;
   Cuckoo sits somewhere, singing so loud;
Swift o'er the meadows glitter the starlings,
   Striking their wings, all the flock at a stroke;
Under the chestnuts new bees are swarming,
   Rising and falling like magical smoke.
Two little children, seeing and hearing,
   Hand in hand wander, shout, laugh, and sing:
Lo, in their bosoms, wild with the marvel,
   Love, like the crocus, is come ere the Spring.
Young men and women, noble and tender,
   Yearn for each other, faith truly plight,
Promise to cherish, comfort and honour;
   Vow that makes duty one with delight.
Oh, but the glory, found in no story,
   Radiance of Eden unquenched by the Fall;
Few may remember, none may reveal it,
   This the first First-love, the first love of all!

Tamerton Church-Tower, and other Poems, 1853

Boon Nature to the woman bows;
   She walks in earth's whole glory clad;
And, chiefest far herself of shows,
   All others help her, and are glad:
No splendour 'neath the sky's proud dome
   But serves for her familiar wear;
The far-fetched diamond finds its home
   Flashing and smouldering in her hair;
For her the seas their pearls reveal;
   Art and strange lands her pomp supply
With purple, chrome, and cochineal,
   Ochre and lapis lazuli;
The worm its golden woof presents;
   Whatever runs, flies, dives, or delves,
All doff for her their ornaments,
   Which suit her better than themselves;
And all, by this their power to give,
   Proving her right to take, proclaim
Her beauty's clear prerogative
   To profit so by Eden's blame.

The Angel in the House, 1863

A Farewell

With all my will, but much against my heart,
We two now part.
My Very Dear,
Our solace is, the sad road lies so clear.
It needs no art,
With faint, averted feet
And many a tear,
In our opposèd paths to persevere.
Go thou to East, I West.
We will not say
There's any hope, it is so far away.

But, O, my Best,
When the one darling of our widowhead,
The nursling Grief,
Is dead,
And no dews blur our eyes
To see the peach-bloom come in evening skies,
Perchance we may,
Where now this night is day,
And even through faith of still averted feet,
Making full circle of our banishment,
Amazëd meet;
The bitter journey to the bourne so sweet
Seasoning the termless feast of our content
With tears of recognition never dry.

The Unknown Eros, 1877

Walt Whitman

From *Children of Adam*

This is the female form,
A divine nimbus exhales from it from head to foot,
It attracts with fierce undeniable attraction,
I am drawn by its breath as if I were no more than a helpless
    vapor, all falls aside but myself and it,
Books, art, religion, time, the visible and solid earth, and what
    was expected of heaven or feared of hell, are now
    consumed,
Mad filaments, ungovernable shoots play out of it, the
    response likewise ungovernable,
Hair, bosom, hips, bend of legs, negligent falling hands all
    diffused, mine too diffused,
Ebb stung by the flow and flow stung by the ebb, love-flesh
    swelling and deliciously aching,

301

Limitless limpid jets of love hot and enormous, quivering jelly
    of love, white-blow and delirious juice,
Bridegroom night of love working surely and softly into the
    prostrate dawn,
Undulating into the willing and yielding day,
Lost in the cleave of the clasping and sweet-fleshed day.

This the nucleus – after the child is born of woman, man is born
    of woman,
This the bath of birth, this the merge of small and large, and
    the outlet again.

Be not ashamed women, your privilege encloses the rest, and is
    the exit of the rest,
You are the gates of the body, and you are the gates of the soul.

The female contains all qualities and tempers them,
She is in her place and moves with perfect balance,
She is all things duly veiled, she is both passive and active,
She is to conceive daughters as well as sons, and sons as well as
    daughters.

As I see my soul reflected in Nature,
As I see through a mist, One with inexpressible completeness,
    sanity, beauty,
See the bent head and arms folded over the breast, the Female I
    see.

Leaves of Grass, 1855

Christina Rossetti
A Birthday

My heart is like a singing bird
    Whose nest is in a watered shoot;
My heart is like an apple tree
    Whose boughs are bent with thickset fruit;

My heart is like a rainbow shell
   That paddles in a halcyon sea;
My heart is gladder than all these
   Because my love is come to me.

Raise me a dais of silk and down;
   Hang it with vair and purple dyes;
Carve it in doves, and pomegranates,
   And peacocks with a hundred eyes;
Work it in gold and silver grapes,
   In leaves, and silver fleurs-de-lys;
Because the birthday of my life
   Is come, my love is come to me.

Goblin Market and Other Poems, 1862

Remember

Remember me when I am gone away,
   Gone far away into the silent land;
   When you can no more hold me by the hand,
Nor I half turn to go, yet turning stay.
Remember me when no more day by day
   You tell me of our future that you planned:
   Only remember me; you understand
It will be late to counsel then or pray.
Yet if you should forget me for a while
   And afterwards remember, do not grieve:
   For if the darkness and corruption leave
   A vestige of the thoughts that once I had,
Better by far you should forget and smile
   Than that you should remember and be sad.

Goblin Market and Other Poems, 1862

Echo

Come to me in the silence of the night;
   Come in the speaking silence of a dream;
Come with soft rounded cheeks and eyes as bright
    As sunlight on a stream;
     Come back in tears,
O memory, hope, love of finished years.

Oh dream how sweet, too sweet, too bitter sweet,
   Whose wakening should have been in Paradise,
Where souls brimful of love abide and meet;
    Where thirsting longing eyes
     Watch the slow door
That opening, letting in, lets out no more.

Yet come to me in dreams, that I may live
   My very life again though cold in death:
Come back to me in dreams, that I may give
    Pulse for pulse, breath for breath:
     Speak low, lean low,
As long ago, my love, how long ago!

Goblin Market and Other Poems, 1862

George Meredith

Sonnets from *Modern Love*

I

By this he knew she wept with waking eyes:
   That, at his hand's light quiver by her head,
   The strange low sobs that shook their common bed
Were called into her with a sharp surprise,
And strangled mute, like little gaping snakes,
   Dreadfully venomous to him. She lay
   Stone-still, and the long darkness flowed away
With muffled pulses. Then, as midnight makes

Her giant heart of Memory and Tears
   Drink the pale drug of silence, and so beat
   Sleep's heavy measure, they from head to feet
Were moveless, looking through their dead black years,
By vain regret scrawled over the blank wall.
   Like sculptured effigies they might be seen
   Upon their marriage-tomb, the sword between;
Each wishing for the sword that severs all.

XVI

In our old shipwrecked days there was an hour,
   When in the firelight steadily aglow,
   Joined slackly, we beheld the red chasm grow
Among the clicking coals. Our library-bower
That eve was left to us: and hushed we sat
   As lovers to whom Time is whispering.
   From sudden-opened doors we heard them sing:
The nodding elders mixed good wine with chat.
Well knew we that Life's greatest treasure lay
   With us, and of it was our talk. 'Ah, yes!
   Love dies!' I said: I never thought it less.
She yearned to me that sentence to unsay.
Then when the fire domed blackening, I found
   Her cheek was salt against my kiss, and swift
   Up the sharp scale of sobs her breast did lift:–
Now am I haunted by that taste! that sound!

XXX

What are we first? First, animals; and next,
   Intelligences at a leap; on whom
   Pale lies the distant shadow of the tomb,
And all that draweth on the tomb for text,
Into which state comes Love, the crowning sun:
   Beneath whose light the shadow loses form.
   We are the lords of life, and life is warm.
Intelligence and instinct now are one.

But Nature says: 'My children most they seem
  When they least know me: therefore I decree
  That they shall suffer.' Swift doth young Love flee:
And we stand wakened, shivering from our dream.
Then if we study Nature we are wise.
  Thus do the few who live but with the day:
  The scientific animals are they. –
Lady, this is my sonnet to your eyes.

XLVII

We saw the swallows gathering in the sky,
  And in the osier-isle we heard their noise,
  We had not to look back on summer joys,
Or forward to a summer of bright dye:
But in the largeness of the evening earth
  Our spirits grew as we went side by side.
  The hour became her husband and my bride.
Love that had robbed us so, thus blessed our dearth!
The pilgrims of the year waxed very loud
  In multitudinous chatterings, as the flood
  Full brown came from the West, and like pale blood
Expanded to the upper crimson cloud.
Love that had robbed us of immortal things,
  This little moment mercifully gave,
  Where I have seen across the twilight wave,
The swan sail with her young beneath her wings.

L

Thus piteously Love closed what he begat:
  The union of this ever-diverse pair!
  These two were rapid falcons in a snare,
Condemned to do the flitting of the bat.
Lovers beneath the singing sky of May,
  They wandered once; clear as the dew on flowers:
  But they fed not on the advancing hours:
Their hearts held cravings for the buried day.

Then each applied to each that fatal knife,
    Deep questioning, which probes to endless dole.
    Ah, what a dusty answer gets the soul
When hot for certainties in this our life! –
In tragic hints here see what evermore
    Moves dark as yonder midnight ocean's force,
    Thundering like ramping hosts of warrior horse,
To throw that faint thin line upon the shore!

Modern Love, 1862

Algernon Charles Swinburne
Rondel

Kissing her hair I sat against her feet,
Wove and unwove it, wound and found it sweet;
Made fast therewith her hands, drew down her eyes,
Deep as deep flowers and dreamy like dim skies;
With her own tresses bound and found her fair,
    Kissing her hair.

Sleep were no sweeter than her face to me,
Sleep of cold sea-bloom under the cold sea;
What pain could get between my face and hers?
What new sweet thing would love not relish worse?
Unless, perhaps, white death had kissed me there,
    Kissing her hair?

Poems and Ballads, 1866

Love and Sleep

Lying asleep between the strokes of night
  I saw my Love lean over my sad bed,
  Pale as the duskiest lily's leaf or head,
Smooth-skinned and dark, with bare throat made to bite,
Too wan for blushing and too warm for white,
  But perfect-coloured without white or red.
  And her lips opened amorously, and said –
I wist not what, saving one word – Delight.
And all her face was honey to my mouth,
  And all her body pasture to mine eyes;
    The long lithe arms and hotter hands than fire,
The quivering flanks, hair smelling of the south,
  The bright light feet, the splendid supple thighs
  And glittering eyelids of my soul's desire.

Poems and Ballads, 1866

A Match

If love were what the rose is,
  And I were like the leaf,
Our lives would grow together
In sad or singing weather,
Blown fields or flowerful closes,
  Green pleasure or grey grief;
If love were what the rose is,
  And I were like the leaf.

If I were what the words are,
  And love were like the tune,
With double sound and single
Delight our lips would mingle,
With kisses glad as birds are
  That get sweet rain at noon;
If I were what the words are
  And love were like the tune.

If you were life, my darling,
   And I your love were death,
We'd shine and snow together
Ere March made sweet the weather
With daffodil and starling
   And hours of fruitful breath;
If you were life, my darling,
   And I your love were death.

If you were thrall to sorrow,
   And I were page to joy,
We'd play for lives and seasons
With loving looks and treasons
And tears of night and morrow
   And laughs of maid and boy;
If you were thrall to sorrow,
   And I were page to joy.

If you were April's lady,
   And I were lord in May,
We'd throw with leaves for hours
And draw for days with flowers,
Till day like night were shady
   And night were bright like day;
If you were April's lady,
   And I were lord in May.

If you were queen of pleasure,
   And I were king of pain,
We'd hunt down love together,
Pluck out his flying-feather,
And teach his feet a measure,
   And find his mouth a rein;
If you were queen of pleasure,
   And I were king of pain.

Poems and Ballads, 1866

A Leave-taking

Let us go hence, my songs; she will not hear.
Let us go hence together without fear;
Keep silence now, for singing-time is over,
And over all old things and all things dear.
She loves not you nor me as all we love her.
Yea, though we sang as angels in her ear,
  She would not hear.

Let us rise up and part; she will not know.
Let us go seaward as the great winds go,
Full of blown sand and foam; what help is here?
There is no help, for all these things are so,
And all the world is bitter as a tear.
And how these things are, though ye strove to show,
  She would not know.

Let us go home and hence; she will not weep.
We gave love many dreams and days to keep,
Flowers without scent, and fruits that would not grow,
Saying 'If thou wilt, thrust in thy sickle and reap.'
All is reaped now; no grass is left to mow
And we that sowed, though all we fell on sleep,
  She would not weep.

Let us go hence and rest; she will not love.
She shall not hear us if we sing hereof,
Nor see love's ways, how sore they are and steep.
Come hence, let be, lie still; it is enough.
Love is a barren sea, bitter and deep;
And though she saw all heaven in flower above,
  She would not love.

Let us give up, go down; she will not care.
Though all the stars made gold of all the air,
And the sea moving saw before it move
One moon-flower making all the foam-flowers fair;

Though all those waves went over us, and drove
Deep down the stifling lips and drowning hair,
  She would not care.

Let us go hence, go hence; she will not see.
Sing all once more together; surely she,
She too, remembering days and words that were,
Will turn a little toward us, sighing; but we,
We are hence, we are gone, as though we had not been there.
Nay, and though all men seeing had pity on me,
  She would not see.

Poems and Ballads, 1866

Sarah Williams

Youth and Maidenhood

Like a drop of water is my heart
  Laid upon her soft and rosy palm,
Turned whichever way her hand doth turn,
  Trembling in an ecstasy of calm.

Like a broken rose-leaf is my heart,
  Held within her close and burning clasp,
Breathing only dying sweetness out,
  Withering beneath the fatal grasp.

Like a vapoury cloudlet is my heart,
  Growing into beauty near the sun,
Gaining rainbow hues in her embrace,
  Melting into tears when it is done.

Like mine own dear harp is this my heart,
  Dumb without the hand that sweeps its strings;
Though the hand be careless or be cruel,
  When it comes my heart breaks forth and sings.

Twilight Hours, 1868

Dante Gabriel Rossetti

This hour be her sweet body all my song,
   Now the same heart-beat blends her gaze with mine,
   One parted fire, Love's silent countersign:
Her arms lie open, throbbing with their throng
Of confluent pulses, bare and fair and strong:
   And her deep-freighted lips expect me now,
   Amid the clustering hair that shrines her brow
Five kisses broad, her neck ten kisses long.

Lo, Love! thy heaven of Beauty; where a sun
   Thou shin'st; and art a white-winged moon to press
   By hidden paths to every hushed recess;
Yea, and with sinuous lightnings here anon
Of passionate change, an instant seen and gone,
   Shalt light the tumult of this loveliness.

      In *The Ashley Library Catalogue*, IX, 1927 (written 1869)

Sudden Light

I have been here before,
   But when or how I cannot tell:
I know the grass beyond the door,
   The sweet keen smell,
The sighing sound, the lights around the shore.

You have been mine before, –
   How long ago I may not know:
But just when at that swallow's soar
   Your neck turned so,
Some veil did fall, – I knew it all of yore.

Then, now, – perchance again!
   O round mine eyes your tresses shake!
Shall we not lie as we have lain
   Thus for Love's sake,
And sleep, and wake, yet never break the chain?

      Poems, 1870

Silent Noon

Your hands lie open in the long fresh grass, –
   The finger-points look through like rosy blooms;
   Your eyes smile peace. The pasture gleams and glooms
'Neath billowing skies that scatter and amass.
All round our nest, far as the eye can pass,
   Are golden kingcup-fields with silver edge
   Where the cow-parsley skirts the hawthorn-hedge.
'Tis visible silence, still as the hour-glass.

Deep in the sun-searched growths the dragon-fly
Hangs like a blue thread loosened from the sky:
   So this winged hour is dropt to us from above.
Oh! clasp we to our hearts, for deathless dower,
This close-companioned inarticulate hour
   When twofold silence was the song of love.

Ballads and Sonnets, 1881

William Morris

October

O Love, turn from the unchanging sea, and gaze
   Down these grey slopes upon the year grown old,
A-dying mid the autumn-scented haze,
   That hangeth o'er the hollow in the wold,
   Where the wind-bitten ancient elms infold
Grey church, long barn, orchard, and red-roofed stead,
Wrought in dead days for men a long while dead.

Come down, O Love; may not our hands still meet,
  Since still we live to-day, forgetting June,
Forgetting May, deeming October sweet –
  O hearken, hearken! through the afternoon,
  The grey tower sings a strange old tinkling tune!
Sweet, sweet, and sad, the toiling year's last breath,
Too satiate of life to strive with death.

And we too – will it not be soft and kind,
  That rest from life, from patience and from pain,
That rest from bliss we know not when we find,
  That rest from love which ne'er the end can gain? –
  Hark, how the tune swells, that erewhile did wane!
Look up, Love! – ah, cling close and never move!
How can I have enough of life and love?

The Earthly Paradise, 1870

Sir Edmund Gosse

Epithalamium

High in the organ-loft, with lilied hair,
  Love plied the pedals with his snowy foot,
  Pouring forth music like the scent of fruit,
And stirring all the incense-laden air;
We knelt before the altar's gold rail, where
  The priest stood robed, with chalice and palm-shoot,
  With music-men who bore citole and lute
Behind us, and the attendant virgins fair,
And so our red aurora flashed to gold,
  Our dawn to sudden sun; and all the while
The high-voiced children trebled clear and cold,
  The censer-boys went swinging down the aisle,
And far above, with fingers strong and sure,
Love closed our lives' triumphant overture.

On Viol and Flute, 1873

Arthur William Edgar O'Shaughnessy

I made another garden, yea,
  For my new Love:
I left the dead rose where it lay
  And set the new above.
Why did my Summer not begin?
  Why did my heart not haste?
My old Love came and walked therein,
  And laid the garden waste.

She entered with her weary smile,
  Just as of old;
She looked around a little while,
  And shivered with the cold:
Her passing touch was death to all,
  Her passing look a blight;
She made the white rose-petals fall,
  And turned the red rose white.

Her pale robe, clinging to the grass,
  Seemed like a snake
That bit the grass and ground, alas!
  And a sad trail did make.
She went up slowly to the gate,
  And then, just as of yore,
She turned back at the last to wait
  And say farewell once more.

Music and Moonlight, 1874

I went to her who loveth me no more,
  And prayed her bear with me, if so she might;
For I had found day after day too sore,
  And tears that would not cease night after night.

And so I prayed her, weeping, that she bore
To let me be with her a little; yea,
   To soothe myself a little with her sight,
Who loved me once, ah! many a night and day.

Then she who loveth me no more, maybe
   She pitied somewhat: and I took a chain
To bind myself to her, and her to me;
   Yea, so that I might call her mine again.
Lo! she forbade me not; but I and she
Fettered her fair limbs, and her neck more fair,
   Chained the fair wasted white of love's domain,
And put gold fetters on her golden hair.

Oh! the vain joy it is to see her lie
   Beside me once again; beyond release,
Her hair, her hand, her body, till she die,
   All mine, for me to do with as I please!
For, after all, I find no chain whereby
To chain her heart to love me as before,
   Nor fetter for her lips, to make them cease
From saying still she loveth me no more.

Music and Moonlight, 1874

Wilfrid Scawen Blunt

I see you, Juliet, still, with your straw hat
Loaded with vines, and with your dear pale face,
On which those thirty years so lightly sat,
And the white outline of your muslin dress.
You wore a little *fichu* trimmed with lace
And crossed in front, as was the fashion then,
Bound at your waist with a broad band or sash,
All white and fresh and virginally plain.

There was a sound of shouting far away
Down in the valley, as they called to us,
And you, with hands clasped seeming still to pray
Patience of fate, stood listening to me thus
With heaving bosom. There a rose lay curled.
It was the reddest rose in all the world.

Love Sonnets of Proteus, 1880

Mathilde Blind

Winding all my life about thee,
    Let me lay my lips on thine;
What is all the world without thee,
    Mine – oh mine!

Let me press my heart out on thee,
    Crush it like a fiery vine,
Spilling sacramental on thee
    Love's red wine,

Let thy strong eyes yearning o'er me
    Draw me with their force divine;
All my soul has gone before me
    Clasping thine.

Irresistibly I follow
    As wherever we may run
Runs our shadow, as the swallow
    Seeks the sun.

Yea, I tremble, swoon, surrender
    All my spirit to thy sway
As a star is drowned in splendour
    Of the day.

The Prophecy of Saint Oran, and Other Poems, 1881

Ah! yesterday was dark and drear,
  My heart was deadly sore;
Without thy love it seemed, my Dear,
  That I could live no more.

And yet I laugh and sing to-day;
  Care or care not for me,
Thou canst not take the love away
  With which I worship thee.

And if to-morrow, Dear, I live,
  My heart I shall not break:
For still I hold it that to give
  Is sweeter than to take.

The Ascent of Man, 1889

John Bowyer Buchanan Nichols
Amoret

Love found you still a child,
Who looked on him and smiled
Scornful with laughter mild
    And knew him not:
Love turned and looked on you,
Love looked and he smiled too,
And all at once you knew
    You knew not what.

Love laughed again, and said
Smiling, 'Be not afraid:
Though lord of all things made,
    I do no wrong:
Like you I love all flowers,
All dusky twilight hours,
Spring sunshine and spring showers,
    Like you am young.'

Love looked into your eyes,
Your clear cold idle eyes,
Said, 'These shall be my prize,
    Their light my light;
These tender lips that move
With laughter soft as love
Shall tremble still and prove
    Love's very might.'

Love took you by the hand
At eve, and bade you stand
At edge of the woodland,
    Where I should pass;
Love sent me thither, sweet,
And brought me to your feet;
He willed that we should meet,
    And so it was.

In *Love in Idleness*, 1883

Halfway in Love

You have come, then; how very clever!
    I thought you would scarcely try;
I was doubtful myself – however
    You have come, and so have I.

How cool it is here, and pretty!
    You are vexed; I'm afraid I'm late;
You've been waiting – O what a pity!
    And it's almost half-past eight.

So it is; I can hear it striking
    Out there in the grey church tower.
Why, I wonder at your liking
    To wait for me half an hour!

I am sorry; what have you been doing
    All the while down here by the pool?
Do you hear that wild-dove cooing?
    How nice it is here, and cool!

How that elder piles and masses
    Her great blooms snowy-sweet;
Do you see through the serried grasses
    The forget-me-nots at your feet?

And the fringe of flags that encloses
    The water; and how the place
Is alive with pink dog-roses
    Soft-coloured like your face!

You like them? shall I pick one
    For a badge and coin of June?
They are lovely, but they prick one
    And they always fade so soon.

Here's your rose. I think love like this is,
    That buds between two sighs,
And flowers between two kisses,
    And when it's gathered dies.

It were surely a grievous thing, love,
    That love should fade in one's sight;
It were better surely to fling love
    Off while its bloom is bright.

The frail life will not linger,
    Best throw the rose away,
Though the thorns having scratched one's finger
    Will hurt for half a day.

What! you'd rather keep it, and see it
    Fade and its petals fall? –
If you will, why Amen, so be it:
    You may be right after all.

In *Love in Idleness*, 1883

Anonymous
The Broken-Hearted Gardener

I'm a broken-hearted Gardener, and don't know what to do,
My love she is inconstant, and a fickle jade, too,
One smile from her lips will never be forgot,
It refreshes, like a shower from a watering pot.
CHORUS: *Oh, Oh! she's a fickle wild rose,*
A damask, a cabbage, a young China Rose.

She's my myrtle, my geranium,
My sun flower, my sweet marjorum.
My honey suckle, my tulip, my violet,
My holly hock, my dahlia, my mignonette.

We grew up together like two apple trees,
And clung to each other like double sweet peas,
Now they're going to trim her, and plant her in a pot,
And I'm left to wither, neglected and forgot.

She's my snowdrop, my ranunculus,
My hyacinth, my gilliflower, my polyanthus,
My heart's ease, my pink water lily,
My buttercup, my daisy, my daffydown dilly.

I'm like a scarlet runner that has lost its stick,
Or a cherry that's left for the dickey to pick,
Like a waterpot I weep, like a paviour I sigh,
Like a mushroom I'll wither, like a cucumber, die.

I'm like a humble bee that don't know where to settle,
And she's a dandelion, and a stinging nettle,
My heart's like a beet root choked with chickweed,
And my head's like a pumpkin running to seed.

I'm a great mind to make myself a felo-de-se,
And finish all my woes on the branch of a tree:
But I won't, for I know at my kicking you'd roar,
And honour my death with a double encore.

In *Modern Street Ballads*, edited by John Ashton, 1888

321

Amy Levy
New Love, New Life

She, who so long has lain
  Stone-stiff with folded wings,
Within my heart again
  The brown bird wakes and sings.

Brown nightingale, whose strain
  Is heard by day, by night,
She sings of joy and pain,
  Of sorrow and delight.

'Tis true, – in other days
  Have I unbarred the door;
He knows the walks and ways –
  Love has been here before.

Love blest and love accurst
  Was here in days long past;
This time is not the first,
  But this time is the last.

A London Plane-Tree and Other Verse, 1889

William Butler Yeats
Down by the Salley Gardens

Down by the salley gardens my love and I did meet;
She passed the salley gardens with little snow-white feet.
She bid me take love easy, as the leaves grow on the tree;
But I, being young and foolish, with her would not agree.

In a field by the river my love and I did stand,
And on my leaning shoulder she laid her snow-white hand.
She bid me take life easy, as the grass grows on the weirs;
But I was young and foolish, and now am full of tears.

Crossways, 1889

When You Are Old

When you are old and grey and full of sleep,
    And nodding by the fire, take down this book,
    And slowly read, and dream of the soft look
Your eyes had once, and of their shadows deep;

How many loved your moments of glad grace,
    And loved your beauty with love false or true,
    But one man loved the pilgrim soul in you,
And loved the sorrows of your changing face;

And bending down beside the glowing bars,
    Murmur, a little sadly, how Love fled
    And paced upon the mountains overhead
And hid his face amid a crowd of stars.

The Rose, 1893

The Lover Tells of the Rose in His Heart

All things uncomely and broken, all things worn out and old,
The cry of a child by the roadway, the creak of a lumbering
    cart,
The heavy steps of the ploughman, splashing the wintry
    mould,
Are wronging your image that blossoms a rose in the deeps of
    my heart.

The wrong of unshapely things is a wrong too great to be told;
I hunger to build them anew and sit on a green knoll apart,
With the earth and the sky and the water, re-made, like a
    casket of gold
For my dreams of your image that blossoms a rose in the deeps
    of my heart.

The Wind among the Reeds, 1899

A Last Confession

What lively lad most pleasured me
Of all that with me lay?
I answer that I gave my soul
And loved in misery,
But had great pleasure with a lad
That I loved bodily.

Flinging from his arms I laughed
To think his passion such
He fancied that I gave a soul
Did but our bodies touch,
And laughed upon his breast to think
Beast gave beast as much.

I gave what other women gave
That stepped out of their clothes,
But when this soul, its body off,
Naked to naked goes,
He it has found shall find therein
What none other knows,

And give his own and take his own
And rule in his own right;
And though it loved in misery
Close and cling so tight,
There's not a bird of day that dare
Extinguish that delight.

Collected Poems, 1933

Robert Bridges

Awake, my heart, to be loved, awake, awake!
The darkness silvers away, the morn doth break,
It leaps in the sky: unrisen lustres slake
The o'ertaken moon. Awake, O heart, awake!

She too that loveth awaketh and hopes for thee;
Her eyes already have sped the shades that flee,
Already they watch the path thy feet shall take:
Awake, O heart, to be loved, awake, awake!

And if thou tarry from her, – if this could be, –
She cometh herself, O heart, to be loved, to thee;
For thee would unashamëd herself forsake:
Awake to be loved, my heart, awake, awake!

Awake, the land is scattered with light, and see,
Uncanopied sleep is flying from field and tree;
And blossoming boughs of April in laughter shake;
Awake, O heart, to be loved, awake, awake!

Lo all things wake and tarry and look for thee:
She looketh and saith, 'O sun, now bring him to me.
Come more adored, O adored, for his coming's sake,
And awake my heart to be loved: awake, awake!'

Shorter Poems, 1890

Albert Chevalier

We've been together now for forty years,
An' it don't seem a day too much;
There ain't a lady livin' in the land
As I'd swop for my dear old Dutch.

  I calls 'er Sal;
'Er proper name is Sairer;
An' yer may find a gal
As you'd consider fairer.
She ain't a angel – she can start
A-jawin' till it makes yer smart;
She's just a *woman*, bless 'er 'eart,
  Is my old gal . . .

We've been together now for forty years,
   An' it don't seem a day too much;
There ain't a lady livin' in the land
   As I'd swop for my dear old Dutch.

   I sees yer, Sal –
Yer pretty ribbons sportin':
Many years now, old gal,
Since them young days of courtin'.
I ain't a coward, still I trust
When we've to part, as part we must,
That Death may come and take me fust
   To wait . . . my pal.

My Old Dutch, 1892

John Leicester Warren, Lord de Tabley
Nuptial Song

Sigh, heart, and break not; rest, lark, and wake not!
   Day I hear coming to draw my Love away.
As mere-waves whisper, and clouds grow crisper,
   Ah! like a rose he will waken up with day!

In moon-light lonely, he is my Love only,
   I share with none when Luna rides in gray.
As dawn-beams quicken, my rivals thicken,
   The light and deed and turmoil of the day.

To watch my sleeper to me is sweeter,
   Than any waking words my Love can say;
In dream he finds me and closer winds me!
   Let him rest by me a little more and stay.

Ah, mine eyes, close not, and though he knows not,
   My lips, on his be tender while you may;
Ere leaves are shaken, and ring-doves waken,
   And infant buds begin to scent new day.

Fair Darkness, measure thine hours, as treasure
  Shed each one slowly from thine urn, I pray;
Hoard in and cover each from my lover;
  I cannot lose him yet: dear night, delay!

Each moment dearer, true-love, lie nearer,
  My hair shall blind thee lest thou see the ray.
My locks encumber thine ears in slumber,
  Lest any bird dare give thee note of day.

He rests so calmly; we lie so warmly;
  Hand within hand, as children after play; –
In shafted amber on roof and chamber
  Dawn enters; my Love wakens; here is day.

Poems Dramatic and Lyrical, 1893

A Song of Faith Forsworn

Take back your suit.
It came when I was weary and distraught
With hunger. Could I guess the fruit you brought?
I ate in mere desire of any food,
Nibbled its edge and nowhere found it good.
Take back your suit.

Take back your love,
It is a bird poached from my neighbour's wood:
Its wings are wet with tears, its beak with blood.
'Tis a strange fowl with feathers like a crow:
Death's raven, it may be, for all we know.
Take back your love.

Take back your gifts.
False is the hand that gave them; and the mind
That planned them, as a hawk spread in the wind
To poise and snatch the trembling mouse below
To ruin where it dares – and then to go.
Take back your gifts.

327

Take back your vows.
Elsewhere you trimmed and taught these lamps to burn;
You bring them stale and dim to serve my turn.
You lit those candles in another shrine,
Guttered and cold you offer them on mine.
Take back your vows.

Take back your words.
What is your love? Leaves on a woodland plain,
Where some are running and where some remain:
What is your faith? Straws on a mountain height,
Dancing like demons on Walpurgis night.
Take back your words.

Take back your lies.
Have them again: they wore a rainbow face,
Hollow with sin and leprous with disgrace;
Their tongue was like a mellow turret bell
To toll hearts burning into wide-lipped hell.
Take back your lies.

Take back your kiss.
Shall I be meek, and lend my lips again
To let this adder daub them with his stain?
Shall I turn cheek to answer, when I hate?
You kiss like Judas in the garden gate!
Take back your kiss.

Take back delight.
A paper boat launched on a heaving pool
To please a child, and folded by a fool;
The wild elms roared: it sailed – a yard or more.
Out went our ship but never came to shore.
Take back delight.

Take back your wreath.
Had it done service on a fairer brow?
Fresh, was it folded round her bosom snow?
Her cast-off weed my breast will never wear:
Your word is 'love me'. My reply 'despair'!
Take back your wreath.

Poems Dramatic and Lyrical, 1893

Arthur Symons

Bianca

Her cheeks are hot, her cheeks are white;
The white girl hardly breathes to-night,
So faint the pulses come and go,
That waken to a smouldering glow
The morbid faintness of her white.

What drowsing heats of sense, desire
Longing and languorous, the fire
Of what white ashes, subtly mesh
The fascinations of her flesh
Into a breathing web of fire?

Only her eyes, only her mouth
Live, in the agony of drouth,
Athirst for that which may not be:
The desert of virginity
Aches in the hotness of her mouth.

I take her hands into my hands,
Silently, and she understands;
I set my lips upon her lips;
Shuddering to her finger-tips
She strains my hands within her hands.

I set my lips on hers; they close
Into a false and phantom rose;
Upon her thirsting lips I rain
A flood of kisses, and in vain;
Her lips inexorably close.

Through her closed lips that cling to mine,
Her hands that hold me and entwine,
Her body that abandoned lies,
Rigid with sterile ecstasies,
A shiver knits her flesh to mine.

Life sucks into a mist remote
Her fainting lips, her throbbing throat;
Her lips that open to my lips,
And, hot against my finger-tips,
The pulses leaping in her throat.

London Nights, 1895

Ernest Dowson

Non Sum Qualis Eram Bonae Sub Regno Cynarae

Last night, ah, yesternight, betwixt her lips and mine
   There fell thy shadow, Cynara! thy breath was shed
Upon my soul between the kisses and the wine;
And I was desolate and sick of an old passion,
   Yea, I was desolate and bowed my head;
I have been faithful to thee, Cynara! in my fashion.

All night upon mine heart I felt her warm heart beat,
   Night-long within mine arms in love and sleep she lay;
Surely the kisses of her bought red mouth were sweet;
But I was desolate and sick of an old passion,
   When I awoke and found the dawn was gray:
I have been faithful to thee, Cynara! in my fashion.

I have forgot much, Cynara! gone with the wind,
   Flung roses, roses, riotously with the throng,
Dancing, to put thy pale lost lilies out of mind;
But I was desolate and sick of an old passion:
   Yea, all the time, because the dance was long:
I have been faithful to thee, Cynara! in my fashion.

I cried for madder music and for stronger wine,
   But when the feast is finished and the lamps expire,
Then falls thy shadow, Cynara! the night is thine;
And I am desolate and sick of an old passion,
   Yea, hungry for the lips of my desire:
I have been faithful to thee, Cynara! in my fashion.

Verses, 1896

The
Moderns

Thomas Hardy

On the Departure Platform

We kissed at the barrier; and passing through
    She left me, and moment by moment got
Smaller and smaller, until to my view
    She was but a spot;

A wee white spot of muslin fluff
    That down the diminishing platform bore
Through hustling crowds of gentle and rough
    To the carriage door.

Under the lamplight's fitful glowers,
    Behind dark groups from far and near,
Whose interests were apart from ours,
    She would disappear,

Then show again, till I ceased to see
    That flexible form, that nebulous white;
And she who was more than my life to me
    Had vanished quite . . .

We have penned new plans since that fair fond day,
    And in season she will appear again –
Perhaps in the same soft white array –
    But never as then!

– 'And why, young man, must eternally fly
    A joy you'll repeat, if you love her well?'
– O friend, nought happens twice thus; why,
    I cannot tell!

Time's Laughingstocks and Other Verses, 1909

The End of the Episode

Indulge no more may we
In this sweet-bitter pastime:
The love-light shines the last time
    Between you, Dear, and me.

There shall remain no trace
Of what so closely tied us,
And blank as ere love eyed us
    Will be our meeting-place.

The flowers and thymy air,
Will they now miss our coming?
The dumbles thin their humming
    To find we haunt not there?

Though fervent was our vow,
Though ruddily ran our pleasure,
Bliss has fulfilled its measure,
    And sees its sentence now.

Ache deep; but make no moans:
Smile out; but stilly suffer:
The paths of love are rougher
    Than thoroughfares of stones.

Time's Laughingstocks and Other Verses, 1909

After a Journey

Hereto I come to view a voiceless ghost;
    Whither, O whither will its whim now draw me?
Up the cliff, down, till I'm lonely, lost,
    And the unseen waters' ejaculations awe me.
Where you will next be there's no knowing,
    Facing round about me everywhere,
        With your nut-coloured hair,
And gray eyes, and rose-flush coming and going.

Yes: I have re-entered your olden haunts at last;
    Through the years, through the dead scenes I have tracked
      you;
What have you now found to say of our past –
    Scanned across the dark space wherein I have lacked you?
Summer gave us sweets, but Autumn wrought division?
    Things were not lastly as firstly well
      With us twain, you tell?
But all's closed now, despite Time's derision.

I see what you are doing: you are leading me on
    To the spots we knew when we haunted here together,
The waterfall, above which the mist-bow shone
    At the then fair hour in the then fair weather,
And the cave just under, with a voice still so hollow
    That it seems to call out to me from forty years ago,
      When you were all aglow,
And not the thin ghost that I now frailly follow!

Ignorant of what there is flitting here to see,
    The waked birds preen and the seals flop lazily;
Soon you will have, Dear, to vanish from me
    For the stars close their shutters and the dawn whitens
      hazily.
Trust me, I mind not, though Life lours,
    The bringing me here; nay, bring me here again!
      I am just the same as when
Our days were a joy, and our paths through flowers.

Satires of Circumstance, 1914

In Time of 'The Breaking of Nations'

    Only a man harrowing clods
      In a slow silent walk
    With an old horse that stumbles and nods
      Half asleep as they stalk.

335

Only thin smoke without flame
From the heaps of couch-grass;
Yet this will go onward the same
Though Dynasties pass.

Yonder a maid and her wight
Come whispering by:
War's annals will cloud into night
Ere their story die.

Moments of Vision and Miscellaneous Verses, 1917 (written in 1915)

When Dead
To —

It will be much better when
I am under the bough;
I shall be more myself, Dear, then,
Than I am now.

No sign of querulousness
To wear you out
Shall I show there: strivings and stress
Be quite without.

This fleeting life-brief blight
Will have gone past
When I resume my old and right
Place in the Vast.

And when you come to me
To show you true,
Doubt not I shall infallibly
Be waiting you.

Human Shows, Far Phantasies, Songs, and Trifles, 1925

Rupert Brooke
The Hill

Breathless, we flung us on the windy hill,
   Laughed in the sun, and kissed the lovely grass.
   You said, 'Through glory and ecstasy we pass;
Wind, sun, and earth remain, the birds sing still,
When we are old, are old. . . .' 'And when we die
   All's over that is ours; and life burns on
Through other lovers, other lips,' said I,
   'Heart of my heart, our heaven is now, is won!'

'We are Earth's best, that learnt her lesson here.
   Life is our cry. We have kept the faith!' we said;
   'We shall go down with unreluctant tread
Rose-crowned into the darkness!' . . . Proud we were,
   And laughed, that had such brave true things to say.
   – And then you suddenly cried, and turned away.

1914 and Other Poems, 1915 (written in 1910)

Beauty and Beauty

When Beauty and Beauty meet
   All naked, fair to fair,
The earth is crying-sweet,
   And scattering-bright the air,
Eddying, dizzying, closing round
   With soft and drunken laughter;
Veiling all that may befall
   After – after–

Where Beauty and Beauty met,
   Earth's still a-tremble there,
And winds are scented yet,
   And memory-soft the air,

337

Bosoming, folding glints of light,
  And shreds of shadowy laughter;
Not the tears that fill the years
  After – after–

1914 and Other Poems, 1915 (written in 1912)

Edmund John

Passional; To E– L–

What does it matter though you shall forget?
Leave it: I hold your warm slim body yet,
Heart against mine, so that your fragrant breath
Falls on my lips, chanting a marvellous song
Most strange and beautiful, though over-long
For one whose heart shall throb itself to death.

I know your lips shall kindle other flames,
Your dawn-lit voice shall whisper distant names:
You, with the kissed hands of Love's acolyte,
The perfume of the night in your wild hair,
Like sad strange incense, like a pagan prayer . . .
I care not, since I hold you here tonight.

Harder, press harder with your scarlet mouth,
That your kiss sear me with the flaming South,
That your frail unstained youth like pain of June
Crush my strong soul your soul's enchantment grips . . .
Cling to my mouth with your young curved Greek lips,
Cling closer till the blood come and life swoon . . .

God, hold the pallid dawn that thou wouldst send
With slow grey fingers that shall spell the end,
When I must leave my soul and you – ah, sweet!
Let me weep here a moment, let me kneel,
And give you tears for Love's, for Sorrow's seal,
And bow my head, and kiss your sad young feet.

Yes, close your eyes, lie still . . . as death . . .
My lips hold yet the memory of your breath . . .
The feverish yellow moon is on the wane;
Closer it comes, silent, and mad, and vast,
With blackness round and dead shapes stealing past,
And splashed with one wild blood-red line of pain.

The Flute of Sardonyx, 1913

D. H. Lawrence
Wedding Morn

The morning breaks like a pomegranate
   In a shining crack of red;
Ah, when tomorrow the dawn comes late
   Whitening across the bed
It will find me watching at the marriage gate
   And waiting while light is shed
On him who is sleeping satiate
   With a sunk, unconscious head.

And when the dawn comes creeping in,
   Cautiously I shall raise
Myself to watch the daylight win
   On my first of days,
As it shows him sleeping a sleep he got
   With me, as under my gaze
He grows distinct, and I see his hot
   Face freed of the wavering blaze.

Then I shall know which image of God
   My man is made toward;
And I shall see my sleeping rod
   Or my life's reward;
And I shall count the stamp and worth
   Of the man I've accepted as mine,
Shall see an image of heaven or of earth
   On his minted metal shine.

Oh, and I long to see him sleep
　In my power utterly;
So I shall know what I have to keep . . .
　I long to see
My love, that spinning coin, laid still
　And plain at the side of me
For me to reckon – for surely he will
　Be wealth of life to me.

And then he will be mine, he will lie
　Revealed to me;
Patent and open beneath my eye
　He will sleep of me;
He will lie negligent, resign
　His truth to me, and I
Shall watch the dawn light up for me
　This fate of mine.

And as I watch the wan light shine
　On his sleep that is filled of me,
On his brow where the curved wisps clot and twine
　Carelessly,
On his lips where the light breaths come and go
　Unconsciously,
On his limbs in sleep at last laid low
　Helplessly,
I shall weep, oh, I shall weep, I know
　For joy or for misery.

Love Poems and Others, 1913

A Young Wife

The pain of loving you
Is almost more than I can bear.

I walk in fear of you.
The darkness starts up where
You stand, and the night comes through
Your eyes when you look at me.

Ah never before did I see
The shadows that live in the sun!

Now every tall glad tree
Turns round its back to the sun
And looks down on the ground, to see
The shadow it used to shun.

At the foot of each glowing thing
A night lies looking up.

Oh, and I want to sing
And dance, but I can't lift up
My eyes from the shadows: dark
They lie spilt round the cup.

What is it? – Hark
The faint fine seethe in the air!

Like the seething sound in a shell!
It is death still seething where
The wild-flower shakes its bell
And the skylark twinkles blue –

The pain of loving you
Is almost more than I can bear.

Look, We have Come Through!, 1917

Flapper

Love has crept out of her sealëd heart
    As a field-bee, black and amber,
    Breaks from the winter-cell, to clamber
Up the warm grass where the sunbeams start.

Mischief has come in her dawning eyes,
    And a glint of coloured iris brings
    Such as lies along the folded wings
Of the bee before he flies.

Who, with a ruffling, careful breath,
    Has opened the wings of the wild young sprite?
    Has fluttered her spirit to stumbling flight
In her eyes, as a young bee stumbleth?

Love makes the burden of her voice.
    The hum of his heavy, staggering wings
    Sets quivering with wisdom the common things
That she says, and her words rejoice.

New Poems, 1918

Song of a Man Who Is Loved

Between her breasts is my home, between her breasts.
Three sides set on me space and fear, but the fourth side rests
Sure and a tower of strength, 'twixt the walls of her breasts.

Having known the world so long, I have never confessed
How it impresses me, how hard the compressed
Rocks seem, and earth, and air uneasy, and waters still ebbing
    west.

All things on the move, going their own little ways, and all
Jostling, people touching and talking and making small
Contacts and bouncing off again, bounce! bounce like a ball!

My flesh is weary with bounce and gone again! –
My ears are weary with words that bounce on them, and then
Bounce off again, meaning nothing. Assertions! Assertions!
   stones, women and men!

Between her breasts is my home, between her breasts.
Three sides set on me chaos and bounce, but the fourth side
   rests
Sure on a haven of peace, between the mounds of her breasts.

I am that I am, and no more than that: but so much
I am, nor will I be bounced out of it. So at last I touch
All that I am-not in softness, sweet softness, for she is such.

And the chaos that bounces and rattles like shrapnel, at least
Has for me a door into peace, warm dawn in the east.
Where her bosom softens towards me, and the turmoil has
   ceased.

So I hope I shall spend eternity
With my face down buried between her breasts;
And my still heart full of security,
And my still hands full of her breasts.

Collected Poems, 1928

Edward Thomas

No One So Much As You

No one so much as you
Loves this my clay,
Or would lament as you
Its dying day.

You know me through and through
Though I have not told,
And though with what you know
You are not bold.

None ever was so fair
As I thought you:
Not a word can I bear
Spoken against you.

All that I ever did
For you seemed coarse
Compared with what I hid
Nor put in force.

My eyes scarce dare meet you
Lest they should prove
I but respond to you
And do not love.

We look and understand,
We cannot speak
Except in trifles and
Words the most weak.

For I at most accept
Your love, regretting
That is all: I have kept
Only a fretting

That I could not return
All that you gave
And could not ever burn
With the love you have,

Till sometimes it did seem
Better it were
Never to see you more
Than linger here

With only gratitude
Instead of love –
A pine in solitude
Cradling a dove.

Collected Poems, 1928 (written before 1917)

John Freeman

Nearness

Thy hand my hand,
Thine eyes my eyes,
All of thee
Caught and confused with me:
My hand thy hand,
My eyes thine eyes,
All of me
Sunken and discovered anew in thee. . .

No: still
A foreign mind,
A thought
By other yet uncaught;
A secret will
Strange as the wind:
The heart of thee
Bewildering with strange fire the heart in me.

Hand touches hand,
Eye to eye beckons,
But who shall guess
Another's loneliness?
Though hand grasp hand,
Though the eye quickens,
Still lone as night
Remain thy spirit and mine, past touch and sight.

Memories of Childhood and Other Poems, 1919

I Have Never Loved You Yet

I have never loved you yet, if now I love.

If Love was born in that bright April sky
And ran unheeding when the sun was high,

345

And slept as the moon sleeps through Autumn nights
While those clear steady stars burn in their heights:

If Love so lived and ran and slept and woke
And ran in beauty when each morning broke,
Love yet was boylike, fervid and unstable,
Teased with romance, not knowing truth from fable.

But Winter after Autumn comes and stills
The petulant waters and the wild mind fills
With silence; and the dark and cold are bitter,
O, bitter to remember past days sweeter.

Then Spring with one warm cloudy finger breaks
The frost and the heart's airless black soil shakes;
Love grown a man uprises, serious, bright
With mind remembering now things dark and light.

O, if young Love was beautiful, Love grown old,
Experienced and grave is not grown cold.
Life's faithful fire in Love's heart burns the clearer
With all that was, is and draws darkling nearer.

I have never loved you yet, if now I love.

Memories of Childhood and Other Poems, 1919

In Those Old Days

In those old days you were called beautiful,
But I have worn the beauty from your face;
The flowerlike bloom has withered on your cheek
With the harsh years, and the fire in your eyes
Burns darker now and deeper, feeding on
Beauty and the remembrance of things gone.
Even your voice is altered when you speak,
Or is grown mute with old anxiety
      For me.

Even as a fire leaps into flame and burns
Leaping and laughing in its lovely flight
And then under the flame a glowing dome
Deepens slowly into blood-like light:–
So did you flame and in flame take delight,
So are you hollow'd now with aching fire.
But I still warm me and make there my home,
Still beauty and youth burn there invisibly
        For me.

Now my lips falling on your silver'd skull,
My fingers in the valleys of your cheeks,
Or my hands in your thin strong hands fast caught,
Your body clutched to mine, mine bent to yours:
Now love undying feeds on love beautiful,
Now, now I am but thought kissing your thought.
– And can it be in your heart's music speaks
A deeper rhythm hearing mine: can it be
        Indeed for me?

Poems New and Old, 1920

Frances Cornford

The New-Born Baby's Song

When I was twenty inches long
I could not hear the thrushes' song;
The radiance of morning skies
Was most displeasing to my eyes.

For loving looks, caressing words,
I cared no more than sun or birds;
But I could bite my mother's breast,
And that made up for all the rest.

Autumn Midnight, 1923

347

The Quarrel

How simple is my burden every day
　　Now you have died, till I am also dead,
The words, 'Forgive me', that I could not say,
　　The words 'I am sorry', that you might have said.

Collected Poems, 1954

Dorothy Parker

Unfortunate Coincidence

By the time you swear you're his,
　　Shivering and sighing,
And he vows his passion is
　　Infinite, undying –
Lady, make a note of this:
　　One of you is lying.

Enough Rope, 1926

Lorenz Hart

My Heart Stood Still

I laughed at sweethearts
　　I met at schools;
All indiscreet hearts
　　Seemed romantic fools.
A house in Iceland
　　Was my heart's domain.
I saw your eyes;
　　Now castles rise in Spain.

I took one look at you,
That's all I meant to do;
  But then my heart stood still!
My feet could step and walk,
My lips could move and talk –
  And yet my heart stood still!
Though not a single word was spoken
I could tell you knew:
That unfelt clasp of hands
Told me so well you knew.
I never lived at all until the thrill
Of that moment when my heart stood still.

Through all my schooldays
  I hated boys.
Those April Fool days
  Brought me loveless joys.
I read my Plato;
  Love I thought a sin,
But since your kiss
  I'm reading Missus Glyn.

I took one look at you,
That's all I meant to do;
  But then my heart stood still!
My feet could step and walk,
My lips could move and talk –
  And yet my heart stood still!
Though not a single word was spoken
I could tell you knew:
That unfelt clasp of hands
Told me so well you knew.
I never lived at all until the thrill
Of that moment when my heart stood still.

In Cochran's *One Dam Thing After Another*, 1927
and *A Connecticut Yankee* (New York), 1927
(set to music by Richard Rodgers)

Robert Graves
Pure Death

We looked, we loved, and therewith instantly
Death became terrible to you and me.
By love we disenthralled our natural terror
From every comfortable philosopher
Or tall, grey doctor of divinity:
Death stood at last in his true rank and order.

It happened soon, so wild of heart were we,
Exchange of gifts grew to a malady:
Their worth rose always higher on each side
Till there seemed nothing but ungivable pride
That yet remained ungiven, and this degree
Callèd a conclusion not to be denied.

Then we at last bethought ourselves, made shift
And simultaneously this final gift
Gave: each with shaking hands unlocks
The sinister, long, brass-bound coffin-box,
Unwraps pure death, with such bewilderment
As greeted our love's first acknowledgement.

Poems, 1927 (revised later)

Counting the Beats

You, love, and I,
(He whispers) you and I,
And if no more than only you and I
What care you or I?

Counting the beats,
Counting the slow heart beats,
The bleeding to death of time in slow heart beats,
Wakeful they lie.

Cloudless day,
Night, and a cloudless day,
Yet the huge storm will burst upon their heads one day
From a bitter sky.

Where shall we be,
(She whispers) where shall we be,
When death strikes home, O where then shall we be
Who were you and I?

Not there but here,
(He whispers) only here,
As we are, here, together, now and here,
Always you and I.

Counting the beats,
Counting the slow heart beats,
The bleeding to death of time in slow heart beats,
Wakeful they lie.

Poems and Satires, 1951

Cole Porter

Let's Do It

When the little Blue-bird,
Who has never said a word,
Starts to sing: 'Spring, Spring!'
When the little Blue-bell,
In the bottom of the dell,
Starts to ring: 'Ding, ding!'
When the little blue clerk,
In the middle of his work,
Starts a tune to the moon up above, –
It is Nature, that's all,
Simply telling us to fall
In love.

And that's why
Birds do it, bees do it,
Even educated fleas do it.
Let's do it,
Let's fall in love.

In Spain the best upper sets do it,
Lithuanians and Letts do it;
Let's do it,
Let's fall in love.

The Dutch in old Amsterdam do it,
Not to mention the Finns.
Folks in Siam do it –
Think of Siamese twins;
Some Argentines, without means, do it,
People say, in Boston, even beans do it;
Let's do it,
Let's fall in love.

Romantic sponges, they say, do it,
Oysters, down in Oyster Bay, do it;
Let's do it,
Let's fall in love.

Cold Cape Cod clams, 'gainst their wish, do it,
Even lazy jelly fish do it,
Let's do it,
Let's fall in love.

Electric eels, I might add, do it
Though it shocks 'em, I know;
Why ask if shad do it?
Waiter, bring me shad roe!

In shallow shoals English soles do it,
Goldfish in the privacy of bowls do it;
Let's do it,
Let's fall in love.

In the revue, *Paris*, 1928 (set to music by the Author)

Conrad Aiken

Annihilation

While the blue noon above us arches
  And the poplar sheds disconsolate leaves,
Tell me again why love bewitches
  And what love gives.

Is it the trembling finger that traces
  The eyebrow's curve, the curve of the cheek?
The mouth that quivers, when the hand caresses
  But cannot speak?

Not, not these, not in these is hidden
  The secret, more than in other things:
Not only the touch of a hand can gladden
  Till the blood sings.

It is the leaf that falls between us,
  The bells that murmur, the shadows that move.
The autumnal sunlight that fades upon us:
  These things are love.

It is the 'No, let us sit here longer,'
  The 'Wait till tomorrow,' the 'Once I knew' –
These trifles, said as I touch your finger
  And the clock strikes two.

The world is intricate, and we are nothing.
  It is the complex world of grass,
The twig on the path, a look of loathing,
  Feelings that pass –

These are the secret! And I could hate you
  When, as I lean for another kiss,
I see in your eyes that I do not meet you,
  And that love is this.

Rock meeting rock can know love better
  Than eyes that stare or lips that touch.
All that we know in love is bitter,
  And it is not much.

John Deth, and Other Poems, 1930

Sir Noël Coward

Someday I'll Find You

When one is lonely the days are long;
  You seem so near
  But never appear.
Each night I sing you a lover's song
  Please try to hear,
  My dear, my dear.

Someday I'll find you,
Moonlight behind you,
True to the dream I am dreaming,
As I draw near you
You'll smile a little smile;
For a little while
We shall stand
Hand in hand.
I'll leave you never,
Love you for ever
All our past sorrow redeeming:
Try to make it true,
Say you love me too;
Someday I'll find you again.

Can't you remember the fun we had?
  Time is so fleet,
  Why shouldn't we meet?
When you're away from me days are sad;
  Life's not complete,
  My sweet, my sweet.

Someday I'll find you,
Moonlight behind you,
True to the dream I am dreaming,
As I draw near you
You'll smile a little smile;
For a little while
We shall stand
Hand in hand.
I'll leave you never,
Love you for ever
All our past sorrow redeeming:
Try to make it true,
Say you love me too;
Someday I'll find you again.

Private Lives, 1930 (set to music by the Author)

Cecil Day Lewis

Do not expect again a phoenix hour,
The triple-towered sky, the dove complaining,
Sudden the rain of gold and heart's first ease
Tranced under trees by the eldritch light of sundown.

By a blazed trail our joy will be returning:
One burning hour throws light a thousand ways,
And hot blood stays into familiar gestures.
The best years wait, the body's plenitude.

Consider then, my lover, this is the end
Of the lark's ascending, the hawk's unearthly hover:
Spring season is over soon and first heatwave;
Grave-browed with cloud ponders the huge horizon.

Draw up the dew. Swell with pacific violence.
Take shape in silence. Grow as the clouds grew.
Beautiful brood the cornlands, and you are heavy;
Leafy the boughs – they also hide big fruit.

From Feathers to Iron, 1931

The Album

I see you, a child
In a garden sheltered for buds and playtime,
Listening as if beguiled
By a fancy beyond your years and the flowering maytime.
The print is faded: soon there will be
No trace of that pose enthralling,
Nor visible echo of my voice distantly calling
'Wait! Wait for me!'

Then I turn the page
To a girl who stands like a questioning iris
By the waterside, at an age
That asks every mirror to tell what the heart's desire is.
The answer she finds in that oracle stream
Only time could affirm or disprove,
Yet I wish I was there to venture a warning, 'Love
Is not what you dream.'

Next you appear
As if garlands of wild felicity crowned you –
Courted, caressed, you wear
Like immortelles the lovers and friends around you.
'They will not last you, rain or shine,
They are but straws and shadows,'
I cry: 'Give not to those charming desperadoes
What was made to be mine.'

One picture is missing –
The last. It would show me a tree stripped bare
By intemperate gales, her amazing
Noonday of blossom spoilt which promised so fair.
Yet, scanning those scenes at your heyday taken,
I tremble, as one who must view
In the crystal a doom he could never deflect – yet, I too
Am fruitlessly shaken.

I close the book;
But the past slides out of its leaves to haunt me
And it seems, wherever I look,
Phantoms of irreclaimable happiness taunt me.
Then I see her, petalled in new-blown hours,
Beside me – 'All you love most there
Has blossomed again,' she murmurs, 'all that you missed there
Has grown to be yours.'

Word Over All, 1943

Hart Crane

Carrier Letter

My hands have not touched water since your hands, –
    No; – nor my lips freed laughter since 'farewell'.
And with the day, distance again expands
    Between us, voiceless as an uncoiled shell.

Yet, – much follows, much endures . . . Trust birds alone:
    A dove's wings clung about my heart last night
With surging gentleness; and the blue stone
    Set in the tryst-ring has but worn more bright.

Collected Poems, 1933

Harold Monro

The Terrible Door

Too long outside your door I have shivered.
You open it? I will not stay.
I'm haunted by your ashen beauty.
Take back your hand. I have gone away.

357

Don't talk, but move to that near corner.
I loathe the long cold shadow here.
We will stand a moment in the lamplight,
Until I watch you hard and near.

Happy release! Good-bye for ever!
Here at the corner we say good-bye.
But if you want me, if you need me
Who waits, at the terrible door, but I?

Collected Poems, 1933

Eric Maschwitz

These Foolish Things

Oh! will you never let me be?
Oh! will you never set me free?
  The ties that bound us
  Are still around us;
There's no escape that I can see.
  And still those little things remain
  That bring me happiness or pain:

A cigarette that bears a lip-stick's traces,
An air-line ticket to romantic places:
And still my heart has wings:
These foolish things
  Remind me of you.

A tinkling piano in the next apartment,
Those stumbling words that told you what my heart meant,
A fair-ground's painted swings:
These foolish things
  Remind me of you.

Gardenia perfume lingering on a pillow,
Wild strawberries only seven francs a kilo;
And still my heart has wings:
These foolish things
  Remind me of you.

The Park at evening when the bell has sounded,
The *Île de France* with all the gulls around it,
The beauty that is Spring's:
These foolish things
  Remind me of you.

First daffodils and long excited cables,
And candelight on little corner tables;
And still my heart has wings:
These foolish things
  Remind me of you.

The smile of Garbo and the scent of roses,
The waiters whistling as the last bar closes,
The song that Crosby sings:
These foolish things
  Remind me of you.

These Foolish Things, 1936 (set to music by Jack Strachey)

W. H. Auden

Lay your sleeping head, my love,
Human on my faithless arm;
Time and fevers burn away,
Individual beauty from
Thoughtful children, and the grave
Proves the child ephemeral:
But in my arms till break of day
Let the living creature lie,
Mortal, guilty, but to me
The entirely beautiful.

Soul and body have no bounds:
To lovers as they lie upon
Her tolerant enchanted slope
In their ordinary swoon,
Grave the vision Venus sends
Of supernatural sympathy,
Universal love and hope;
While an abstract insight wakes
Among the glaciers and the rocks
The hermit's sensual ecstasy.

Certainty, fidelity
On the stroke of midnight pass
Like vibrations of a bell,
And fashionable madmen raise
Their pedantic boring cry:
Every farthing of the cost,
All the dreaded cards foretell,
Shall be paid, but from this night
Not a whisper, not a thought,
Not a kiss nor look be lost.

Beauty, midnight, vision dies:
Let the winds of dawn that blow
Softly round your dreaming head
Such a day of sweetness show
Eye and knocking heart may bless,
Find the mortal world enough;
Noons of dryness see you fed
By the involuntary powers,
Nights of insult let you pass
Watched by every human love.

Another Time, 1940

My second thoughts condemn
And wonder how I dare
To look you in the eye.
What right have I to swear
Even at one a.m.
To love you till I die?

Earth meets too many crimes
For fibs to interest her;
If I can give my word,
Forgiveness can recur
Any number of times
In Time. Which is absurd.

Tempus fugit. Quite.
So finish up your drink.
All flesh is grass. It is.
But who on earth can think
With heavy heart or light
Of what will come of this?

Collected Shorter Poems, 1960

Louis MacNeice

Les Sylphides

Life in a day: he took his girl to the ballet:
Being shortsighted himself could hardly see it –
  The white skirts in the grey
  Glade and the swell of the music
  Lifting the white sails.

Calyx upon calyx, canterbury bells in the breeze
The flowers on the left mirror to the flowers on the right
  And the naked arms above
  The powdered faces moving
  Like seaweed in a pool.

361

Now, he thought, we are floating – ageless, oarless –
Now there is no separation, from now on
   You will be wearing white
   Satin and a red sash
   Under the waltzing trees.

But the music stopped, the dancers took their curtain,
The river had come to a lock – a shuffle of programmes –
   And we cannot continue down-
   Stream unless we are ready
   To enter the lock and drop.

So they were married – to be the more together –
And found they were never again so much together,
   Divided by the morning tea,
   By the evening paper,
   By children and tradesmen's bills.

Waking at times in the night she found assurance
In his regular breathing but wondered whether
   It was really worth it and where
   The river had flowed away
   And where were the white flowers.

Plant and Phantom, 1941

Robert Frost

Never Again Would Birds' Song Be the Same

He would declare and could himself believe
   That the birds there in all the garden round
From having heard the daylong voice of Eve
   Had added to their own an oversound,
Her tone of meaning but without the words.
   Admittedly an eloquence so soft
Could only have had an influence on birds
   When call or laughter carried it aloft.

Be that as may be, she was in their song.
　　Moreover her voice upon their voices crossed
Had now persisted in the woods so long
　　That probably it never would be lost.
Never again would birds' song be the same.
And to do that to birds was why she came.

A Witness Tree, 1943

Alun Lewis

Goodbye

So we must say Goodbye, my darling,
And go, as lovers go, for ever;
Tonight remains, to pack and fix on labels
And make an end of lying down together.

I put a final shilling in the gas,
And watch you slip your dress below your knees
And lie so still I hear your rustling comb
Modulate the autumn in the trees.

And all the countless things I shall remember
Lay mummy-cloths of silence round my head;
I fill the carafe with a drink of water;
You say 'We paid a guinea for this bed,'

And then, 'We'll leave some gas, a little warmth
For the next resident, and these dry flowers,'
And turn your face away, afraid to speak
The big word, that Eternity is ours.

Your kisses close my eyes and yet you stare
As though God struck a child with nameless fears;
Perhaps the water glitters and discloses
Time's chalice and its limpid useless tears.

Everything we renounce except our selves;
Selfishness is the last of all to go;
Our sighs are exhalations of the earth,
Our footprints leave a track across the snow.

We made the universe to be our home,
Our nostrils took the wind to be our breath,
Our hearts are massive towers of delight,
We stride across the seven seas of death.

Yet when all's done you'll keep the emerald
I placed upon your finger in the street;
And I will keep the patches that you sewed
On my old battledress tonight, my sweet.

Ha! Ha! Among the Trumpets, 1945 (written before 1944)

Dylan Thomas

On the Marriage of a Virgin

Waking alone in a multitude of loves when morning's light
Surprised in the opening of her nightlong eyes
His golden yesterday asleep upon the iris
And this day's sun leapt up the sky out of her thighs
Was miraculous virginity old as loaves and fishes,
Though the moment of a miracle is unending lightning
And the shipyards of Galilee's footprints hide a navy of doves.

No longer will the vibrations of the sun desire on
Her deepsea pillow where once she married alone,
Her heart all ears and eyes, lips catching the avalanche
Of the golden ghost who ringed with his streams her mercury
     bone,
Who under the lids of her windows hoisted his golden luggage,

For a man sleeps where fire leapt down and she learns through
   his arm
That other sun, the jealous coursing of the unrivalled blood.

Deaths and Entrances, 1946

Laurie Lee
First Love

That was her beginning, an apparition
of rose in the unbreathed airs of his love,
her heart revealed by the wash of summer
sprung from her childhood's shallow stream.

Then it was that she put up her hair,
inscribed her eyes with a look of grief,
while her limbs grew as curious as coral branches,
her breast full of secrets.

But the boy, confused in his day's desire,
was searching for herons, his fingers bathed
in the green of walnuts, or watching at night
the Great Bear spin from the maypole star.

It was then that he paused in the death of a game,
felt the hook of her hair on his swimming throat,
saw her mouth at large in the dark river
flushed like a salmon.

But he covered his face and hid his joy
in a wild-goose web of false directions,
and hunted the woods for eggs and glow-worms,
for rabbits tasteless as moss.

And she walked in fields where the crocuses
branded her feet, and mares' tails sprang
from the prancing lake, and the salty grasses
surged round her stranded body.

The Bloom of Candles, 1947

Sir John Betjeman

Indoor Games near Newbury

In among the silver birches winding ways of tarmac wander
And the signs to Bussock Bottom, Tussock Wood and Windy
    Brake,
Gabled lodges, tile-hung churches, catch the lights of our
    Lagonda
As we drive to Wendy's party, lemon curd and Christmas cake.
Rich the makes of motor whirring, past the pine-plantation
    purring
                Come up, Hupmobile, Delage!
Short the way your chauffeurs travel, crunching over private
    gravel
                Each from out his warm garáge.

Oh but Wendy, when the carpet yielded to my indoor pumps
There you stood, your gold hair streaming, handsome in the
    hall-light gleaming
There you looked and there you led me off into the game of
    clumps
Then the new Victrola playing and your funny uncle saying
'Choose your partners for a fox-trot! Dance until it's *tea* o'clock!
'Come on, young 'uns, foot it featly!' Was it chance that paired
    us neatly,
                I, who loved you so completely,
You, who pressed me closely to you, hard against your party
    frock?

'Meet me when you've finished eating!' So we met and no one
    found us.
Oh that dark and furry cupboard while the rest played hide
    and seek!

Holding hands our two hearts beating in the bedroom silence
   round us,
Holding hands and hardly hearing sudden footstep, thud and
   shriek.
Love that lay too deep for kissing – 'Where *is* Wendy? Wendy's
   missing!'
          Love so pure it *had* to end,
Love so strong that I was frightened when you gripped my
   fingers tight and
          Hugging, whispered 'I'm your friend.'

Good-bye Wendy! Send the fairies, pinewood elf and larch tree
   gnome,
Spingle-spangled stars are peeping at the lush Lagonda
   creeping
Down the winding ways of tarmac to the leaded lights of home.
There, among the silver birches, all the bells of all the churches
Sounded in the bath-waste running out into the frosty air.
Wendy speeded my undressing, Wendy is the sheet's caressing
          Wendy bending gives a blessing,
Holds me as I drift to dreamland, safe inside my slumberwear.

                            Selected Poems, 1948

In a Bath Teashop

'Let us not speak, for the love we bear one another –
   Let us hold hands and look.'
She, such a very ordinary little woman;
   He, such a thumping crook;
But both, for a moment, little lower than the angels
   In the teashop's ingle-nook.

                            Selected Poems, 1948

Gerald Bullett

First Love

When I was in my fourteenth year,
And captain of the third eleven,
I fell in love with Guenevere,
And hovered at the gate of heaven.
She wasn't more than twenty-seven.

I partnered her, by happy chance,
At tennis, losing every game.
No shadow dimmed her careless glance,
No teasing word, no hint of blame,
Brightlier burned my secret flame.

Nothing I asked but to adore,
In dumb surrender, shy and stiff:
But ah, she gave me how much more,
A benison beyond belief!
'Just hold my racquet for a jiff.'

Windows on a Vanished Time, 1955

Alan Jay Lerner

I've Grown Accustomed to Her Face

I've grown accustomed to her face:
    She almost makes the day begin.
I've grown accustomed to the tune
She whistles night and noon.
Her smiles, her frowns, her ups, her downs,
Are second nature to me now,
    Like breathing out and breathing in.

I was serenely independent and content before we met;
Surely I could always be that way again, and yet
I've grown accustomed to her looks,
Accustomed to her voice,
Accustomed to her face.

I've grown accustomed to her face:
   She almost makes the day begin.
I've gotten used to hear her say
'Good morning' every day.
Her joys, her woes, her highs, her lows,
Are second nature to me now,
   Like breathing out and breathing in.

I'm very grateful she's a woman and so easy to forget:
Rather like a habit one can always break, and yet
I've grown accustomed to the trace
Of something in the air:
Accustomed to her face.

In *My Fair Lady*, 1956 (set to music by Frederick Loewe)

Laurence Whistler

Hotel Bedroom

Tenderness of evening sky: the light shrinking.
The mirror lifting a dulled eye to the cornice.
Breath of a city: multitude of delicate sounds
Off an unfamiliar horizon. The blind-cord stirring
Unevenly, a pendant on the breast of twilight.

We have slept for some minutes, I discover – resuming now
In a room shades darker; and lie together, inert
In a kind of atonement, desire left to sleep on,

Almost like a bed-fellow, a third. And we,
In a moment of unsought grace, perfectly rhyming together
A kind of plenary indulgence, are excused
All inquietude, all anxiety; and take pleasure
In the silhouette of the wardrobe – observing, too,
How the basin taps are marvellously defined
By twin faint stars. And meditate on the world
Beyond these murmuring horizons, where nations await
No judgement, only sentence – our world being
This moment, small and safe in a hired room,
And this nude room as rich to explore as the world.

The luggage waits to be opened on the stool.
The floor-boards speak discreetly in the corridor.
The cord moves, pendant in the rhythm of compassion.

We shall never lie here again. Already the room
Overlooks our one-night tenure; vacantly exists
For tomorrow, always for tomorrow; hears already
The rapid portering footsteps pause, and drop their burden;
Then the brisk engagement of the lock – sees
Faces, not ours, that enter glancing around them
The same unspoken comment: 'Here, the exception.
This will never be home.' We are virtually gone already –
Might almost never have come. We moved too lightly
Through the public mind of this room – appeared too briefly
In the long exposure of the dark impersonal lens,
To be more, in that darkening eye, than ghosts.

Tenderness of the fugitive; of the immaterial.
Of the soon-deleted; of the fond once-in-a-while.
Of a blind-cord moving, softly, softly,
In time with the low breathing of maternal twilight.
Of rhyming together, once in an endless while.

The View from this Window, 1956
(text from *To Celebrate Her Living*, 1967)

Patrick Kavanagh
In Memory of My Mother

I do not think of you lying in the wet clay
Of a Managhan graveyard; I see
You walking down a lane among the poplars
On your way to the station, or happily
Going to a second Mass on a summer Sunday –
You meet me and you say:
'Don't forget to see about the cattle –'
Among your earthiest words the angels stray.

And I think of you walking along a headland
Of green oats in June,
So full of repose, so rich with life –
And I see us meeting at the end of a town
On a fair day by accident, after
The bargains are all made and we can walk
Together through the shops and stalls and markets
Free in the oriental streets of thought.

O you are not lying in the wet clay,
For it is a harvest evening now and we
Are piling up the ricks against the moonlight
And you smile up at us – eternally.

Collected Poems, 1964 (written in 1956)

Ralph Hodgson
Silver Wedding

In the middle of the night
He started up
At a cry from his sleeping Bride –
A bat from some ruin
In a heart he'd never searched
Nay, hardly seen inside:

371

'Want me and take me
For the woman that I am
And not for her that died,
The lovely chit nineteen
I one time was,
And am no more' – she cried.

The Skylark and Other Poems, 1959

George Barker

Summer Song: I

I looked into my heart to write
  And found a desert there.
But when I looked again I heard
Howling and proud in every word
  The hyena despair.

Great summer sun, great summer sun,
  All loss burns in trophies;
And in the cold sheet of the sky
Lifelong the fishlipped lovers lie
  Kissing catastrophes.

O loving garden where I lay
  When under the breasted tree
My son stood up behind my eyes
And groaned: Remember that the price
  Is vinegar for me.

Great summer sun, great summer sun,
  Turn back to the designer:
I would not be the one to start
The breaking day and the breaking heart
  For all the grief in China.

My one, my one, my only love,
    Hide, hide your face in a leaf,
And let the hot tear falling burn
The stupid heart that will not learn
    The everywhere of grief.

Great summer sun, great summer sun,
    Turn back to the never-never
Cloud-cuckoo, happy, far-off land
Where all the love is true love, and
    True love goes on for ever.

Collected Poems, 1957

Philip Larkin

An Arundel Tomb

Side by side, their faces blurred,
The earl and countess lie in stone,
Their proper habits vaguely shown
As jointed armour, stiffened pleat,
And that faint hint of the absurd –
The little dogs under their feet.

Such plainness of the pre-baroque
Hardly involves the eye, until
It meets his left-hand gauntlet, still
Clasped empty in the other; and
One sees, with a sharp tender shock,
His hand withdrawn, holding her hand.

They would not think to lie so long.
Such faithfulness in effigy
Was just a detail friends would see:
A sculptor's sweet commissioned grace
Thrown off in helping to prolong
The Latin names around the base.

373

They would not guess how early in
Their supine stationary voyage
The air would change to soundless damage,
Turn the old tenantry away;
How soon succeeding eyes begin
To look, not read. Rigidly they

Persisted, linked, through lengths and breadths
Of time. Snow fell, undated. Light
Each summer thronged the glass. A bright
Litter of birdcalls strewed the same
Bone-riddled ground. And up the paths
The endless altered people came,

Washing at their identity.
Now, helpless in the hollow of
An unarmorial age, a trough
Of smoke in slow suspended skeins
Above their scrap of history,
Only an attitude remains:

Time has transfigured them into
Untruth. The stone fidelity
They hardly meant has come to be
Their final blazon, and to prove
Our almost-instinct almost true:
What will survive of us is love.

The Whitsun Weddings, 1964

F. Pratt Green
The Old Couple

The old couple in the brand-new bungalow,
Drugged with the milk of municipal kindness,
Fumble their way to bed. Oldness at odds
With newness, they nag each other to show
Nothing is altered, despite the strangeness
Of being divorced in sleep by twin-beds,
Side by side like the Departed, above them
The grass-green of candlewick bedspreads.

In a dead neighbourhood, where it is rare
For hooligans to shout or dogs to bark,
A footfall in the quiet air is crisper
Than home-made bread; and the budgerigar
Bats an eyelid, as sensitive to disturbance
As a distant needle is to an earthquake
In the Great Deep, then balances in sleep.
It is silence keeps the old couple awake.

Too old for loving now, but not for love,
The old couple lie, several feet apart,
Their chesty breathing like a muted duet
On wind instruments, trying to think of
Things to hang on to, such as the tinkle
That a budgerigar makes when it shifts
Its feather weight from one leg to another,
The way, on windy nights, linoleum lifts.

The Old Couple, 1976 (first printed in *New Poems*, 1969)

Biographical Notes

The following notes are intended to provide factual biographical information and some indication of the activities of the poets. There is no attempt at critical evaluation of their work.

AIKEN, CONRAD POTTER (1899–1973), was born in Georgia and was a contemporary of T. S. Eliot at Harvard. He published a number of books of verse between 1914 (*Earth Triumphant*) and his *Collected Poems* in 1961. His *Selected Poems* won the Pulitzer Prize in 1929. He also wrote several novels of an experimental kind.

ANDREWES, DR FRANCIS (*fl.*1629). Little is known of this writer, several of whose poems, dated 1629, appear in the Harleian MS quoted. The Valentine poem was formerly attributed to Lancelot Andrews, Bishop of Winchester. Norman Ault, in *Seventeenth-Century Lyrics*, was the first editor to quote it completely.

ARNOLD, MATTHEW (1822–88), was the son of Thomas Arnold, the famous headmaster of Rugby School. He spent most of his life as an Inspector of Schools. His chief poems were *The Strayed Reveller* (1849), *Empedocles on Etna* (1852), 'Sohrab and Rustum' and 'The Scholar-Gipsy' (1853), and 'Balder Dead' (1853). 'Dover Beach' was published in 1867. He was Professor of Poetry at Oxford from 1857 to 1867.

ATTERBURY, FRANCIS (1662–1732), a political and theological controversialist, became Bishop of Rochester. He was imprisoned in 1720 for alleged participation in a Jacobite plot, and later went to live in France.

AUDEN, WYSTAN HUGH (1907–73), read English at Oxford. His earliest verse, including *Poems* (1930) and *The Orators* (1932), was influenced by Eliot. Later he became the leader of a group of left-wing poets, including Spender, Day Lewis and Louis MacNeice, whose work had a strong political element. He collaborated with Christopher Isherwood in verse dramas, and the two went to live in America in 1939. In 1946 he became an American citizen, though he returned to live in England before his death.

AYRES, PHILIP (1638–1712), was a tutor in the family of Montagu Garrard Drake, of Amersham, and claimed to be a friend of Dryden.

377

He was a miscellaneous writer, but his *Lyric Poems* (1687) contained eloquent and distinctive verse.

A.W. are the initials appended to some eighty poems in a manuscript of *A Poetical Rapsody*, 1602, by its editor Francis Davison. Although the poems are of great merit no definite attribution has ever been advanced for them, though the editor said they were written 'almost twenty years since' by a 'dear friend'. In the printed book some are subscribed 'Anomos'. It is one of the great unsolved mysteries of Elizabethan poetry.

BAKER, HENRY (1698–1774), was a Fellow of the Royal Society who helped to develop the microscope and invented an ingenious method for teaching the deaf and dumb. He married Daniel Defoe's daughter. He published two volumes of *Original Poems* (1725 and 1726).

BARKER, GEORGE GRANVILLE (b. 1913), published seven volumes of sometimes obscure verse before his *Collected Poems* of 1957. He also wrote an autobiographical poem, *The True Confession of George Barker* (1950), which has aroused controversy, two books of fiction, and two plays.

BARNES, BARNABE (?1569–1609), educated at Brasenose College, Oxford, wrote much verse, including *Parthenophil and Parthenophe*, (1593), a collection of sonnets, madrigals, elegies and odes, and *A Divine Centurie of Spirituall Sonnets* (1595). Little is known of his life.

BAYLY, THOMAS HAYNES (1797–1839), was a prolific writer of songs, ballads and no less than thirty-six pieces for the stage. His 'drawing-room songs', for which he often wrote the music himself, were prodigiously popular throughout the Victorian era and have subsequently tended to be ridiculed. He had, however, undoubted gifts as a sentimental or satirical versifier.

BEDDOES, THOMAS LOVELL (1803–49), a poet with a taste for the macabre, is chiefly known for his drama in the Elizabethan manner, *Death's Jest-Book*, rewritten several times before he committed suicide.

BEDINGFIELD, WILLIAM (*fl.* 1720–33), is an obscure figure of whom little is known other than that he was a contributor to Hammond's miscellany (1720) and was a subscriber to Mary Masters' *Poems on Several Occasions* (1733), where he was described as 'of the Inner Temple'.

378

BEHN, APHRA (1640–89), was brought up in the West Indies, married a City merchant and was received at Court. Charles II employed her as a government spy. After her husband died in 1666 she became the first professional woman author, producing fifteen plays including *The City Heiress* (1682), novels, including *Oroonoko* (1678), a poetic *Miscellany* (1685), and her own *Poems Upon Several Occasions*, 1684.

BEST, CHARLES (?1570–?1627), is only known as a contributor of poems to Francis Davison's *Poetical Rapsodie* (1602).

BETJEMAN, SIR JOHN (b. 1906), was a contemporary of W. H. Auden at Oxford, but his poetry pursued an entirely idiosyncratic course, being traditional in technique and much concerned with domestic 'twentyish themes, often seen through satirical eyes. His first book of verse was published in 1933, his *Collected Verse* in 1958. *Summoned by Bells*, a verse autobiography, was published in 1960. He has written much on architecture, churches and conservation of buildings. He was knighted in 1969 and became Poet Laureate in 1972. He has had great success as a broadcaster.

BETTERTON, THOMAS (?1635–1710), joined Davenant's company of actors in 1661, wrote several plays, including *The Prophetess* (1690) based on an opera by Beaumont and Fletcher, and produced Congreve's *Love for Love* and plays by Vanbrugh. He was a noted actor in his day. The lyric quoted here has been attributed also to Dryden, who certainly wrote the Prologue to *The Prophetess*.

BISHOP, SAMUEL (1731–95), became Headmaster of Merchant Taylors' School. He wrote a number of poems in Latin, and his *Poetical Works*, published in 1796, made two very handsome quarto volumes dedicated to the King. Many of his poems, including one on 'The Game of Cricket', and another 'On Drunkenness', were recited on Prize Days at his school.

BLAKE, WILLIAM (1757–1827), was an engraver who illustrated his own 'prophetic' books, such as *The Book of Thel* (1789), *The Marriage of Heaven and Hell* (1790), *Visions of the Daughters of Albion* (1793), *The Book of Urizen* (1794), *Milton* and *Jerusalem* (1804). His earliest poems were published conventionally in *Poetical Sketches* (1783), followed by the illustrated *Songs of Innocence* in 1789. His later minor poems were not published in his lifetime.

379

BLIND, MATHILDE (1841–96), daughter of a banker, was born at Mannheim, but came to England as a child. She became a friend and supporter of Mazzini, and met Swinburne and Madox Brown. She translated the diary of Marie Bashkirtseff, and was active in the campaign for women's rights.

BLUNT, WILFRID SCAWEN (1840–1922), was a flamboyant traveller, orientalist, and champion of lost causes. He was married to Lady Anne Noel, a descendant of Byron and a brilliant Arabic scholar, but that did not stand in the way of Blunt's enthusiasm for lady-killing. His chief book of verse, *Sonnets and Songs by Proteus* (1875), was evidence of his protean gifts in this area.

BOOTH, BARTON (1681–1733), was an actor whose only 'poetical pieces' were printed in his biography, published in 1733. The poem included here, however, had already appeared in the popular song-book, *The Hive*.

BOSWORTH, WILLIAM (1607–?1650), belonged to a Cambridgeshire family living at Boxworth. He published no books during his lifetime, but a collected volume of his verse was published by a friend in 1651.

BOYCE, SAMUEL (d. 1775). Very little is known of this accomplished minor poet, but he may have been related to Dr William Boyce, the musician, whose name appears in the list of subscribers to his *Poems on Several Occasions* (1757), along with those of David Garrick, Dr Johnson, Joshua Reynolds and Peg Woffington. Boyce's songs were evidently popular at Ranelagh, Vauxhall and the other pleasure gardens, and they occur often in the song books of the latter half of the eighteenth century.

BRETON, NICHOLAS (?1545–?1626), son of a wealthy merchant, was a prolific writer of poems, romances, dialogues and essays. Surprisingly little is known of his life except that the Countess of Pembroke was one of his patrons.

BRIDGES, ROBERT SEYMOUR (1844–1930), published *Shorter Poems* between 1873 and 1893, and longer poems in the 'nineties. He was appointed Poet Laureate in 1913, and published *The Testament of Beauty* in 1929. His anthology, *The Spirit of Man*, was published in 1916.

BRONTË, EMILY (1818–48), sister of Charlotte and Anne Brontë, was the daughter of Patrick Brontë, curate of Haworth in Yorkshire from 1820 to 1861. Some of her poems appeared in *Poems by Currer, Ellis and Acton Bell*, pseudonymously, in 1846. She published *Wuthering Heights* in 1847. Many of her poems were not published until years after her death.

BROOKE, LORD (*see* Greville).

BROOKE, RUPERT CHAWNER (1887–1915), son of a housemaster at Rugby School, went to King's College, Cambridge, and settled at the Old Vicarage, Grantchester. Among his friends were Gosse, John Drinkwater, Walter de la Mare, W. H. Davies and the Asquiths. He became a Fellow of King's, and planned with Harold Monro the anthology, *Georgian Poetry*, later edited by his friend Edward Marsh. In 1913 he travelled in the South Seas, and in 1914 joined the Royal Naval Division. He was sent to the Dardanelles and died of septicaemia in Scyros, where he was buried. His *1914 and Other Poems* caught the prevailing mood of wartime self-sacrifice: 'If I should die . . .'

BROOME, WILLIAM (1689–1745), was Chaplain to Lord Cornwallis, of Eye, in Suffolk. He was one of Pope's collaborators in the translation of *The Odyssey*. In later editions of his *Poems* the 'Rosebud' poem was addressed to 'the Right Honourable the Lady Jane Wharton'.

BROWNING, ELIZABETH BARRETT (1806–61), an invalid from the age of fifteen, married Robert Browning against the wishes of her tyrannical father. *Aurora Leigh*, 1857, was a long novel in verse. Her *Sonnets from the Portuguese*, love poems addressed to her husband, who nicknamed her 'the little Portuguese',were published in 1844.

BROWNING, ROBERT (1812–89), married Elizabeth Barrett in 1846 and lived in devoted happiness with her in Italy until her death fifteen years later, when he returned to London. An intellectual poet, who expressed himself chiefly through the dramatic monologue, he had a large and strikingly original output of verse, including *Bells and Pomegranates* (1841), *Dramatis Personae* (1864) and *The Ring and the Book* (1868–9).

BUCKINGHAM, DUKE OF (*see* Sheffield).

BULLETT, GERALD WILLIAM (1893–1958), studied English at Cambridge after serving in the Royal Flying Corps in the First World

War. He wrote a number of novels, including *The History of Egg Pandervil* (1928), *The Jury* (1935), *The Snare of the Fowler* (1936) and *A Man of Forty* (1939), and many short stories. He worked as a publisher, literary editor and reviewer, and published two interesting anthologies: *The English Galaxy* (1933) and *The Testament of Light* (1932). He published several volumes of lyric poetry which have been undeservedly neglected by critics.

BURNS, ROBERT (1759–96), the son of an Ayrshire cottar, wrote many of his early poems whilst still working as a farmer. The Kilmarnock edition of his poems was published in 1786. Publication of the second edition brought him £500 and enabled him to marry Jean Armour, one of his many loves, and settle on a farm at Ellisland. After the failure of his farm he became an exciseman.

BYRON, GEORGE GORDON, LORD (1788–1824), began to write when at Cambridge, and produced a vast output of verse, despite constant travel, many love affairs, and entanglement in Greek politics. The first two cantos of *Childe Harold's Pilgrimage* were published in 1812; *Don Juan* was published between 1819 and 1824. He married an heiress, Anne Isabella Milbanke, in 1815, but left her in 1816 to live abroad, for some time with the Shelleys. He died of fever at Missolonghi, having joined the Greek insurgents.

CAMPION, THOMAS (1567–?1619), was a poet, musician and 'Doctor of Phisicke'. After collaborating with his fellow composer Rosseter in 1601 he published four *Bookes of Songes and Ayres* of which the words and music were all his own work. He wrote a number of masques for the Court and *Observations in the Art of English Poesie* (1602). As a poet he was almost forgotten until A. H. Bullen collected his works in 1889.

CAREW, THOMAS (?1595–?1639), went into the Law but 'was fonder of roving after hounds and hawks'. He became Gentleman of the Privy Chamber to Charles I. He was a friend of Dryden, Suckling and Davenant. He wrote a masque (1633). His collected poems were not published until after his death.

CAREY, HENRY (?1687–1743), is chiefly remembered as the author of the words and music of 'Sally in our Alley'. He also invented the nickname of his fellow poet Ambrose Philips – Namby Pamby. He was reputedly the son of George Savile, Marquess of Halifax.

CAVENDISH, WILLIAM, DUKE OF NEWCASTLE (1592–1676). A friend of Charles I, he fought in the Royalist cause, and fled after the battle of Marston Moor in 1644 to France, where he met and married a maid of honour to Queen Henrietta Maria. He returned to England at the Restoration, and published two well-known books on the management of horses. His poems, a number of which were written to his wife before and after he married her, under the title of *The Phanseys*, remained in manuscript in the British Museum until published in 1956.

CHAPMAN, GEORGE (?1559–?1634), is chiefly known for the translation of Homer commemorated in Keats's sonnet, but he was renowned as a scholar and dramatist and was perhaps the 'rival poet' referred to in Shakespeare's *Sonnets*. He collaborated with Jonson and Marston and wrote a continuation of Marlowe's *Hero and Leander* in 1598.

CHARLES II, KING (1630–85). There is controversy as to whether the song quoted can be attributed to the King, as was done by Sir John Hawkins and Horace Walpole. It has also been attributed to Dryden.

CHEEKE, THOMAS (*fl.* 1688–1701), appears not to have published separately under his own name, but only to have contributed to song-books and miscellanies.

CHESTERFIELD, EARL OF (*see* Stanhope).

CHETTLE, HENRY (?1562–?1607), was a printer, pamphleteer and dramatist. He was author or joint-author of over forty plays, and wrote an elegy on the death of Queen Elizabeth.

CHEVALIER, ALBERT (1861–1923), was a music-hall artiste specializing in costermonger acts. He wrote many sketches, songs and monologues.

CHURCHYARD,THOMAS (?1520–1604), at one time a page to Henry, Earl of Surrey, became an itinerant soldier in Scotland, Ireland, France and the Low Countries, and a minor figure at Court. His best-known works are 'Shore's Wife', in *A Mirror for Magistrates* (1559), and *The Worthiness of Wales* (1587).

CLARE, JOHN (1793–1864), was the son of a Northamptonshire labourer. His *Poems Descriptive of Rural Life* were published in 1820 and led him for a time to be lionized in literary circles. This was followed by *The Village Minstrel* (1821), *The Shepherd's Calendar* (1827) and *The Rural Muse* (1835). He married in 1820, and, with a family of seven children, was always in financial straits. His health broke down; he suffered from delusions – his thoughts often returning to a girl he had known in his youth – and he spent the last twenty-three years of his life in the Northampton Asylum, where some of his finest poems were written.

COLERIDGE, HARTLEY (1796–1849), was the eldest son of Samuel Taylor Coleridge. Abandoning a career as a schoolmaster he went to live at Grasmere in the Lake District. His collected poems, including some beautiful if melancholy sonnets, were published in 1851 by his brother Derwent.

COLERIDGE, SARA (1802–52), was the daughter of Samuel Taylor Coleridge, and author of *Phantasmion* (1837), a romantic fairy tale.

COLLINS, WILLIAM (1721–59), is chiefly known for his *Odes* (1747), including the Ode to Evening, the Ode to Simplicity, and the Ode beginning 'How sleep the brave'. He became insane.

CONCANEN, MATTHEW (1701–49), was an Irish poet who first published his *Poems upon Several Occasions* in Dublin in 1722. He had published in the previous year *A Match at Foot-ball* (in verse). He came to London and in 1724 edited a miscellany to which Swift contributed.

CONGREVE, WILLIAM (1670–1729), a fellow student with Swift at Trinity College, Dublin, entered the Middle Temple, but soon abandoned law for literature. *The Old Bachelor* (1693), *The Double Dealer* (1694), *Love for Love* (1695) and *The Way of the World* (1700) are a brilliant quartette of artificial comedies. But Congreve maintained that his social life – he was a friend of Steele and Pope and Voltaire, and was deeply attached to the Duchess of Marlborough – was of more importance to him than the stage. The actress Mrs Bracegirdle was believed to be his mistress.

CONSTABLE, HENRY (1562–1613), was a friend of Sir Philip Sidney. He became a Roman Catholic and for a time was a papal envoy to Edinburgh. In 1603 for a time he was imprisoned in the Tower of London. His *Diana*, a collection of sonnets, was published in 1592, and he contributed to *England's Helicon* (1600).

COOPER, MYLES (?1737–85), became Chaplain of Queen's College, Oxford, and in 1763 President of King's College, New York, which grew fast in importance under his vigorous control. Despite his great contributions to cultural activities in America he was forced to flee from a revolutionary mob and sail for England in 1775. His well-turned verses were published when he was twenty-four and still at Oxford. They are addressed not only to Delia, but also to Amanda, Celia, Chloe, and Sylvia. He complimented 'Myra' as well as Delia on her singing. He never married.

CORNFORD, FRANCES CROFTS (1886–1960), was a grand-daughter of Charles Darwin. She was born in Cambridge and married a Cambridge Professor of Ancient Philosophy. She published six volumes of poetry between 1915 and 1948, and was awarded the Queen's Medal for Poetry in 1959.

COTTON, CHARLES (1630–87), is best known as the author of the dialogue between 'Piscator' and 'Viator', written in 1676, which was added to the fifth edition of Izaak Walton's *Compleat Angler*. He also translated Montaigne's *Essays* (1685) and wrote burlesques of Virgil and Lucian. Although his *Poems* were not published until 1689 most of his love lyrics were written in the 1660s.

COWARD, SIR NOËL PIERCE (1899–1973), actor, singer, dramatist, composer and poet, was the outstanding all-round theatrical figure of his time. His plays included *The Vortex* (1923), *Hay Fever* (1925), *Private Lives* (1930), *Cavalcade* (1931) and *Blithe Spirit* (1941). He wrote and composed revues for Charles B. Cochran in the 'twenties, and wrote and composed the musical plays *Bitter Sweet* (1929), *Conversation Piece* (1934) and *Sail Away* (1961). He published two volumes of autobiography and a book of verse, *Not Yet the Dodo* (1967).

COWLEY, ABRAHAM (1618–67). Thrown out of his fellowship at Cambridge by the Parliamentarians, he became a Royalist spy. Amongst a large output of pastoral drama, Pindaric Odes and sacred epics, *The Mistress* (1647) became one of the best-known love sequences of the seventeenth century.

COWPER, WILLIAM (1731–1800), suffered from fits of depression, and lived most of his life in retirement at Huntingdon with Morley and Mary Unwin, and, after Morley Unwin's death, with his widow at

Olney and Weston Underwood. In 1782 he wrote *John Gilpin* and in 1784 *The Task*. He also wrote many well-known hymns.

CRANE, HAROLD HART (1899–1932), born in Ohio, worked in a munitions factory during the First World War, and then became a reporter. He lived an undisciplined life and committed suicide at sea. His poems, which owed something to the Imagist movement, were mostly published in *White Buildings* (1926) and *The Bridge* (1930), the latter being a mystical interpretation of American history.

CROWNE, JOHN (?1640–?1703) came to London, apparently from Nova Scotia, in 1665 and wrote several tragedies and comedies, the latter including *Sir Courtly Nice* (1785) and *The English Frier* (1690).

CUNNINGHAM, JOHN (1729–73), was a strolling player, born in Dublin, who settled in Newcastle. His pastoral poems engaged the interest of Shenstone, and some of his ballads were very popular.

CUTTS, JOHN, LORD (1661–1707) was a soldier of some distinction, serving William of Orange and Queen Anne in various theatres of war in Europe and Ireland. His *Poetical Exercises* was published in 1687. He was given an Irish peerage in 1690.

DANIEL, SAMUEL (1562–1619). The son of a music master in Somerset, Daniel became tutor to William Herbert, third Earl of Pembroke. Apart from the sonnets to *Delia* (1592), which are some of the most accomplished of their time, he wrote an epic about the Lancastrian Civil Wars, several tragedies, and masques for the court, including *Hymen's Triumph* (1615).

DARLEY, GEORGE (1795–1846), was a member of the staff of the *London Magazine*. He published *Sylvia: or The May Queen* in 1827. His *Nepenthe* was privately printed in 1839.

DAVENANT, SIR WILLIAM (1606–68), reputedly a godson of Shakespeare, was a strong Royalist and was several times imprisoned by the Parliamentarians. He wrote comedies, tragedies and court masques, established the 'Duke's Theatrical Company' of actors in 1660, and was granted the patent under which Covent Garden opera house still operates.

DAVIES, SIR JOHN (1569–1626), was a solicitor and attorney-general for Ireland, subsequently appointed lord chief justice of the King's Bench. *Orchestra* (1596) was a didactic poem in seven-line stanzas reducing natural phenomena to an ordered motion or 'dancing'. He also wrote *Astraea*, a collection of acrostics on the name Elizabeth (1599) and a philosophical poem, *Nosce Teipsum*.

DAVISON, FRANCIS (?1575–?1619), son of William Davison, Secretary of State to Queen Elizabeth, and a friend of Essex, was the editor, with his brother Walter, of the important miscellany, *A Poetical Rapsody* (1602).

DAY LEWIS, CECIL (1904–72), started his working life as a school-master, then became an editor and publisher. He was a member of the left-wing group of poets headed by W. H. Auden, but later developed a more personal and traditional lyrical gift. He held the Chair of Poetry at Oxford from 1951 to 1955 and in 1968 was appointed Poet Laureate. Apart from writing poetry – his *Collected Poems* were published in 1954 – he wrote very successful detective stories under the pseudonym of Nicholas Blake. He was married twice, latterly to Jill Balcon, the actress.

DE TABLEY, LORD (*see* Warren).

DE VERE, EDWARD, EARL OF OXFORD (1550–1604), succeeded to the hereditary office of Lord Great Chamberlain in 1562 at the age of twelve. He became a favourite of Queen Elizabeth. He was tutored by his uncle, Arthur Golding, the translator, and was said to have written plays as well as poems. He has even been put forward as a possible author of Shakespeare's plays. He had a chequered marriage to Anne Cecil, daughter of the Queen's chief Minister of State, and had a love affair with Anne Vavasour, one of the Queen's Ladies in Waiting.

DODSLEY, ROBERT (1703–64), was the outstanding bookseller-publisher of the eighteenth century, whose *Collection of Poems by Several Hands* (1748–58) contained many of the most important poems of the period. He himself wrote *The Muse in Livery, or the Footman's Miscellany* (1732), *Beauty: or the Art of Charming* (1735), *Trifles* (1745) and *The Art of Preaching* (1746).

DONNE, JOHN (?1572–1631), son of a London ironmonger, was brought up as a Roman Catholic. He accompanied Essex on his expedition to Cadiz in 1596, and was secretary to Sir Thomas Egerton, Lord Keeper of the Great Seal, until he was dismissed, having married secretly in 1601. Having joined the Church of

England he was ordained in 1615, was appointed Chaplain to James I, and in 1621 became Dean of St Paul's and a famous preacher. His poems were not collected and published until 1633.

DORSET, EARL OF (*see* Sackville).

DOWLAND, JOHN (?1563–1626), lutenist and composer, published three books of *Songes or Ayres of Foure Partes with Tablature for the Lute* in 1597, 1600 and 1603. In 1625 he was appointed lutenist to King Charles I. Some of the lyrics he set to music are very beautiful, but their authorship is unknown.

DOWSON, ERNEST (1867–1900), was a key figure in the English Decadent movement of the 'nineties, who died, worn out by his excesses, at the age of thirty-three. His chief collection of poems was *Verses* (1896). The son of an East End dock owner, Dowson had a somewhat lurid and glamorized affair with the daughter of a Polish restaurateur in Soho. Though a minor talent, he had a gift for musical and memorable lines.

DRAKE, JAMES (*fl.* 1734), put together a curious hot-potch entitled *The Humours of New Tunbridge Wells at Islington* (1734) which was dedicated to Voltaire. Professor Case listed it as a book of composite authorship, but the Preface indicates that it is all, except for Voltaire's Ode, the work of Drake, who claimed to be 'the first Englishman who has transfus'd Chinese and Gascoon poetry into his Native Language'. The book contains examples of these 'transfusions'.

DRAYTON, MICHAEL (1563–1631). Born in Warwickshire, Drayton is said to have been a friend of Shakespeare and Ben Jonson. He wrote a mass of verse, including historical epics and pastoral poetry and *Poly-Olbion*, a folk-history and geographical survey of Britain, published between 1613 and 1622.

DRYDEN, JOHN (1631–1700), although a friend of Oliver Cromwell, become the acknowledged leader of the writers of the Restoration. Of his many plays the best was probably *All for Love* (1678), but he interpolated love lyrics of outstanding beauty in several of his plays. In 1668 he published an important *Essay of Dramatic Poesy*, and in 1670 he was appointed Poet Laureate. Later he wrote several satirical poems, *Absalom and Achitophel* (1681), *MacFlecknoe* (1682) and *The Hind and the Panther* (1687). He was converted to Roman

Catholicism in 1686. The last part of his life (when he was deprived of the Laureateship) was chiefly devoted to translations. His famous second *Ode for St Cecilia's Day* was published in 1687.

DUKE, RICHARD (1658–1711), was a friend of Dryden. 'He was one of the wits', wrote Swift, 'but turned parson and left it.' The poems quoted here are decidedly non-parsonical, but the *DNB* records that Duke's 'clerical life was blameless'.

D'URFEY, THOMAS (1653–1723), was a prolific and popular poet and dramatist. He was on intimate terms with Charles II and James II. In 1719 he published a collection of songs and ballads entitled *Wit and Mirth, or Pills to Purge Melancholy* in which many of his own songs appeared.

DYER, LADY CATHERINE (d. 1654), was the wife of Sir William Dyer, of Colmworth in Bedfordshire. The verses quoted are what she herself wrote, to be inscribed after her death on the alabaster and marble monument depicting her husband, herself and their seven children, in the parish church of Colmworth.

DYER, SIR EDWARD (d. 1607), held various posts at Court, to which he was introduced by the Earl of Leicester. He translated Theocritus; and Sidney's pastoral, 'Join, mates, in mirth with me', was addressed to him and Fulke Greville. He is best known for his poem beginning 'My mind to me a kingdom is'. His verse is known only through miscellanies and manuscripts.

'EPHELIA' (*fl.* 1679) has not been identified with any certainty though Sir Edmund Gosse suggested that she was a daughter of the poetess Katherine Phillips, the 'Matchless Orinda'. Her *Female Poems on Several Occasions* were published in 1679. The J.G., for whom she confessed so hopeless a love, apparently jilted her and found other consolations in Africa.

ELIZABETH I, QUEEN (1533–1603). Whether the moving verses attributed to her were in fact written by the Queen is unlikely to be proved. But in the Bodleian manuscript from which they are derived they are headed by the words: 'Verses made by the Queen when she was supposed to be in love with Montague.' Little is known of Montague except that he was chosen by the Queen for a special mission to the Court of Spain in 1561, as one 'whom she highly esteemed for his great prudence and wisdom'.

ETHEREGE, SIR GEORGE (?1634–?1691), spent his early years in France. He became one of the Restoration Wits. His *The Comical Revenge, or Love in a Tub* (1664) was partly written in rhymed heroics but the comic underplot in prose has been regarded as the foundation of the comedy of Congreve and Farquhar. He also produced *She Would If She Could* (1668) and *The Man of Mode* (1676). He led a dissolute life and died in France.

FARQUHAR, GEORGE (1678–1707), Irish dramatist, wrote *The Constant Couple* (1700), *Sir Harry Wildair* (1701), *The Recruiting Officer* (1706), and *The Beaux' Stratagem* (1707). He died in poverty. His plays have been revived again and again.

FAWKES, FRANCIS (1720–77), a clergyman, was an accomplished translator of Anacreon and co-editor, with William Woty, of *The Poetical Calendar* (1763). His patron appears to have been Archbishop Herring, Archbishop of Canterbury. His *Original Poems and Translations* (1761) included the well-known poem about the Toby Jug.

FENTON, ELIJAH (1683–1730), is chiefly known as collaborator with Pope in his translation of the *Odyssey*. He was a corpulent man who liked, as a woman who waited on him said, 'to lie a-bed and be fed with a spoon'. Lord Orrery, who was his pupil, said 'he died of a great chair and two bottles of port a day'. Nevertheless Dr Johnson summed him up as 'an excellent versifyer and a good poet'.

FIELD, NATHANIEL (1587–1633), acted in plays by Shakespeare, Ben Jonson (*Bartholomew Fair*) and Beaumont and Fletcher. He wrote two comedies, *A Woman's a Weathercock* (1612) and *Amends for Ladies* (1618) and collaborated in Massinger's *The Fatal Dowry* (1632).

FIELDING, HENRY (1707–54). The author of the famous novels, *Joseph Andrews* (1742), *Tom Jones* (1749) and *Amelia* (1751), and a number of successful plays, wrote few poems. They are contained in his *Miscellanies*, 1743.

FINCH, ANNE, COUNTESS OF WINCHILSEA (1661–1720), was a writer of pleasant 'occasional' verse, with a more genuine concern for Nature than most of her contemporaries. She was a friend of Pope. Curiously, her charming poem 'The Sigh', though it had appeared in a miscellany in 1710, was not included in her own volume of *Miscellany Poems on Several Occasions* (1713).

FLETCHER, GILES (?1549–1611), a Fellow of King's College, Cambridge, went as an envoy to Russia in 1588 and later wrote a book about that country, which was not published in its entirety until 1856. His *Licia* (1593) was one of the first collections of sonnets published after Sidney's *Astrophel and Stella*.

FLETCHER, JOHN (1579–1625), the nephew of Giles Fletcher, collaborated with Francis Beaumont from 1606 to 1616 in the production of a number of plays including *The Knight of the Burning Pestle* (1609). He wrote many plays on his own, and collaborated with Jonson, Middleton, Massinger, and probably also with Shakespeare, in *The Two Noble Kinsmen*, published in 1634.

FREEMAN, JOHN (1880–1929), left school at the age of twelve and became an insurance clerk. By 1927 he was Secretary and a Director of an insurance company. Usually regarded as one of the 'Georgian Poets', he published several volumes of verse between 1909 and 1928, and his *Poems New and Old* won the Hawthornden Prize in 1920. He was probably a much finer poet than present-day opinion grants.

FROST, ROBERT LEE (1875–1963), born in San Francisco, was a teacher, editor and farmer before coming to England in 1912, when he met and was much influenced by Edward Thomas, Walter de la Mare and other poets. His first book of verse was *A Boy's Will* (1913). He returned to the United States in 1915 and published some ten volumes of verse, being four times awarded the Pulitzer Prize for Poetry. Much of his poetry is concerned with rural life and observation of nature.

GASCOIGNE, GEORGE (?1525–77), was a pioneer in several literary forms. His *Supposes*, acted in 1566, is regarded as the earliest English comedy in prose. He published *Posies* in 1575, and a satire, *The Steele Glas*, in 1576.

GAY, JOHN (1685–1732), not only wrote the perpetually popular *Beggar's Opera* (1728), *Polly* (1729), and the libretto for Handel's *Acis and Galatea* (1732), but published poems on *Rural Sports* (1713), *The Shepherd's Week* (1714), and *Trivia* (1716), which was a description of a walk through the City of London. He also wrote two volumes of *Fables* (1727 and 1738). On his monument in Westminster Abbey is inscribed the epitaph written by himself:

> Life is a jest, and all things show it;
> I thought so once, but now I know it.

GLAPTHORNE, HENRY (*fl.* 1639–42), wrote a number of plays, but very little is known of his life. He published *Poems* in 1639, several being addressed to a lady called Lucinda. In 1643 he published *Whitehall, a Poem, with Elegies*, dedicated to 'my noble Friend and Gossip, Captain Richard Lovelace'.

GODOLPHIN, SIDNEY (1610–43), was a Member of Parliament and an adherent of Strafford. He was one of the last Royalists to leave the House on the outbreak of the Civil War, in which he was killed. He contributed various poems to miscellanies.

GOLDSMITH, OLIVER (1730–74), author of the novel, *The Vicar of Wakefield* (1766), the play, *She Stoops to Conquer* (1773) and the didactic poem, *The Deserted Village* (1770), wrote a variety of hack books and was an assiduous journalist. He was a doctor, a friend of Johnson, and a member of 'The Club'. He had a gift for light verse which was not exercised as often as it might have been.

GOSSE, SIR EDMUND WILLIAM (1849–1928), was the son of Philip Gosse, a zoologist. His childhood was vividly described in his *Father and Son*, first published anonymously in 1907. He started life as a librarian, eventually becoming Librarian to the House of Lords. He became well known as a literary critic and was on terms of intimate friendship with many outstanding authors of his day, including Swinburne, Stevenson and Henry James. He published a number of literary studies and biographies.

GRANVILLE, GEORGE, LORD LANSDOWNE (1667–1735), became Secretary of State in 1710, when he was raised to the peerage. After the accession of George I he was imprisoned in the Tower for two years as a suspected Jacobite, and he later lived in France. He wrote several plays before he took up politics. Most of his poems to 'Mira', the Countess of Newburgh, to whom he wrote verses before he was twenty-three, appeared in the apparently unauthorized *Poems Upon Several Occasions* in 1712. In 1732 he revised them considerably for his *Genuine Works*. He was a patron of Pope, and had a very real lyrical gift of his own when young, though Dr Johnson wrote off his verses to Mira with the comment that 'they have little in them of the sentiments of a lover, or the language of a poet'.

GRAVES, RICHARD (1715–1804), was a clergyman who was one of Shenstone's circle of friends, and wrote a picaresque novel, *The Spiritual Quixote, or The Summer's Ramble of Mr Geoffry Wildgoose* (1772).

His poems were mostly contained in *Euphrosyne, or Amusements on the Road of Life* (1776).

GRAVES, ROBERT RANKE (b. 1895), son of the writer Alfred Perceval Graves, served in the Great War in the same regiment as Siegfried Sassoon. *Goodbye to All That* (1929) recorded some of his war experiences. After the War, and again after the Second World War, he went to live in Majorca. Apart from publishing several volumes of poems, which fully justified his election as Professor of Poetry at Oxford, 1961–66, he has written several novels on classical themes, including *I, Claudius* (1934) and *Count Belisarius* (1938).

GREEN, FREDERICK PRATT (b. 1903), is a retired Methodist minister who has an international reputation as a hymn writer. His publications include *This Unlikely Earth* (1952), *The Skating Parson* (1963) and *The Old Couple* (1976).

GREENE, ROBERT (?1560–92), led a roving and dissolute life and wrote a number of plays including *Friar Bacon and Friar Bungay* (1594). He may have had some share in some of the plays of Shakespeare, of whose success he was very jealous. The best of his lyrics occur in his various romances.

GREVILLE, 1st LORD BROOKE (1554–1628), a favourite of Queen Elizabeth and a friend of Sir Philip Sidney, Sir Francis Bacon and William Camden, was a prominent politician and was granted Warwick Castle and Knole Park by James I. He wrote a biography of Sidney and several tragedies, and a remarkable collection of love poems called *Caelica*, none of which were published until after his death. He was murdered by his manservant.

GRIFFIN, BARTHOLOMEW (d. 1602) appears to have been an attorney. His series of sixty-two delightful sonnets entitled *Fidessa, more chaste than kinde*, was published in 1596 and is now of extreme rarity. It was addressed to 'The Gentlemen of the Inns of Court' and the author promised them shortly 'A Pastoral, yet unfinished'. I can find no trace of this, or any other poems by him, having been published.

HARDY, THOMAS (1840–1928), trained as an architect, and lived most of his life in Dorset, where he wrote, between 1870 and 1897, the novels for which he is famous. He spent the ten years from 1897 writing an epic drama, *The Dynasts*. Thereafter he concentrated upon shorter lyric poems. He became estranged from his first wife, who

393

was mentally unstable, but wrote some of his most beautiful love poems about her after her death, when he was seventy-two.

HART, LORENZ (1895–1943), wrote the words and Richard Rodgers wrote the music for many of the outstanding songs for musical plays and revues between 1924 and 1943, including *The Girl Friend* (1926), *A Connecticut Yankee*, *The Boys from Syracuse* and *Pal Joey* (1940). They also wrote songs for Charles B. Cochran's London revues, including 'My Heart Stood Still', for *One Dam Thing After Another* (1927). This song originated in a near taxi crash in Paris when Hart involuntarily uttered the words 'My heart stood still!'

HAUSTED, PETER (d. 1645), dramatist and divine, was Rector of Hadham in Hertfordshire and Vicar of Gretton in Northampton-shire, and became chaplain to the Earl of Northampton during the Civil War.

HERBERT, EDWARD, LORD, OF CHERBURY (1583–1648), philosopher, historian and diplomatist, was the elder brother of George Herbert, the poet. His *De Veritate*, written in Latin (1624) is the first purely metaphysical work written by an Englishman. His *Life of Henry VIII* was published in 1649. His poetry was interesting as using a metre later employed by Tennyson in *In Memoriam*.

HERRICK, ROBERT (1591–1674), was incumbent of Dean Prior, in Devon, from 1629 to 1647, when he was ejected until restored to his living after the Restoration. His chief collection of poems was *Hesperides* (1648), to which was added a collection of religious poems, *Noble Numbers*.

HEYRICK, THOMAS (1649–94), was Curate of Market Harborough. His *Miscellany Poems*, published at Cambridge in 1691, reveal an interesting metaphysical talent which has been surprisingly neg-lected by the anthologists.

HEYWOOD, THOMAS (d. 1650), was a member of the Queen's Com-pany of Players and wrote many plays, of which the best known is *A Woman Kilde with Kindnesse*, produced in 1603. Many of his plays have been lost.

HODGSON, RALPH (1871–1962), originally one of the 'Georgian Poets', became famous for 'The Bull' and 'The Song of Honour', both included in his *Poems* (1917). In 1924 he became a professor of

English in Japan, and from 1937 he lived in the United States. His *Collected Poems* were published in 1961.

HOOKES, NICHOLAS (1628–1712) was a contemporary of Dryden at Westminster and Cambridge. His series of poems, *Amanda* (1653), was described by him as 'a Sacrifice to an unknowne Goddesse, or a Free-Will offering of a Loving Heart to a Sweet-heart.' The 'Sweet-heart', he tells us in his preface, was an entirely imaginary person.

JENKYN, PATHERICKE (*fl.* 1661) appears to have published nothing other than a very small octavo book of poems, largely love poems, entitled *Amorea. The Lost Lover or The Idea of Love and Misfortune. Being Poems, Sonets, Songs, Odes, Pastoral, Elegies, Lyrick Poems, and Epigrams. Never before printed* (1661).

JENYNS, SOAME (1704–87), was a Member of Parliament who wrote two serious treatises: *A Free Enquiry in the Nature and Origin of Evil* (1757) and *A View of the Internal Evidence of the Christian Religion* (1776), which were widely read. His *Poems* (1752) and collected *Works* (1790) included a number of delightful and stylish amatory conceits in verse.

JOHN, EDMUND (1883–1917), was of Welsh ancestry. He travelled widely in France, Germany, Cuba and Italy. He volunteered for service with the Artists' Rifles in the Great War but in 1916 was invalided out with heart disease. He went to Italy with his wife, but died there. His first book, *The Flute of Sardonyx*, had an enthusiastic preface by Stephen Phillips, and was very well received despite what now appear to be strong homosexual implications. His only other publication was a somewhat turgid *Symphonie Symbolique*, published after his death.

JOHNSON, ESTHER (1681–1728), was Swift's 'Stella', to whom he was devoted and wrote the *Journal to Stella*. The poem 'Jealousy, by a Lady' has been attributed to her with some reason, especially as Concanen's miscellany, in which it first appeared (it was several times reprinted elsewhere) contained much material of Irish origin. In his *Observations* (1754) Delany, another of the contributors to Concanen's miscellany, said he was shown the poem in manuscript under promise of secrecy, but could not let it go until he 'had got it by heart'.

395

JONES, ROBERT (*fl.* 1597–1614), was a lutenist who published five *Bookes of Songes and Ayres* between 1600 and 1610, the last two being entitled *A Musicall Dreame* (1609) and *The Muse's Gardin of Delights* (1610). He also published a *Set of Madrigals* in 1607. There is no evidence that he wrote (or did not write) the words of the songs he set to music.

JONSON, BEN (?1572–1637). After a short period of soldiering in Flanders he joined Henslowe's company of actors. He wrote many plays, of which *Every Man in His Humour* (1598) had Shakespeare in the cast. *Volpone* (1606), *The Alchemist* (1610) and *Bartholomew Fayre* (1614) were other outstanding plays which are still revived. He was granted a pension by James I in 1616, becoming in effect Poet Laureate. In later years he wrote and produced many masques. His friends included Bacon, Chapman, Beaumont, Fletcher, Donne, Herrick and Suckling. *Underwoods* (1640) was one of his chief volumes of verse.

KAVANAGH, PATRICK (1906–67), was an Irish poet and a familiar figure in the Dublin scene during the 1940s and 1950s. In his younger days, as he wrote later, he 'literally starved in Dublin', and during the 1939–45 War he 'did a gossip column for a newspaper for 4 guineas a week'.

KING, HENRY (1592–1669), was a friend of Izaak Walton, Donne and Jonson. He became Bishop of Chichester, but was deprived of his office during the Commonwealth. His poetical works were published in 1657, under the title *Poems, Elegies, Paradoxes and Sonnets*.

LANSDOWNE, LORD (*see* Granville).

LARKIN, PHILIP ARTHUR (b. 1922), became Librarian of Hull University in 1955. His output of poetry has been small, but influential: *The North Ship* (1945), *The Less Deceived* (1955), *The Whitsun Weddings* (1964), and *High Windows* (1974). He has also written two novels and a book on jazz, and has edited *The Oxford Book of Twentieth-Century Verse*. He was awarded the Queen's Medal for Poetry in 1975.

LAWRENCE, DAVID HERBERT (1885–1930), was the son of a Nottinghamshire coalminer. He became a schoolmaster and went to London in 1908. His first novel, *The White Peacock*, was published in 1911, the year when his mother died. The mother-son relationship is the theme of *Sons and Lovers* (1913), with which he became famous. In

1912 he ran away with the German-born wife of an English professor, and they lived a nomadic life from then on. Further novels included *The Rainbow* (1915), *The Plumed Serpent* (1926) and *Lady Chatterley's Lover*, published in Florence in 1928 but not until 1961 in England in its entirety. Throughout his writing life Lawrence continued to write poems.

LEE, LAURIE (b. 1914), was born at Slad near Stroud, his early days being the subject of his book *Cider with Rosie* (1959). He worked for the GPO Film Unit, 1939–40, and for the Crown Film Unit, 1941–3. He was Caption-Writer in Chief for the Festival of Britain. His first book of verse was *The Sun My Monument* (1944). It was followed by *The Bloom of Candles* (1947) and *My Many-Coated Man* (1955). *As I Walked out One Midsummer Morning* (1969) was a second volume of autobiography.

LEIGH, RICHARD (b. 1649), lived in Staffordshire and went to Oxford. He seems to have become a doctor, and apart from his *Poems* (1675) he is only known to have written a pamphlet attacking *The Conquest of Granada* and other plays by Dryden, and a pamphlet attacking Marvell. In his own book of poems there are at least six or seven love lyrics of great charm and accomplishment.

LERNER, ALAN JAY (b. 1918) is famous for his collaboration with the composer Frederick Loewe in the musical adaptation of Shaw's *Pygmalion*, *My Fair Lady*, produced first in New York in 1956. They were also responsible for *Brigadoon* (1947) and *Camelot* (1960). Lerner also collaborated with Kurt Weill, and with André Previn in *Gigi* (1973).

LEVY, AMY, (1861–89), was of Jewish ancestry and educated at Newnham College, Cambridge, where a pamphlet of her verse, *Xantippe*, was published in 1881. This showed extraordinary promise, which was largely fulfilled in *A Minor Poet and other Verse* (1884). She published a controversial novel about Jewish life, *Reuben Sachs*, in 1889. Much of her work is infused with melancholy, and she committed suicide within a week of correcting the proofs of her last book of verse, *A London Plane Tree* (1889).

LEWIS, ALUN (1915–44), was born near Aberdare, joined the Army in 1940, and served in India and Burma, where he was killed. Two volumes of his poetry were published: *Raider's Dawn* in 1942 and *Ha! Ha! Among the Trumpets* posthumously in 1945. He also wrote short stories, *The Last Inspection* (1943). A number of his letters from India were published, with some stories, under the title *In the Green Tree*.

LILLIAT, JOHN (? 1550–?1599), was the author of several poems, in his hand and signed by him, which are in a MS volume in the Bodleian Library. One of these poems is the one taken here from Robert Jones's song book.

LLOYD, ROBERT (1733–64), was a playwright who wrote a poem on *The Actor* (1760) and published a quarto collection of *Poems* in 1762. He was a friend of Charles Churchill, Bonnell Thornton and John Wilkes.

LODGE, THOMAS (?1558–1625), was the son of a Lord Mayor of London, and became a lawyer. His *Defence of Poetry, Music and Stage Plays* was published in 1579, and thereafter he wrote many pamphlets, romances and plays. His pastoral romance *Rosalynde* was the basis of Shakespeare's *As You Like It*. His poems mostly appeared in *Phillis* (1593). He became a Roman Catholic and qualified as a physician in 1603.

LOVELACE, RICHARD (1618–58), came of a rich Kentish family and became a soldier and a courtier at the Court of Charles I. He was imprisoned in 1642 for his support of the King, and again in 1648 on his return from France, when 'Lucasta', his betrothed Lucy Sacheverell, had, assuming his death, married another man. Lovelace died in penury, having prepared his *Lucasta: Epodes, Odes, Sonnets, Songs, etc.* for press whilst in prison. His brother published further verses after his death.

LYLY, JOHN (?1554–1606), was a Member of Parliament and had a post at Court in which he was responsible for Court entertainments and the training of actors. He wrote several plays, such as *Alexander and Campaspe* (1584) and *Midas* (1592), which contain attractive lyrics, but his best-known work was *Euphues* (1578–80), a prose romance written in a peculiar style which has given rise to the word 'Euphuism'.

LYTTELTON, GEORGE, LORD LYTTELTON (1709–73), who was for a time Chancellor of the Exchequer, was a friend of Pope and a generous patron of literature. James Thomson dedicated *The Seasons* (1726–30) to him. Apart from writing *The Progress of Love* (1732) in youth and *Dialogues of the Dead* (1760) in middle age, he contributed several elegant trifles to Dodsley's *Collection of Poems*. The 'Miss Lucy F.——' to whom he addressed charming poems was Lucy Fortescue, whom he married in 1741, but who died in childbed five years later, to be mourned by Lyttelton in a monody, *To the Memory of A Lady lately deceased* (1747). In his later years he 'adorned' – as Dr Johnson put it – the family seat at Hagley in Worcestershire 'by a house of great elegance and expence, and by much attention to the decoration of his park'.

MABBE, JAMES (1572–?1642), was a lay prebendary of Wells and a translator of Cervantes.

MACNEICE, LOUIS (1907–63), was born in Belfast but went to Oxford University where he was a contemporary and friend of Auden, Spender and Day Lewis. After lecturing in Birmingham, London and Cornell University he became a producer for the BBC and wrote several plays for radio. He published twelve collections of verse and an autobiography, *The Strings Are False*.

MARLOWE, CHRISTOPHER (1564–93), son of a Canterbury shoemaker, was educated at Cambridge, and then joined the Earl of Nottingham's theatre company. His chief plays were *Tamburlaine* (1587), *Dr Faustus* (published in 1604), *The Jew of Malta* (published in 1633), and *Edward II* (1594). It has been suggested that he was part author of Shakespeare's *Titus Andronicus*. He was reputedly a government agent, and died in a tavern brawl.

MARVELL, ANDREW (1621–78) was born near Hull and became tutor to the daughter of Lord Fairfax, in Yorkshire. Here he wrote poems in praise of gardens and country life. In 1653 he became tutor to Cromwell's ward, William Dutton, and later Milton's assistant in the Latin Secretaryship to the Council. After the Restoration he entered Parliament and wrote several political satires in verse. Most of his poems were not published until 1681.

MASCHWITZ, ERIC (1901–69), joined the BBC in 1926 and edited the *Radio Times* from 1927 to 1933, when he became Director of Variety. He served as a Secret Agent during the 1939–45 War. He was head of Light Entertainment for Television from 1958 to 1961. He wrote plays, revues and musical plays, including *Balalaika* (1936) and *Goodnight, Vienna* (1946). He wrote the words of the song 'A Nightingale Sang in Berkeley Square'.

MAYNE, JASPER (1604–72), dramatist and Archdeacon of Chichester, wrote a play called *The City Match* (1639), which was seen and condemned by Samuel Pepys thirty years later as 'but a silly play'. *The Amorous War* was better stuff.

MEREDITH, GEORGE (1828–1909), was a journalist and publisher's reader, and a friend of Swinburne, Rossetti and the Pre-Raphaelites. Most of his work was fiction, including *The Ordeal of Richard Feverel* (1859), *Evan Harrington* (1860) and *The Egoist* (1879). He was the model for the famous painting 'The Death of Chatterton', by Thomas Wallis, who ran away with Meredith's wife in 1858. His *Modern Love* (1862) is a long series of sonnets expressing the strains and distresses of an unhappy marriage.

MILTON, JOHN (1608–74), wrote *Comus* (1634), *Lycidas* (1637) and others of his well-known longer poems whilst living with his father in Buckinghamshire. In 1642 he married Mary Powell, who left him after six weeks, when he wrote several pamphlets on divorce. He became Latin Secretary to the Council after the execution of Charles I. He was reconciled to his wife, who bore him three daughters. After her death he married again, his second wife dying in 1658. *Paradise Lost* was completed in 1663 and *Paradise Regained* was published in 1671. In his latter years he went blind.

MOORE, THOMAS (1779–1852), issued a volume of *Poetical Works* under the pseudonym of Thomas Little in 1801, but became well known as an Irish lyricist with *Irish Melodies* (1807–35). His *Loves of the Angels* (1823) was a long poem that aroused controversy. He also wrote humorous books and biographies. He was a musician as well as a poet.

MORRIS, WILLIAM (1834–96), a pioneer Socialist, founder of the Arts and Crafts movement, printer, designer of fabrics and wallpapers, made his first impact as a poet with his *Defence of Guenevere and Other Poems* in 1858. *The Life and Death of Jason* (1867), in heroic couplets, and *The Earthly Paradise* (1868–70), in Chaucerian metres, were narrative poems on classical themes. *The Dream of John Ball* (1888) and *News from Nowhere* (1891) expressed his political ideas. After his wife's affair with Rossetti he concentrated mostly on the productions of the Kelmscott Press.

MUNDAY, ANTHONY (1553–1633), wrote or collaborated in a number of plays, wrote City pageants, and translated popular romances. He also contributed to *England's Helicon* (1600).

NEWCASTLE, DUKE OF (*see* Cavendish).

NICHOLS, JOHN BOWYER BUCHANAN (1859–1939), won the Newdigate Prize Poem at Oxford in 1883, and wrote three volumes of verse in collaboration with his fellow undergraduates, H. C. Beeching and J. W. Mackail: *Secundae* (1879), *Love in Idleness* (1883) and *Love's Looking Glass* (1891). His *Collected Poems* were published in 1943. He became a painter and art critic. He was the father of the poet, Robert Nichols.

NOEL, HENRY (*fl.* 1653). I can find no information about this writer though the poem which Lawes set to music appeared in several miscellanies of the period.

NUGENT, ROBERT, EARL NUGENT (1702–88), contributed fourteen witty and polished epigrams in verse to the second volume of Dodsley's *Collection of Poems* (1748). He had published a collection of *Odes and Epistles* in 1739.

OLDMIXON, JOHN (1673–1742), a Whig historian and hack, incurred the hostility of Pope, who pilloried him in *The Dunciad* for his *Essay on Criticism*, prefixed to the 1727 edition of his *Critical History of England*. His *Poems on Several Occasions* (1696) contain a number of elegantly phrased trifles expressing a genial cynicism.

O'SHAUGHNESSY, ARTHUR WILLIAM EDGAR (1844–81), was for a time an assistant in the natural history department of the British Museum. His *Epic of Women, and Other Poems* (1870) had a good reception. *Music and Moonlight* (1874) was written under Pre-Raphaelite influence, and was marked by a strong love-hate attitude to women.

OTWAY, THOMAS (1652–85), was a prolific playwright, his outstanding tragedy, in blank verse, being *Venice Preserved* (1682). He also wrote prologues, epilogues and a few 'occasional' poems. For many years he maintained an unrequited passion for the actress, Mrs Barry, who performed in his play, *Alcibiades* (1675).

OXFORD, EARL OF (*see* De Vere).

PARKER, DOROTHY ROTHSCHILD (1893–1967), journalist, short story writer and Hollywood screenwriter, was a prominent member of the group of critics and wits who met regularly for lunch at the Algonquin Hotel in New York in the 'twenties and 'thirties. She contributed to *Vogue, Vanity Fair* and the *New Yorker*. Her three volumes of verse were collected in *Not So Deep as a Well* in 1936.

PARNELL, THOMAS (1679–1718), became Archdeacon of Clogher in Ireland. He was a friend of Swift and Pope. His poems were published by Pope posthumously in 1722.

PATMORE, COVENTRY KERSEY DIGHTON (1823–96), was an assistant librarian in the British Museum, and a friend of Tennyson, Ruskin and the Pre-Raphaelite painters. *The Angel in the House*, a long poem in praise of married love, was published in four parts between 1854 and 1862. After the death of his first wife in 1862 he married a Roman Catholic and adopted the Catholic faith. In 1877 he published *The Unknown Eros*. After his second wife's death in 1880 he married for a third time, and when nearly seventy he became devoted to the poet Alice Meynell (who rejected his advances).

PATTISON, WILLIAM (1706–27), died at the age of twenty-one in the house of Edmund Curll, the bookseller, who employed several youthful hacks. It was alleged that Curll had starved him to death, but in fact he died of smallpox. His two volumes of *Poetical Works*, the second of which was entitled *Cupid's Metamorphoses, or Love in All Shapes*, were published in 1728 with a distinguished list of subscribers including Pope.

PEELE, GEORGE (?1558–97), son of a clerk of Christ's Hospital, became a playwright and actor. Amongst many plays, pastorals and pageants which he wrote the best-known is *The Arraignement of Paris* (1584). Before dying in distress he wrote much miscellaneous verse, his best lyrics being scattered through his plays.

PHILIPS, AMBROSE (?1675–1749), was immortalized by Henry Carey as 'Namby-Pamby' because of the babyish diction of one of his poems. He was, however, a considerable literary figure in his time, wrote a successful play, *The Distrest Mother* (1712), and quarrelled with Pope as to the respective merits of their *Pastorals*.

POE, EDGAR ALLAN (1809–49). Born at Boston, Mass., of actor parents, he was educated partly in England and partly at the University of Virginia. After a period in the US army he became a journalist. He edited the *Southern Literary Messenger* in which some of

published in 1593 and 1594, and his *Sonnets* in 1609, though most of them had probably been written between 1593 and 1600.

SHEFFIELD, JOHN, DUKE OF BUCKINGHAM (1648–1721), held high governmental office, but is chiefly remembered as the author of *An Essay on Satire*, published anonymously, which was attributed to Dryden and led to Dryden being beaten up by masked men at the Earl of Rochester's instigation. He was a patron of Dryden and a friend of Pope. His poems were not collected until 1721 and 1723.

SHELLEY, PERCY BYSSHE (1792–1822), began to write poetry at Eton and Oxford, whence he was sent down for publishing a pamphlet on *The Necessity of Atheism*. In the same year, 1811, he married Harriet Westbrook, who was aged sixteen, and from whom he separated three years later. He left England in 1814 with Mary Wollstonecraft, whom he married after Harriet drowned herself. He travelled constantly in Italy, often with Byron. *The Cenci* was published in 1819 and *Prometheus Unbound* in 1820. His odes 'To a Skylark' and 'To the West Wind' were written in 1819. He was drowned whilst sailing near Spezzia.

SHENSTONE, WILLIAM (1714–63), author of *The Schoolmistress* (1742), was a friend of many of the leading writers of his time. He was a prolific writer of elegies, odes, songs and ballads, including 'Jemmy Dawson', but his chief claim to fame is probably the creation of his famous garden at the Leasowes, near Halesowen. Like some other elegant amorists in verse he was a bachelor. But he had an admirable housekeeper, Mrs Arnold.

SHERIDAN, RICHARD BRINSLEY (1751–1816), was not only a successful dramatist and a theatre manager but a notable Member of Parliament. His plays included *The Rivals* (1775), *The Duenna* (1775), *A Trip to Scarborough* (1777), *The School for Scandal* (1777) and *The Critic* (1779). His theatre in Drury Lane was destroyed by fire in 1809. Rebuked by a friend for calmly drinking as he watched the flames from a window in Covent Garden, he protested: 'Surely a man may be allowed to drink a glass of wine by his own fireside.'

SHIRLEY, JAMES (1596–1666), wrote some forty dramas including *The Maid's Revenge* (1626), *The Traitor* (1631), *Love's Cruelty* (1631) and *The Cardinall* (1641). He wrote also comedies of social humour and *The Contention of Ajax and Ulysses* (1659), a dramatic piece that ends with the well-known lines:

> The glories of our blood and state
> Are shadows, not substantial things.

He died in the Fire of London.

SIDNEY, SIR PHILIP (1554–86), courtier, diplomat and soldier, was a friend of Spenser (who dedicated *The Shepherd's Calendar* to him) and of Fulke Greville, Dyer, and other poets. He addressed his series of sonnets known as *Astrophel and Stella* to Penelope Devereux, daughter of the 1st Earl of Essex, who in 1580 was married, against her will, to Lord Rich. Whether or not Sidney was as devoted to her as the sonnets suggest is a matter of doubt. In 1583 he married Frances, daughter of Sir Francis Walsingham. His *Arcadia*, a pastoral prose romance incorporating some poems, was not published until after his death. He was killed at Zutphen, reputedly passing a cup of water to another wounded man. His *Apology for Poetry* was also not published until after his death. His work had a strong influence on other poets for many years.

SMITH, ALEXANDER (1830–67), a lace-pattern designer in Glasgow, published *Poems* in 1853, including 'A Life-Drama', and some sonnets on the Crimean War in 1855. *City Poems* (1857) contained a sombre verse picture of life in Glasgow and 'A Boy's Poem', a vivid recollection of his working-class childhood.

SMITH, JOHN (*fl.* 1713). Hardly anything is known of this accomplished, if not notably original, poet despite the fact that he published a substantial book of *Poems upon Several Occasions* in 1713.

SOMERVILE, WILLIAM (1675–1742), was a Warwickshire squire who wrote a once-popular fox-hunting epic in blank verse, *The Chase* (1735), *Hobbinol* (1740), a mock-heroic account of rural games, and *Field Sports* (1742), a poem on hawking. Dr Johnson said of him that 'he writes very well for a gentleman'.

SPENCER, WILLIAM ROBERT (1769–1834), poet and wit, was a grandson of the third Duke of Marlborough, and a popular man in London Society, enjoying the friendship of Pitt, Fox, Sheridan and Sydney Smith. His wife's first husband was said to have committed suicide in order that Spencer could marry her.

SPENSER, EDMUND (?1552–99), who was born in London, though he lived for some years in Ireland, was a friend of Sir Philip Sidney and other men of letters, and was regarded by his contemporaries as the greatest poet of his time. A pastoral, *The Shepherd's Calendar*, was published in 1579, and *The Faerie Queene* between 1590 and 1596. *Epithalamion*, written on the occasion of his marriage in 1594, was published in the following year together with his collection of sonnets, *Amoretti*. His castle in Ireland was burnt during an insurrection in 1598, and he died in poverty in London.

STANHOPE, PHILIP DORMER, EARL OF CHESTERFIELD (1694–1773). The politician and diplomatist who became famous for his *Letters* to his natural son (and for giving his name to a certain kind of sofa) contributed some characteristically witty and cynical poems to Dodsley's *Collection of Poems*.

STANLEY, THOMAS (1625–78), was a kinsman of the Earl of Derby. He wrote a *History of Philosophy* (1655–62) and translated Aeschylus and Theocritus.

STRODE, WILLIAM (1602–45), became a Canon of Christ Church, Oxford, in 1638. His tragi-comedy, *The Floating Island*, was performed before Charles I and his Queen at Oxford in 1636. His poems were uncollected until the twentieth century.

SUCKLING, SIR JOHN (1609–42), inherited large estates, travelled and soldiered on the Continent, then came to Court in London and lived in great style. He wrote a play, *Aglaura* (1637), containing the famous line 'Why so pale and wan, fond lover?', and his poems were collected in a volume entitled *Fragmenta Aurea* (1646). He was a friend of Ben Jonson and Carew. He is believed to have committed suicide in Paris.

SWINBURNE, ALGERNON CHARLES (1837–1909). Swinburne's somewhat disreputable private life, developing into masochistic adventures with prostitutes, has perhaps tended to blur appreciation of his extraordinary poetic facility and gift for memorable lines. Having launched his poetic career with a classical drama, *Atalanta in Calydon* (1865) he continued with *Poems and Ballads* (1866), and *Songs before Sunrise* (1871), a second series of *Poems and Ballads* (1878) and *Studies in Song* (1880), apart from writing romantic dramas about Mary Queen of Scots and a romantic poem in rhymed couplets, *Tristram of Lyonesse* (1882).

SYLVESTER, JOSHUA (1563–1618). The initials I.S. appended to a poem in *A Poetical Rapsody* (1602) have been taken – with very little supporting evidence – to denote Joshua Sylvester, translator of *Divine Weekes and Workes* from the French of Du Bartas (1608).

SYMONS, ARTHUR (1865–1945), was an outstanding figure in the 'Nineties movement, and his poetry had a morbid eroticism that raised it above most of the pretty-pretty verse of the Decadents. Much of his erotic verse was concerned with 'ladies of the town'. He had a nervous breakdown in 1908 which destroyed his already failing talents.

TENNYSON, ALFRED, LORD (1809–92), son of a Lincolnshire parson, was one of the most prolific and certainly the most popular, of Victorian poets. His intimate undergraduate friend, A. H. Hallam, who died suddenly at the age of twenty-two, was the subject of his long autobiographical poem, *In Memoriam*, begun in 1833 but not published till 1850, in which year Tennyson was appointed Poet Laureate. His chief poems included *The Princess* (1847), his Ode on the death of Wellington, and 'The Charge of the Light Brigade' (1854), *Maud* (1855), *Idylls of the King* (1859) and *Enoch Arden* (1864). He also wrote several verse dramas. He did not marry until 1850.

THOMAS, DYLAN MARLAIS (1914–53), was born in Swansea and educated at the grammar school where his father was senior English master. For a time he was a reporter on the *South Wales Evening Post*. His first book, *Eighteen Poems* (1934) was praised by Edith Sitwell. This was followed by *Twenty-five Poems* in 1936. Rejected for war service, he worked for the BBC. In 1940 he published *Portrait of the Artist as a Young Dog* and in 1946 another book of verse, *Deaths and Entrances*. *Under Milk Wood* was written for broadcasting and first performed in 1954. He died, partly as a result of heavy drinking, during a lecture tour of the USA, where his 'surreal' verse had a huge vogue.

THOMAS, PHILIP EDWARD (1878–1917), lived mostly in Kent, having married whilst still an undergraduate. He made a meagre living by hack journalism and writing books about the countryside. He wrote no poetry until 1912. He enlisted as a private in the army on the outbreak of the Great War and was killed at Arras. His tortured nature and difficult domestic life were vividly described in two biographical books by his widow, Helen, *As It Was* and *World Without End*.

THURSTON, JOSEPH (*fl.* 1729), is one of those minor poets of no importance in literary history who nonetheless wrote a number of graceful lyrics which were reprinted frequently in the song books of the eighteenth century. He also wrote a satirical poem on *The Toilette* (1730).

TOFTE, ROBERT (d. 1620), was chiefly known as a translator from the classics and Italian. His book of sonnets, *Laura* (1597) was in praise of a lady of the name of Caryll, though its successor, *Alba* (1598), was dedicated to Mistress Anne Herne. Tofte was familiarly known amongst his friends as 'Robin Redbreast', a name referred to several times in his books.

TUNSTALL, WILLIAM (*fl.* 1716). Little is known of this writer except that he was taken prisoner at Preston in the Jacobite rising of 1715, and that he contributed to *Poems of Love and Gallantry: Written by the Prisoners in the Marshalsea and Newgate* (1716). Most of his and his fellow-prisoners' poems were addressed to 'Ladies about Court and Town'.

VANBRUGH, SIR JOHN (1664–1726), dramatist and architect, was an outstanding creative talent of the Restoration and Queen Anne period. His comedies included *The Relapse, or Virtue in Danger* (1697), *The Provok'd Wife* (1697) and *The Confederacy* (1705). As an architect he designed Castle Howard, Blenheim Palace, and his own Haymarket Theatre, earning for himself the apt epitaph:

> Lie heavy on him, Earth, for he,
> Laid many a heavy load on thee.

WALLER, EDMUND (1606–87), lived at Beaconsfield in Buckinghamshire. In 1631 he married a London heiress who died in 1634. He entered Parliament and became a Royalist, for which he was fined and imprisoned. He was restored to favour at the Restoration. He addressed love poems, as 'Sacharissa', to Lady Dorothy Sidney, but married Mary Bracey in 1644. He continued to write polished verse in his later years, including a well-known lyric on old age and six cantos *Of Divine Love* (1685). His poems ran through many editions in the seventeenth and eighteenth centuries.

WALSH, WILLIAM (1663–1708), was a Member of Parliament and a man of fashion, ostentatiously splendid in his dress. He declared that there was not one folly he had not committed in his devotion to women, with the exception of marriage. He wrote a 'Dialogue concerning Women,' which was included in his posthumous *Works* (1736).

WARREN, JOHN BYRNE LEICESTER, LORD DE TABLEY (1835–95), a well-to-do dilettante with special interest in botany and numismatics, published two tragedies and some poems on classical themes, but his *Poems Dramatic and Lyrical* (1893) included several lyrics of eloquence and power.

WATSON, THOMAS (?1557–92), published several collections of sonnets, to some extent based on classical and Italian originals. He contributed to *The Phoenix Nest* (1593) and *England's Helicon* (1600), and his *Tears of Fancie* (1593) was a series of sixty sonnets modelled on Petrarch and Ronsard.

WELSTED, LEONARD (1688–1747), figures in no history of English literature though his chief publication, *Epistles, Odes, etc.* (1724) opened with 'A Dissertation concerning the Perfection of the English Language, the State of Poetry, etc.', and contained a translation of Longinus on the Sublime. As with so many of the minor writers of the period, however, the '*etc.*' included a few deft and elegant trifles, such as the one printed here.

WHISTLER, LAURENCE (b. 1912), is now chiefly known as an engraver on glass, on which subject he has published three books, the last being *The Image on the Glass* (1975). He has always written poetry, however, his most recent books being *The View from This Window* (1956), *Audible Silence* (1961) and *To Celebrate Her Living* (1967). Many of his poems concern his first wife, the actress Jill Furse, who died in 1944, and was the subject of his autobiographical book, *The Initials in the Heart* (1964). He has also written books on Vanbrugh's architecture and on the work of his brother Rex, the artist.

WHITMAN, WALT (1818–92), was born in Long Island and became a printer in New York. He also worked as a schoolmaster and a war correspondent and as a volunteer hospital nurse. His *Leaves of Grass*, first published in 1855, was an entirely original collection of reflections on life in rhythmic sentences of varying length. His highly emotional, if sometimes muddled, thoughts on beauty, sex, American ideals, slavery and death are America's most distinctive contribution to English poetry of the past 150 years.

WILLIAMS, SARAH (1841–68), was an invalid who died young. She contributed verses and stories to *Good Words* and *Argosy* under the pseudonym of 'Sadie', but her more serious poems would probably have been lost if they had not been collected after her death by her one-time teacher at Queen's College.

WILMOT, JOHN, EARL OF ROCHESTER (1647–80), was the most notorious and most talented of the Restoration Rakes. After travelling in France and serving with the Fleet he became Gentleman of the King's Bedchamber and a boon companion of the King, who periodically dismissed him in disgrace. He wrote a *Satire against Mankind* (1675), some scurrilous and pornographic verse, and a number of beautiful love lyrics. Despite his amorous frolics he remained deeply devoted to the wife who stayed at his country home.

WINCHILSEA, COUNTESS OF (*see* Finch).

WITHER, GEORGE (1588–1667), poet and pamphleteer, was twice imprisoned in the Marshalsea for his satirical writings. He served under Charles I in the Civil War in Scotland, but then became a Puritan and a Parliamentarian, being given posts by Cromwell. He was imprisoned again at the Restoration.

WORDSWORTH, WILLIAM (1770–1850), was the leader, with his close friend Coleridge, of the Romantic Movement in English literature. Their *Lyrical Ballads* (1798) marked a break with the artificial poetic diction of the eighteenth century and a new approach to Nature, which was the chief theme of much of Wordsworth's poetry. Although he had a daughter by a French woman with whom he fell in love as a young man, and later married Mary Hutchinson, of Penrith, in 1802, he wrote relatively little love poetry. *The Prelude*, begun in 1799 but not published until after his death, is largely autobiographical. He was deeply devoted to his sister Dorothy, with whom he lived from 1813 until his death, at Grasmere.

WOTY, WILLIAM (?1731–91), was co-editor, with Francis Fawkes, of *The Poetical Calendar* (1763). In his first collection of verse, *The Shrubs of Parnassus* (1760), the author's name is given as 'J. Copywell, of Lincoln's Inn, Esq.' Despite this pseudonymity the subscribers included Fielding, Garrick, Dr Johnson, Smollett and John Wilkes.

411

YALDEN, THE REV. THOMAS (1670–1736), was a friend of Addison and Congreve. Dr Johnson said of his poems that 'they deserve perusal, though they are not always exactly polished'.

YEATS, WILLIAM BUTLER (1865–1939), was the acknowledged leader of the Irish literary revival and the Irish theatre around the turn of the century. His best-known plays are *The Countess Cathleen* (1892) and *The Land of Heart's Desire* (1894). He published many volumes of lyrical verse, from the *Poems* of 1895 and *The Wind among the Reeds* (1899) to *The Trembling of the Veil* (1922). He was acknowledged as the outstanding lyrical poet of his time.

YONGE, SIR WILLIAM (d. 1755), was one of the Commissioners of the Treasury under Walpole. He contributed to several miscellanies and in 1730 he and Matthew Concanen turned Brome's *The Jovial Crew* into a comic opera by the addition of a number of songs.

Acknowledgments

The editor and publishers wish to thank the following for permission to reproduce copyright works:

CONRAD AIKEN 'Annihilation' from *Collected Poems* by Conrad Aiken. Copyright © 1953, 1970 by Conrad Aiken. Reprinted by permission of Oxford University Press, Inc.

W. H. AUDEN 'Lay your sleeping head, my love' and 'My second thoughts condemn' reprinted by permission of Faber and Faber Ltd from *Collected Poems* by W. H. Auden, and of Random House, Inc. from *W. H. Auden: Collected Poems* by W. H. Auden, edited by Edward Mendelson. 'Lay your sleeping head, my love', copyright 1940 and renewed 1968 by W. H. Auden; 'My second thoughts condemn', copyright 1945 by W. H. Auden.

GEORGE BARKER 'Summer Song: I' reprinted by permission of Faber and Faber Ltd from *Collected Poems* by George Barker.

JOHN BETJEMAN 'Indoor Games Near Newbury' and 'In a Bath Teashop' reprinted by permission of John Murray (Publishers) Ltd from *Collected Poems* by John Betjeman.

GERALD BULLETT 'First Love' reprinted by permission of A. D. Peters and Co. Ltd from *Windows on a Vanished Time*, published by Michael Joseph.

FRANCES CORNFORD 'The New-born Baby's Song' and 'The Quarrel' reprinted by permission of the Hutchinson Publishing Group Ltd from *Autumn Midnight*, 1923 and *Collected Poems*, 1954.

NOËL COWARD 'Someday I'll Find You' from *Private Lives* reproduced by kind permission of Chappell Music Ltd. Copyright © 1930 by Chappell and Co., Ltd. Copyright renewed. International copyright secured. All rights reserved. Used by permission.

HART CRANE 'Carrier Letter' reprinted from *The Complete Poems and Selected Letters and Prose of Hart Crane* edited by Brom Weber, by permission of Oxford University Press and of Liveright Publishing

413

Corporation. Copyright 1933, © 1958, 1966 by Liveright Publishing Corporation.

CECIL DAY LEWIS 'Do Not Expect Again a Phoenix Hour' from *From Feathers to Iron*, 1931 and 'The Album' from *Collected Poems*, 1954, published by the Hogarth Press and reprinted by permission of the Executors of the Estate of C. Day Lewis and Jonathan Cape Ltd.

ROBERT FROST 'Never Again Would Birds' Song Be the Same' from *The Poetry of Robert Frost* edited by Edward Connery Lathem and reprinted by permission of Jonathan Cape Ltd and Holt, Rinehart and Winston, Publishers. Copyright 1942 by Robert Frost. Copyright © 1969 by Holt, Rinehart and Winston. Copyright © 1970 by Lesley Frost Ballantine.

ROBERT GRAVES 'Pure Death' from *Poems*, 1927, and 'Counting the Beats' from *Poems and Satires*, 1951, reprinted by kind permission of Robert Graves.

F. PRATT GREEN 'The Old Couple' from *New Poems*, 1965, reprinted by kind permission of F. Pratt Green.

LORENZ HART 'My Heart Stood Still' from *A Connecticut Yankee*, reproduced by kind permission of Chappell Music Ltd and of Warner Bros Music, © 1927 Warner Bros Inc. Copyright renewed. All rights reserved. Used by permission.

RALPH HODGSON 'Silver Wedding' from *The Skylark and Other Poems*, 1959, reproduced by permission of Mrs Hodgson and Macmillan, London and Basingstoke.

PATRICK KAVANAGH 'In Memory of My Mother' from *Collected Poems*, 1964, reproduced by kind permission of Mrs Katherine B. Kavanagh.

PHILIP LARKIN 'An Arundel Tomb' from *The Whitsun Weddings*, 1964, reproduced by permission of Faber and Faber Ltd.

D. H. LAWRENCE 'Wedding Morn', 'A Young Wife', 'Flapper' and 'Song of a Man Who Is Loved' reproduced from *The Complete Poems of D. H. Lawrence* edited by Vivian de Sola Pinto and F. Warren Roberts and published by William Heinemann Ltd and Viking Penguin Inc., copyright © 1964, 1971 by Angelo Ravagli and C. M. Weekley, Executors of the Estate of Frieda Lawrence Ravagli.

Reprinted by permission of Laurence Pollinger Ltd, Viking Penguin Inc. and the Estate of the late Mrs Frieda Lawrence Ravagli.

LAURIE LEE 'First Love' from *The Bloom of Candles*, 1947, reprinted by kind permission of Laurie Lee.

ALAN JAY LERNER 'I've Grown Accustomed to Her Face' from *My Fair Lady*, © 1956 Alan Jay Lerner and Frederick Loewe, reproduced by kind permission of Chappell Music Ltd and of Chappell and Co. Inc., owner of publication and allied rights. International copyright secured. All rights reserved. Used by permission.

ALUN LEWIS 'Goodbye' from *Ha! Ha! Among the Trumpets*, 1945, reproduced by permission of George Allen and Unwin (Publishers) Ltd.

LOUIS MACNEICE 'Les Sylphides' reprinted by permission of Faber and Faber Ltd from *The Collected Poems of Louis MacNeice*.

ERIC MASCHWITZ 'These Foolish Things' © copyright 1936 by Boosey and Co. Ltd. Reprint by permission of Boosey and Hawkes Music Publishers Limited. Copyright renewed. Publication rights for the USA and Canada controlled by Bourne Co. Used by permission.

HAROLD MONRO 'The Terrible Door' from *Collected Poems*, 1933, reproduced by permission of Gerald Duckworth and Co., Ltd.

J. B. B. NICHOLS 'Amoret' and 'Halfway in Love' from *Love in Idleness*, 1883, reproduced by kind permission of the Estate of the late J. B. B. Nichols.

DOROTHY PARKER 'Unfortunate Coincidence' reproduced by permission of Gerald Duckworth and Co., Ltd from *Enough Rope*, 1926, and of Viking Penguin Inc. from *The Portable Dorothy Parker*, copyright 1926, 1954 by Dorothy Parker.

COLE PORTER 'Let's Do It' from *Paris* reproduced by kind permission of Chappell Music Ltd, © Harms Inc. (Warner Bros), and of Warner Bros Music, © 1928 Warner Bros Inc. Copyright renewed. All rights reserved. Used by permission.

DYLAN THOMAS 'On the Marriage of a Virgin' reproduced by permission of the Trustees for the Copyrights of the Late Dylan Thomas and J. M. Dent & Sons Ltd from *Deaths and Entrances*, 1946, and of New Directions Publishing Corporation from *The Poems of Dylan*

Thomas. Copyright 1946 by New Directions Publishing Corporation. Reprinted by permission of New Directions.

LAURENCE WHISTLER 'Hotel Bedroom' from *The View from this Window*, 1956, reproduced by kind permission of Laurence Whistler.

W. B. YEATS 'Down by the Salley Gardens', 'When You Are Old', 'The Lover Tells of a Rose in His Heart' and 'A Last Confession' reproduced from *The Collected Poems of W. B. Yeats* by permission of M. B. Yeats, Anne Yeats and Macmillan London Limited. Reprinted with the permission of Macmillan Publishing Co., Inc. from *Collected Poems* by W. B. Yeats. 'Down by the Salley Gardens', 'When You Are Old', 'The Lover Tells of a Rose in His Heart' copyright 1906 by Macmillan Publishing Co., Inc., renewed 1934 by William Butler Yeats; 'A Last Confession' copyright 1933 by Macmillan Publishing Co., Inc., renewed 1961 by Bertha Georgie Yeats.

Index of Authors

Index of First Lines